D0714027

About this Series: General Editor, Abdullahi A. An-Na'im

The present book is the outcome of two related research projects led by Professor Abdullahi A. An-Na'im at the School of Law, Emory University, and funded by the Ford Foundation. Both projects deploy the notion of cultural transformation to promote human rights in African and Islamic societies. The first explores this notion in theoretical terms and then focuses on issues of women and land in Africa from customary, religious and statutory rights perspectives, with a view to linking research to advocacy, for securing the rights of women to own or control land as a vital economic resource. The second project is a global study of Islamic family law, including some country studies and thematic studies, from a human rights perspective. Four volumes are being published at this stage of these on-going projects:

VOLUME I *Cultural Transformation and Human Rights in Africa*, edited by Abdullahi A. An-Na'im

VOLUME II *Islamic Family Law in a Changing World: A Global Resource Book*, edited by Abdullahi A. An-Na'im

VOLUME III *Women and Land in Africa: Linking Research to Advocacy*, edited by L. Muthoni Wanyeki

VOLUME IV *Islamic Family Law in Comparative Perspective*, edited by Lynn Welchman

Cultural Transformation and Human Rights in Africa

edited by
Abdullahi A. An-Na'im

Zed Books Ltd
LONDON • NEW YORK

Cultural Transformation and Human Rights in Africa was first published by
Zed Books Ltd, 7 Cynthia Street, London N1 9JF, UK and Room 400,
175 Fifth Avenue, New York, NY 10010, USA in 2002.

Distributed in the USA exclusively by Palgrave, a division of St Martin's
Press, LLC, 175 Fifth Avenue, New York, NY 10010, USA

Editorial copyright © Law and Religion Program, Emory University, 2002
Individual chapters copyright © individual authors, 2002

Cover designed by Andrew Corbett
Set in Monotype Baskerville and Univers Black by Ewan Smith, London
Printed and bound in Malaysia

The rights of the contributors to be identified as the authors of this work
have been asserted by them in accordance with the Copyright, Designs and
Patents Act, 1988.

A catalogue record for this book is available from the British Library
Library of Congress Cataloging-in-Publication Data: available

ISBN 1 84277 090 x cased
ISBN 1 84277 091 8 limp

Contents

About the Contributors

Hussaina Jummai Abdullah holds a Bachelor's degree in sociology from the Ahmadu Bello University, Zaria, a Master's degree in sociology from the University of Lagos and a doctorate in sociology and social anthropology from the University of Hull in the UK. She has long-standing experience working on women's issues, ranging from her academic writings on women and democratization, labour and religion to consultancies she has undertaken for CUSO, the ILO, the UNFPA, SIDA and the Swedish NGO Foundation for Human Rights. She was employed as the foundation programme officer of the UNIFEM Anglophone West Africa office in Lagos, Nigeria.

Abdullahi Ahmed An-Na'im LLB (Khartoum), LLB (LLM) and Diploma in Criminology (Cambridge), PhD (Edinburgh), is a Charles Howard Candler Professor of Law at Emory University and former executive director of Human Rights Watch/Africa. Dr An-Na'im is a widely acclaimed authority on human rights, Islam and African politics, and has participated in con-ferences and panels around the world. He has taught human rights and comparative law in universities in Europe, North America and Africa, in-cluding in his native Sudan, and has received several prestigious fellowships and grants to support his work. Dr An-Na'im's numerous publications include *Toward an Islamic Reformation: Civil Liberties, Human Rights and International Law*, and three edited volumes: *Human Rights in Africa: Cross-Cultural Perspectives*; *Human Rights in Cross-Cultural Perspectives: Quest for Consensus*; and *Human Rights and Religious Values: An Uneasy Relationship?*

Florence Butegwa is a WGLI graduate and Global Center partner. She is recognized as having played an essential role in placing women's human rights on the regional and international agenda. Her work as a lawyer, teacher, theoretician and author is considered an important and valuable contribution to the present and future of women's human rights. She was the founder and coordinator of Women in Law and Development Africa (WiLDAF), a network of women lawyers and women's rights activists in eighteen countries. Florence Butegwa is a member of the African Commission on Human and Peoples'

Rights and has served as the Edith and Irving Laurie New Jersey Chair in women's studies at Douglass College, Rutgers University, 1999–2000. She is currently director of Associates for Change, a human/women's rights NGO based in Uganda.

Martin Leon Chanock, BA (Hons) LLB, Witwatersrand; PhD, Cambridge. Martin Chanock's fields of research include legal colonization and globalization, constitutionalism and constitutional law, African and South African law, and law and cultural heritage. His publications include *The Making of South African Legal Culture, Law, Custom and Social Order* and 'A Post-Calvinist Catechism or a Post-Marxist Manifesto? Intersecting Narratives in the South African Bill of Rights Debate', in P. Alston (ed.), *Promoting Human Rights by Bills of Rights*. Professor Chanock has taught at universities in Central and West Africa, England and the USA and has held visiting appointments at Harvard, London, Cambridge and Wellesley. He is currently a professor in the Law and Legal Studies Department, La Trobe University, Australia.

Jeffrey B. Hammond received the BA magna cum laude in 1997 from Harding University. In 2001, he received the Master of Theological Studies from Emory University, Candler School of Theology, and the JD from Emory University School of Law. Mr Hammond was awarded the Herman Dooyeweerd Award by the Law and Religion Program of Emory University. His Masters thesis was about how American lawyers used Christian theology during the mid-twentieth century. His current research interests are in theological ethics, jurisprudence and religion and politics. Mr Hammond currently practises law in Nashville, Tennessee. He is married and has one daughter.

Makau Mutua is Professor of Law and director of the Human Rights Center at the State University of New York at Buffalo School of Law where he teaches international human rights, international business transactions and international law. Professor Mutua has been a visiting professor at Harvard Law School, the University of Iowa College of Law, and the University of Puerto Rico School of Law. He was educated at the University of Nairobi, the University of Dar es Salaam, and at Harvard Law School, where he became a Doctor of Juridical Science in 1987. Professor Mutua was co-chair of the 2000 annual meeting of the American Society of International Law. He has written numerous scholarly articles exploring topical subjects in international law, human rights and religion. In addition, he has authored dozens of articles for popular publications such as the *New York Times* and the *Washington Post*.

Celestine Nyamu-Musembi is a Kenyan lawyer and a recent graduate of the SJD programme at Harvard Law School. Her work focuses on gender, culture and property relations in the context of legal pluralism. She based her doctoral work on empirical research she conducted in Makueni district, Kenya. She has published articles on gender equality within the family and effective human rights responses to the cultural legitimization of gender hierarchy.

Akinyi Nzioki holds a doctorate in anthropology from the University of Nairobi, Institute of African Studies. She is an active member of the women's movement, both in Kenya and Eastern African Region and has made a substantial contribution in terms of action-oriented research and in other activist-oriented fora within the African region. She has carried out research on several topics: reproductive health, women and technology, food production and security, women's land rights, women's entrepreneurship, credit for women, women's human rights and violence against women. Currently she is the principal researcher, coordinating a research programme for the Eastern African Sub-Regional Support Initiative (EASSI) on 'Women's Land Rights', covering Ethiopia, Eritrea, Kenya, Uganda, Tanzania and Rwanda. She is employed by the Royal Netherlands Embassy as a gender expert.

Issa G. Shivji is a professor of law at the University of Dar es Salaam, Tanzania, where he has taught for the last thirty years. He has written extensively on political economy, land and constitutional law. He is the founding executive director of the Land Rights Research and Resources Institute. Professor Shivji chaired the Presidential Commission of Inquiry into Land Matters, the first of its kind in Tanzania. Its report is published by the Scandinavian Institute of African Studies and is considered a pioneer work on land tenure in Africa. Professor Shivji has undertaken a number of consultancies on land for the UNDP in Eritrea and Zimbabwe and is currently working on village governance in Tanzania.

INTRODUCTION

Abdullahi A. An-Na'im

§ THE challenge facing the human rights paradigm, as discussed in the first chapter of this book, is how to ensure that people enjoy the same rights within their communities, while respecting the cultural autonomy of those communities. As Albie Sachs, the South African jurist, put it, human rights are the right to be the same and the right to be different.[1] This profound insight leads to the next question of how to realize this delicate balance: how can all people be treated in the same way, without distinction on such grounds as race, gender, religion or belief (that is, without discrimination), while respecting their equally important right to distinctive personal and collective identity? In other words, how is the inherent tension between these two competing claims or entitlements to be mediated, for instance, by respecting the integrity of a community without permitting it to practise discrimination against women or minorities? Is such mediation supposed to work in the same or similar ways in all human societies throughout the world, or do considerations such as culture and context make a difference, and to what extent? In cases where it is impossible to reconcile the demands or implications of these two sides of the formula, which side should have priority over the other? Is the choice that one makes, whether in favour of the right to be the same or the right to be different, supposed to apply in all cases where conflict arises, or should the balancing of the two be attempted, and choices be made in each context?

Upon reflection, one can readily appreciate that there are many universally shared values and ideals, as well as specific universally expected behavioural responses to certain stimuli that evoke fear, tension, discomfort, pleasure, and so forth. If this is true, then how does one explain numerous and clear cultural differences within and among various societies and communities? Part of the answer, it seems to me, is the tension between the universal human need for being (or to be perceived as being) different from others, both individually and collectively, on the one hand, and the power of cultural discourse to mobilize people and motivate them to act in certain ways, on the other. The first psychological factor leads individuals, within their communities on both sides of a given cultural divide, to emphasize the differences they perceive in order to vindicate their need to be individually and collectively different from other people and their communities. The second social and political dimension means that the ruling elite and leaders of social movements will probably seek to promote their objectives by emphasizing differences between various types of groups in support of the policies they seek to implement. It should be emphasized here that people tend to presume the factual validity of their own perceptions of difference, regardless of what some disinterested person might observe. In other words, perceptions of difference are intended by those who articulate them, and taken by the target constituencies, to be sufficiently real to motivate action by individuals and communities.

These and related issues and concerns were explored in relation to African societies through an interdisciplinary research project implemented during 1996–98 by the Law and Religion Program of Emory University, under a generous grant from the Ford Foundation, to examine the processes and dynamics of cultural transformation in Africa from a human rights perspective. Here is a brief explanation of the basic concept and main activities of that project, followed by a discussion of the rationale and organization of this book.

The Cultural Transformation Approach

As explained in its original proposal, the objective of this project, entitled Cultural Transformation in Africa: Religious, Legal and Human Rights Dimensions, is to promote an empirically sound, yet visionary and dynamic, understanding of the relationships between religion, law and human rights in African societies, with a view to formulating concrete policy recommendations, law reform proposals and practical strategies for the greater protection of human rights throughout the continent. The working concept of the project took a broad and dynamic view of religion to include local or indigenous belief systems and customary practices, and of law to encompass customary and religious law as well as state civil law and enforcement institutions and processes. It also emphasized that conceptions of human rights should draw on local cultural and legal norms and institutions, and address locally set priorities in the definition and effective implementation of individual and collective claims and entitlement.

No single project can, of course, completely encompass the wide varieties of perspectives, academic disciplines and scholarly approaches required to address the full range and implications of all aspects of change and transformation in contemporary Africa. However, to ensure that the selection of agenda and the focus for the project were not arbitrary or capricious, the project directors conducted numerous consultations about possible directions for research and analysis, especially at an informal meeting at Emory University, Atlanta, USA, in June 1996 and a workshop at the University of Cape Town, South Africa, in March 1997.[2] In addition to clarifying conceptual and programmatic choices of focus for the project, those discussions emphasized the need to render the best possible scholarship in the service of policy and action. This resulted in the adoption of what we call the complete or integrated model, whereby the object is not only to arrive at valid conclusions and make appropriate recommendations, but also to do so in ways that are conducive to influencing policy-making and implementation at the local, national and international level.

In its original conception, as clarified and developed during its implementation, the project attempted to apply a human rights paradigm in uncovering the actual realities and exploring the possibilities of the role of religion and law in the processes of cultural transformation. In so doing, however, the project sought to draw on positive aspects of this tripartite relationship, as well as addressing its negative dimensions. On the positive side, a human rights paradigm is necessary for mediating the processes of the social construction of rights by supporting the creation of political and social 'space' for more inclusive and equitable processes of change. It can also guide those processes and their outcome into greater conformity with internationally recognized human rights norms, as locally specified and legitimated. But such a useful paradigm, in turn, needs to be supported through religious justification and legal implementation and enforcement. On the negative side, certain religious beliefs and institutions have often been seen as inconsistent with the universality of human rights or as obstacles to the effective implementation of those rights. Similarly, legal norms and institutions have often been used to entrench oppression and provide formalistic justification for the violation of human rights. Each side of this tripartite relationship can be stated as follows.

As abstract ideals of human dignity and economic and social justice, human rights norms depend upon the religious vision and commitment of specific communities to give them content and coherence, and to motivate voluntary compliance with their dictates. Religious visions and commitments are also needed for generating the political will to enforce legal norms and implement concrete policies, as and when necessary for the protection and promotion of human rights standards. But many forms of religion, in Africa and elsewhere, seem to work contrary to the values of equality, justice and peace contemplated by a human rights paradigm. They are often used to legitimate and support many forms of violence and injustice, like the oppression of women, abuse of children, persecution of minorities and dissidents within the community of believers, and aggression against non-believers. Despite these conflicts and tensions between human rights and some prevalent perceptions of religion, there is strong need for reconciliation and mutual support because of the organic interdependence of the two. While human rights regimes in and of themselves provide no panacea for all the problems of any society, or those of the world at large, they are a critical part of any solution. On the other hand, while religions are not easy allies to engage, the struggle for human rights cannot be won without them, particularly in the African context.

Thus, participants in the project were encouraged to take a broad and dialectic view of the role of religion in the cultural dynamics of change, especially from a human rights perspective. The underlying premise of this approach is the view that religious beliefs and practice are constantly changing and evolving in every society. Since such transformations occur through internal discourse and cross-cultural dialogue, as discussed in the first chapter of this book, human rights advocates should engage in such discourse and dialogue with a view to promoting those aspects of religious belief and practice that are supportive of human rights in the society in question.[3] This dialectic conception of the relationship between religion and cultural change raises possibilities of transforming the negative dynamics of this relationship in situations such as those in Algeria, Nigeria and Sudan in the 1990s. Similarly, internal discourse and cross-cultural dialogue can be deployed to promote the human rights of women and children, to reinforce the claims of excluded persons and groups, and to support the demands of persecuted ethnic and religious minorities for economic, social and cultural rights.

The possibility of a constructive relationship between religion and human rights in the context of cultural transformation must find its concrete and practical expression and application through the legal norms and institutions of the modern African state. The legal protection of human rights by the state is needed by activists and scholars who are seeking to guide and direct the processes of cultural transformation in favour of the greater protection of human rights in general. In addition, legal action by the state is also necessary for implementing and securing gains made by human rights advocates. That is, law plays a vitally important role in sustaining a human rights paradigm, both during the process of cultural transformation and in relation to its outcomes.

Yet, as many African societies have experienced since independence, oppressive and corrupt ruling elites abuse legal systems. Law enforcement organs and personnel often exceed and abuse their powers with impunity, and manage to perpetuate an institutional culture of violence and repression, in the 'normal' administration of criminal justice or in the field of social policy and so-called state security. Abusive and discriminatory practices against women and children are legitimized and enforced by family or personal law regimes, including property and inheritance law. Legal norms and institutions are used in so-called democratic regimes as well as in autocratic or authoritarian regimes to legitimate and perpetuate policies and practices of political exclusion and marginalization of minorities or economically disadvantaged groups throughout Africa.

These and other negative manifestations and uses of the law reflect and reinforce social judgements that are often predicated on religious and moral values and traditions of the community at large. The abuse of the law and the legal process, however gross and frequent, does not necessitate or justify wholesale abandonment of these institutions. Similar to the case of religion, the relationship between law and human rights in the context of cultural transformation in Africa must also be accurately characterized with a view to proposing effective ways of making it more conducive to the protection and promotion of human rights.

The project sought to include in its conception of human rights what Africans themselves accept as the normative standards they wish to establish and implement through their local struggles, as well as a clear understanding of the context within which those visions and perspectives can be realized in practice. Instead of taking human rights as a given, or a concept already definitively settled by the international community, the project sought to open up the concept, its normative content, priorities and implementation mechanisms for further discussion and clarification. Thus, a particular early focus of the project was the exploration of ways of clarifying and substantiating demands for the protection of economic, social and cultural rights. After decades of neglect in traditional human rights discourse, and excessive politicization in the polemics of the Cold War, internationally recognized economic, social and cultural rights are at serious risk of total oblivion in this age of economic liberation and structural adjustment programmes in Africa. Yet any human rights paradigm is unlikely to have much significance for Africans if it does not include concerns about their fundamental economic, social and cultural claims/entitlement in the mediation and guidance of the local definition and implementation of rights. Neither the protection of civil and political rights, nor the pursuit of developmental and environmental objectives, will be meaningful in Africa without the incorporation of basic guarantees of economic, social and cultural rights.

Moreover, to achieve the protection of the economic and social human rights of women and children, the project attempted to contribute to developing ways of challenging existing customary and religious laws of inheritance and land tenure that apply in most African countries. This is by no means an easy task, as it will certainly be resisted by the guardians of the status quo in the name of 'protecting' traditional African culture and/or religion. It is therefore imperative that these claims be challenged and tested by African scholars and activists who enjoy internal legitimacy and credibility within their communities.

This 'internal' approach, it seems to the directors of the project, is essential in view of current debates about the universality versus cultural relativity or contextual specificity of human rights. The project sought neither to ignore the issues underlying the challenges to the universality of human rights in the present cultural and political context of African societies, nor to concede the high moral ground to radical and negative relativism that seeks to repudiate the principle of universality itself. On the one hand, the project took the present international and regional human rights standards and implementation mechanisms as a very important and useful, though not necessarily definitive or exhaustive, framework for the internal and cross-cultural social construction of rights at the local, African and global levels. On the other hand, rather than assume a certain set of norms and implementation mechanisms, especially an externally imposed one, the project emphasized the importance of internally produced conceptions, priorities and implementation of human rights. This social construction of rights does not mean that the processes we are concerned with are wholly and exclusively internal to a given society, as external and cross-cultural influence and exchange are inevitable, and often desirable. Rather, the point is that agents of external influence should be aware of the nature and dynamics of internal processes, and respectful of their integrity. Scholars, professionals and activists abroad must be educated about and assisted in their efforts to support local African actors in the social construction of rights, at both the internal and cross-cultural, local and global, level.

As reflected in some chapters of this book, some participants in this project expressed reservations about the utility of a 'human rights paradigm' in examining the nature and implications of cultural transformation in Africa. The question was forcefully raised, at both the Atlanta and Cape Town meetings, whether the project should focus on a 'rights discourse' or deploy 'other languages of resistance'. While taking this view seriously, the directors of the project still felt that there are good reasons for keeping a human rights paradigm as a framework for the project as a whole. It is true that the rural and urban poor of Africa may not use a 'rights language' to identify and demand satisfaction of their economic, social and cultural claims. Instead, they may define and rank the importance of such claims in terms that are more familiar in their own local and cultural contexts. But experience clearly indicates that both rural and urban populations need to articulate their demands for individual and collective justice in 'rights language', for those demands to be recognized and satisfied. Applying a human rights paradigm is necessary in view of the concrete realities of the economic and social policy of nation-states which are inescapably linked to international relations and trade, financial institutions, regional and international security systems, and so forth. A rights approach is essential for dealing with this complex web of local and global dimensions of life today. A particularly compelling concern in this regard, as discussed in the first chapter of this book, is the reality of the state and its extensive powers which profoundly affect every aspect of people's private as well as public lives. Since those powers are supposed to be limited and regulated through a rights paradigm according to the European models of the post-colonial state in Africa, it follows that such a paradigm should be applied to the independent African state as well.

Nevertheless, as already noted, the project was conceived from the beginning as an effort to verify and clarify the utility of a human rights paradigm with a view to adapting it to fundamental African concerns. Far from taking such a paradigm as a given, the project sought to open up the human rights concept, and its normative content, priorities and mechanisms for further discussion and clarification in the African context. In this way, it was hoped to provide an opportunity to challenge common assumptions about the role of customary and religious norms and practices in relation to the universality of human rights, especially regarding the promotion and protection of the economic, social and cultural rights of women.

The Rationale and Organization of this Book

Given the strong emphasis of the above-mentioned project on the possibilities of the local promotion of human rights through the processes of cultural transformation, the primary focus of this book is on the theoretical clarification and illustration of the creative possibilities, as well as the difficulties and limitations, of this relationship. The first chapter, by Abdullahi An-Na'im and Jeffrey Hammond, sets the scene through a discussion of the meaning and significance of the human rights paradigm, and attempts to clarify the notions of culture and transformation, in order to reflect on the combination of all these elements together in the present context of African societies. By emphasizing the profound impact of culture on the articulation and implementation of human rights in all societies, on the one hand, and the dynamic nature of cultural transformation, on the other, the authors argue for the need consciously to utilize the latter in the widest possible and most sustainable protection of human rights in African societies. This is imperative, An-Na'im and Hammond suggest, for the mediation of the profound paradox of ensuring effective domestic (national) protection of internationally recognized human rights norms through international supervision, without violating national sovereignty as a fundamental collective human right. For the protection of human rights to be the product of the free exercise of self-determination, rather than in spite of it, these rights must be rooted and legitimized within the local cultures of African societies.

While accepting the Western origins of the modern concept of human rights, and emphasizing the impact of global power relations in the articulation and implementation of this concept, An-Na'im and Hammond argue for the need to promote genuine universality for human rights standards throughout the world. According to these authors, although every culture, whether so-called Western and non-Western, has its own difficulties or problems with some aspect or another of the human rights paradigm, the inevitability of cultural transformation opens possibilities for reconciliation between human rights norms and opposing cultural norms or practices. For this to happen, however, awareness of the nature and dynamics of conflicts and tensions between these two normative systems should be combined with deliberate strategies for achieving widely accepted and sustainable reconciliation between them. For this reason, the authors emphasize the role of human agency in the processes of cultural transformation.

General theoretical reflection continues in the second chapter with Martin Chanock's general assessment of rights in Africa. Chanock asserts that any construction of new rights depends on an active revolution in culture, not just a passive resignation to rights slowly evolving over time. He also argues that rights cannot necessarily be seen within a universalist framework, but that general 'universal-like' concerns should inform our cultural analyses of rights, while emphasizing the relevance of nation and class in understanding categories of rights. Moreover, Chanock maintains that it is the colonial framework that underlies the weakness of conceptions and protection of rights in African societies, rather than the cultures of those societies as such, and explores the role of the state in the protection of rights, or lack thereof. While noting the inherent tension between the role of the state as the primary violator of rights and as the supposed medium of their protection, he suggests that there is greater need for the protection of rights in the context of the marginalized state. He also examines the relevance of a rights paradigm to issues of family relations and land use, as individual concerns, despite their common association with culture and religion.

Makau Mutua, in Chapter 3, calls for taking African cultures seriously in a dynamic and genuinely universal process of creating a valid conception of human rights, without conceding the claims of cultural relativism. In fact, he rejects the term 'cultural relativism' itself, as it is promoted by those who resist the construction of a multi-cultural human rights corpus, usually from an ethnocentric bias that is symptomatic of the moral imperialism of the West. Instead of asserting the primacy of one culture over others, or arguing that only one cultural expression and historical experience constitutes human rights, Mutua views each experience as a contributor to the whole. He maintains that the language of duty in African societies, as reflected in the African Charter of Human and Peoples' Rights of 1981, offers a different meaning for individual/state-society relations: while people have rights, they also bear duties. The resolution of a claim is an opportunity for society to contemplate the complex web of individual and community duties and rights to seek a balance between the competing claims of the individual and society.

In Chapter 4, Florence Butegwa brings a specific focus to bear on the relationship between cultural transformation and the human rights of women in African societies. She calls for reconceptualizing the dilemma of either tolerating the marginalization of women, or perceiving their struggles for human dignity and rights as an attack on the core of social solidarity and communal integrity. The key to such reconceptualization, Butegwa suggests, is the mediation of differences between allegedly deeply entrenched aspects of African cultures, and recent advances in the theory and practice of human rights which provide women a level playing field, for instance, in their struggle for more equitable use and control of land and other economic resources. In her view, such 'bottom-up' dynamism is also important for promoting greater state compliance with their obligations under international human rights treaties.

In Chapter 5, Celestine Nyamu-Musembi follows through on her earlier call to women's rights actors to respond to the cultural legitimization of gender hierarchy to show that local norms and practices produce and redefine ideas about human rights. She draws from the practices of administrative and informal social institutions at the local level and identifies features that are favourable to the realization of gender equality and features that impede such realization. The author illustrates her arguments with examples from her research in Kenya on gender relations and access to and control of property, especially land.

Chapter 6, by Hussaina Abdullah, focuses on the role of human agency in the mediation of the conflict between cultural/religious factors and the promotion of human rights in the Nigerian context of concurrent growth of human rights advocacy and religious renewal. In analysing current women's organizations, Abdullah lauds Women in Nigeria (WIN) for its unapologetic advocacy of women's human rights. While appreciating the culture-specific advocacy strategies of the Federation of Muslim Women's Association in Nigeria (FOMWAN), which seeks to empower Muslim women without necessarily striving for equality with men, Abdullah suggests that FOMWAN's efforts have been hampered by its hostility to other women's rights organizations. She concludes by calling for unity among Nigerian women's rights organizations, despite their different approaches to the promotion of human rights in their society and communities.

The next two chapters, by Issa Shivji and Elizabeth Akinyi Nzioki, are devoted to issues of land tenure regimes as structural dimensions of cultural transformation. In Chapter 7, Shivji examines in detail a recent major effort at reform of land tenure in Tanzania through the work of the Presidential Commission on Land Matters. Noting how the Commission had to confront the colonial origins of the official land tenure system, whereby the governor held ultimate control over the land, regardless of customary law or practice, Shivji examines how the draft Land Act, a product of the Commission, now entrenches ultimate power over land in the Tanzanian state, while leaving the day-to-day administration to the authority of village officials. A particularly relevant aspect of the Commission's work is how it proposed the formalization of the role of the traditional system of dispute resolution by a group of elders. This discussion brings into sharp relief the tension between traditional practices and institutions, on the one hand, and the role of the modern state, on the other, in relation to issues of social and economic justice.

In Chapter 8, Akinyi Nzioki examines land tenure reform in Kenya, where 80 per cent of the population is directly dependent on agriculture. According to Nzioki, women comprise half of Kenya's agricultural producers, yet they can have access to land only through male family members. She explains that earlier traditional systems of land tenure used to stress inclusive uses, whereby the person's needs determined her access to land. Though land was ultimately held by the head of the family, members had a strong sense of their own rights, and were not silenced when they demanded to use a piece of property. Women did have considerable use rights, though they never held titles in their own hands, since land was almost inevitably allocated to males. During the post-colonial period, legislative reforms centred on three specific goals: adjudication, consolidation and title registration. Nzioki also presents her own study of women's responses to the land registration process. In her particular case study, she found that women owned only 11.8 per cent of the land in her study area, and the majority of those women were widows. Even more startling was the finding that only 3.2 per cent of the daughters in the study area inherited land. But, as was to be expected, 78.6 per cent of the women had access to the land to cultivate it for their families. And, adding injury to the insult of the death of women landowners, 66.4 per cent of women surveyed cannot mortgage land to raise money for themselves or their families.

The publication of this collection of essays is intended to introduce readers to some of the general issues of cultural transformation and human rights in African societies, to be followed with a second volume containing some case studies on issues of women and land in particular. A more systematic and comprehensive coverage of the subject has been attempted through the project, as outlined earlier, but not all commissioned draft papers were appropriate, or revised in good time, for publication in this volume. It is nevertheless hoped that this selection will generate sufficient interest in the proposed conceptualization and methodology of the relationship between cultural transformation and human rights in all societies, especially African societies today.

Notes

1. Justice Albie Sachs of the Constitutional Court of South Africa said this during a presentation I attended on the occasion of the first meeting of the International Council for Human Rights Policy, Cairo, Egypt, 25 June 1997.

2. This project was implemented between June 1996 and May 1998, under the direction of Professors Abdullahi A. An-Na'im, John Witte Jr and Johan van der Vyver of the Emory University School of Law. The directors are grateful to Professor Mahmood Mamdani, the chair of the Centre for African Studies at the University of Cape Town, and his staff for the successful implementation of the Cape Town workshop. The directors are also grateful to Ms Florence Butegwa and Ms Taaka Awori of Associates for Change, Kapala, Uganda, for organizing the Entebbe workshop. Both these events are mentioned in the following review of the activities of the project.

3. For a theoretical formulation and application of this approach see, generally, A. A. An-Na'im and F. M. Deng (eds), *Human Rights in Africa: Cross-Cultural Perspectives*, Washington, DC: Brookings Institution, 1990; and A. A. An-Na'im (ed.), *Human Rights in Cross-Cultural Perspectives: Quest for Consensus*, Philadelphia: University of Pennsylvania Press, 1992.

ONE

Cultural Transformation and Human Rights in African Societies

Abdullahi A. An-Na'im and Jeffrey Hammond

§ THE premise of this book can be summarized in four propositions. First, culture profoundly affects the articulation and implementation of human rights in all societies because of its formative and constant influence on human motivation and behaviour. Second, while this does not mean that culture is the sole determinant of all human activities, the ability of members of a cultural tradition to take alternative courses of action is conditioned by the broad parameters of their culture. Third, every culture is constantly changing through the interactions of a wide variety of actors and factors at different levels of society. This internal discourse within each culture includes the activities of non-elite actors who contribute to cultural change through different patterns of behaviour and other forms of non-verbal communication, as well as the more visible and articulate forms of interaction by elite and openly active social actors. In other words, people are generally predisposed to act in culturally sanctioned ways, but they are to varying degrees agents of change in the transformation of their own culture. Fourth, the speed and sustainability of change in particular ways tends to vary with such factors as the level of entrenchment of the values and institutions in question, degree of stability in the circumstances of conditions of the society, and ability and willingness of social actors to engage in deliberate strategies of cultural transformation.

By the term cultural transformation we are referring to the dynamics of change as internal processes of societal adaptation by a variety of actors in response to a wide range of stimuli at different levels, rather than simply the product of internal hegemony or external imposition. With due regard to the impact of differentials in power relations within each society, and in relation to external actors and forces, the notion of cultural transformation incorporates the whole process as an indigenous expression of a people's right to self-determination. Moreover, we use the term transformation in order to de-emphasize the internal/external dichotomy in cross-cultural dialogue because externally initiated change is unsustainable except to the extent that it is internalized by the people concerned. Such an understanding of cultural change, we believe, is crucial for the theoretical validity and practical application of human rights norms in all societies throughout the world.

From this perspective, the objective of the present book is to explore the possibilities of utilizing the dynamic of cultural transformation for the promotion of human rights in present-day African societies. We hope to contribute to the achievement of this objective by clarifying a way of analysis that was first presented elsewhere (An-Na'im and Deng [eds] 1990; An-Na'im [ed.] 1992), and illustrating its application in relation to selected issues for some African societies, instead of attempting a comprehensive examination of the full range of human rights norms, or coverage of the whole continent. Although certain African societies are the primary focus of this book, some comparative study of parallel developments in other parts of the world can improve our understanding of the relationship between cultural transformation and human rights in the global context. Since African cultures are transforming in interaction with other cultures, including broader global trends and emerging transnational 'third cultures' which extend beyond all national boundaries (Featherstone 1990: 1), it is important to understand these processes as elements of cross-cultural dialogue, as discussed below.

We begin this chapter with a brief explanation of what we call the human rights paradigm in order to underscore its paradoxical yet imperative nature in setting universal standards which are unlikely to prevail without due regard for local cultural legitimacy and contextual understanding of these rights. The second section will be devoted to a general clarification of the nature of culture and the dynamics of cultural transformation. This is followed in the third section by a discussion of the context and dynamics of transformation in post-colonial African countries.

The Human Rights Paradigm in Context

Traditionally, human rights norms are supposed to be provided for in national constitutions and laws for domestic application by the judicial and executive organs of the state as a matter of national sovereignty. But because experience has shown that the state cannot be trusted sufficiently to protect the rights of all persons and groups within its territorial jurisdiction, the idea of international protection emerged as a means of ensuring certain minimum human rights standards everywhere. The term 'human rights paradigm' is used here to indicate that traditional notions of state sovereignty over its citizens and territory must somehow be reconciled with the need to respect and protect universal human rights as rights due to every human being by virtue of his or her humanity, without distinction on such grounds as race, sex, belief, language or national origin. This concept found its first and most authoritative expression in the Charter of the United Nations of 1945, and the Universal Declaration of Human Rights of 1948, as subsequently elaborated in many multilateral treaties and other international instruments.[1] It is clear by now that at least the basic idea of this paradigm has been established beyond dispute through developments within the global United Nations (UN) system, the European, Inter-American and African regional systems, and the work of national and international non-governmental organizations (Steiner and Alston 1996).

However, the human rights paradigm is premised on a complex paradox. First, the idea of international supervision of domestic human rights protection is apparently inconsistent with the right to self-determination, as discussed below. Second, the normative and institutional arrangements for such international supervision are supposed to be produced and sanctioned by processes beyond the exclusive control of individual states and their societies. Yet, these internal entities continue to play a crucial role in the interpretation and implementation of human rights norms. In other words, while being a means of ensuring the protection of certain minimum human rights at the domestic level, international protection still requires the cooperation of the state in limiting its own ability to treat as it pleases all persons who are subject to its domestic jurisdiction. The solution that we propose is to work through cultural transformation to ensure that necessary local variations in the implementation of human rights are consistent with the universal validity of these rights.

It is true that the paradox of depending on the state to regulate itself also faces the domestic constitutional and legal protection of human rights. But an important difference between constitutional and international protection of human rights is that, for good and bad, the former is the product of internal dynamics, whereas the latter attempts to influence those domestic dynamics from outside the country in favour of upholding certain minimum standards. In other words, whatever level of constitutional protection may exist in a country at any time is the product of the configuration of political forces, social conditions, economic resources, institutional capacity and other domestic factors. In contrast, the human rights paradigm by definition seeks to improve the quality of domestic protection by overcoming internal opposition to the protection of human rights within the country in question. The tension between national sovereignty and the application of internationally recognized human rights norms raises a dilemma. While people want the wide recognition of the global authority of human rights to translate into the ability to stop the massive and persistent violations, they are unlikely to accept this desirable outcome if it is to be achieved by violating their national sovereignty.

Since this cannot and should not be done through external imposition, the very nature of the human rights paradigm requires its proponents to generate sufficient political support within each country to overcome the lack or weakness of sufficient domestic constitutional protection of human rights. This can be done, we suggest, through a deliberate effort at building an overlapping consensus around the normative content and implementation mechanisms of human rights.[2] The project of the universality of human rights is to be realized through a confluence of internal societal responses to injustice and oppression, instead of attempting to transplant a fully developed and conclusive concept and its implementation mechanisms from one society to another. The way to get a universal idea accepted locally is to present it in local terms, which can best be done by local people. Conversely, local acceptance enriches the universal idea (Daniel 1975: 211) by giving it meaning and relevance to people's lives.

This complex paradox is the necessary consequence of the fundamental principle of state sovereignty on which the present international system is premised, as entrenched in the Charter of the United Nations and reiterated in numerous instruments.[3] Indeed, state sovereignty is the practical expression of the principle of self-determination, which has itself been proclaimed a fundamental human right by the first Article of both the International Covenant on Economic, Social and Cultural Rights of 1966, and the International Covenant on Civil and Political Rights, also of 1966. In addition to the fact that it is unlikely that states will deliberately relinquish their own autonomy by abandoning traditional notions of sovereignty or allow them to be undermined by other actors, a frontal attack on the principle of sovereignty can also be counterproductive for the protection of human rights. State sovereignty remains the essential expression of the fundamental right to self-determination, the practical vehicle of domestic policy, and the necessary medium of international relations. A more realistic objective, it seems to us, is to diminish the negative consequence of the paradox of self-regulation by infusing the human rights ethos into the fabric of the state itself and the global context in which it operates. Gross and massive violations of human rights should end through the free exercise, rather than breach, of the right to self-determination. To contribute to this paradigm shift, we are focusing on the internal dynamic of transformation to see how it can be used to make the protection of human rights part of the cultural self-identity of the people in question. Opponents of the human rights paradigm often seek to undermine its high moral, political and legal standing by attempting to dismiss it as a product of Western philosophical and political developments.[4] In terms of origins, the Universal Declaration was drafted and adopted in 1946–48, when there were only four African members of the United Nations (Egypt, Ethiopia, Liberia and South Africa). At that time, the rest of Africa was colonized by the same powers that were proclaiming the universality of human rights as defined through their own cultural assumptions and constitutional experiences. It is true that African and Asian states adopted the principle of universality of human rights, but they had to do so on the basis of the normative framework established by the UN Charter and Universal Declaration (An-Na'im 1990: 350). The question is therefore often raised of how Western conceptions of human rights can be accepted as universal. The answer we propose is first to appreciate that the specific origin of an idea or institute does not mean that it cannot achieve universal acceptance. This is clearly true of European models of the nation-state which are now accepted by all societies throughout the world. Second, we suggest that those of us who are committed to the universality of human rights should work for its global acceptance through cultural transformation towards the local legitimation of international standards.

Part of the process of influencing the course of cultural transformation in favour of the stronger protection of human rights as a matter of the free expression by the people of their right to self-determination is to insist that a genuine commitment to the protection of human rights is inherent to the *raison d'être* of any state. For African states, this was not only the premise of their struggle for self-determination from colonial rule, but has also been repeatedly proclaimed in national constitutions and policy statements after independence. The other side of this coin, however, is that since discharging any obligation is a matter of national sovereignty, the government of each country should be entitled to interpret and implement human rights norms in accordance with its own national circumstances, including relevant cultural and contextual factors. This claim must be conceded, the argument goes, not only because of the lack of effective international mechanisms for the implementation and protection of human rights, but also out of respect for the people's right to self-determination. In other words, it can be said that, at its present stage of development, the international system is not able to ensure enforcement of human rights at the national level. Moreover, to seek enforcement through applying external pressure, instead of supporting internal initiatives in that regard, would play into the hands of those seeking to discredit international efforts and undermine the universality of human rights.

Therefore, the unavoidable risk of this linkage between human rights and self-determination is that the latter might be cited to justify, or rationalize, the repudiation of the alleged benefit of the universality of human rights on grounds of upholding the national priorities of political stability and economic development, or out of purported respect for the integrity of national culture. This situation presents human rights advocates with a serious dilemma. On the one hand, claims of contextual and cultural relativity are likely to sound very plausible to the national constituencies to whom they are normally addressed. On the other hand, human rights are meaningless unless they are universal in the sense of being due to every human being by virtue of that person's humanity. How can one acknowledge and address national priorities as well as cultural and contextual factors without allowing that to be the means for repudiating the principle of universality? In exploring the role of cultural transformation in response to this question we are not in the least suggesting that this should be the only approach. We do believe, however, that an understanding of culture and its transformation is relevant to the effective deployment of other approaches and strategies.

Clearly, many factors affect the implementation of human rights, such as the level and quality of political commitment to the implementation of administrative, educational and other policies, allocation of economic resources, and civil society activism. Legal protection is particularly important not only for the judicial enforcement of these rights as legal entitlements, thereby sustaining the efficacy and credibility of all other mechanisms and processes, but also for the development and application of operational definitions of each human right, and the mediation of competing claims of rights. But there is a clear cultural dimension to all these factors and strategies because, as explained in the next section, culture is the framework for understanding the human motivation and behaviour that underlie political commitment, determination of priorities for allocation of resources and direction of civil society activism. For example, legal protection of rights presupposes a certain degree of political stability, institutional capacity, and the willingness and ability of the public at large to resort to the courts for the enforcement of their rights. Legal protection also assumes the prevalence of a certain conception of the rule of law, independence of the judiciary, and executive compliance with judicial determinations. Each of these prerequisites has its clear cultural dimension. In the final analysis, cultural factors are crucial for the development of the political will to initiate and sustain any approach, whether in favour of or against the protection of human rights. The issue therefore becomes how to promote political will that is consistently supportive of the systematic protection of human rights.

Part of the way to address this issue, we suggest, is for human rights to be seen as the present expression of a long history of struggle for social justice and resistance to oppression in all human societies, rather than simply the product of so-called Western political philosophy and experiences (Mamdani 1990: 359, 360). That is not to say, of course, that all human societies have actually articulated and applied human rights norms in the modern sense of the term. Rather, the point here is to broaden the historical basis of the modern concept of human rights by seeing it as a specific manifestation of shared experiences of all the peoples of the world in seeking solutions to their own political and social problems. This perception of the shared heritage of human rights in that basic sense is likely to encourage a feeling of 'ownership' and relevance of these rights by people in different parts of the world because they reflect their own history, current experience and aspirations. Rejecting claims of exclusive Western 'authorship' of human rights in this way reinforces the authority of these rights as a common standard of achievement for all humanity, which is the essence of their universality.

Moreover, the present articulation of human rights emerged in Western countries in response to particular models of the centralized powers of the nation-state and certain forms of economic development. Since these models now prevail in all parts of the world through colonialism and its aftermath, the same articulation of rights would probably be necessary everywhere for the same reasons those formulations were adopted by Western societies. Generally speaking, all human rights (whether so-called economic, social and cultural, or civil and political) are designed to help people to ensure that the centralized powers and economic resources of the state are used in full accord with their human dignity and for the satisfaction of their basic needs. For example, freedom of expression and association are essential for effective participation in the determination and implementation of public policies regarding the provision of education, health care and other essential services. Trade union rights are necessary for the protection of the human dignity and well-being of workers under certain types of relations of production, commonly known as capitalist or free-market ideology, wherever those relations may prevail in the world. It is instructive in this regard to note that ruling elites in developing countries are happy to exercise the extensive centralized powers of the state, but refuse to accept what long experience has shown to be necessary safeguards against the abuse of those powers.

To say that human rights are necessary safeguards wherever Western models of the state and economic development prevail does not mean that earlier or present Western formulations will remain definitive everywhere in the world. The universalization of Western models of state structures and powers, economic development and social policy does not mean that they were replicated everywhere according to the same precise and static blueprint. In addition to initial modification and adaptation to local conditions in different parts of the world, those models are still constantly evolving and adapting to changing local and global conditions everywhere, including Western Europe and North America. It would therefore seem to follow logically that the human rights response must also change over time and from one place to another. On the other hand, however, formulations of rights which have proven their relevance and effectiveness should not be discarded without a convincing critique and the presentation of better alternatives. That is the subject of cross-cultural dialogue. For example, Islamic or East Asian societies may raise objections to some of the present formulations of human rights standards, but that should be done in ways that other societies can appreciate, even if they are unable to accept such a critique, including suggested alternative formulations, instead of simply applying a blanket claim of incompatibility of these standards with Islamic or Asian values.

By seeing human rights as the product of a long history of struggle for social justice and resistance to oppression that is constantly adapting to changing conditions in order better to achieve its objectives, one can appreciate the possibilities of mediation. To the extent that the structures and processes of social injustice and oppression are specific to each society, there is the pull of cultural and contextual relativism – the claim that a society should live by its own norms and values rather than those of other societies. As certain aspects of local particularities diminish under the force of growing globalization, the push for universal human rights as a common response tends to increase. But the tension between the relative and the universal will remain because globalization tends to reflect the current unequal power relations between developed and developing countries. Although it cannot be permanently resolved, this tension can be mediated once it is realized that upholding the universality of human rights as a highly desirable objective does not mean that it should be taken as either an accomplished fact or a static and immutable phenomenon.

To conclude this section, we suggest that given the inherent paradox of expecting the state to protect its citizens against the excesses of its own power, and the need to reconcile or mediate competing claims on the limited resources of the state itself, it is necessary to address the underlying structural root causes of human rights violations as well as to redress such violations as and when they occur. In other words, we are calling for the proactive deployment of a variety of measures and policies to achieve the actual realization of human rights in a systematic and comprehensive manner, in addition to effective enforcement and protection in individual cases. A proactive approach to addressing underlying causes of human rights violations is particularly important in the African context because of the difficulties of legal protection in the narrow technical sense (An-Na'im 2001). It is in this light that we will continue, in subsequent sections of this chapter, to elaborate on the role of culture and cultural transformation in the promotion and protection of human rights in African societies today.

Culture and Cultural Transformation

We do not propose to engage in an elaborate discussion of culture in general, or some specialized aspect of cultural studies, which is a vast and fast-growing interdisciplinary field. Instead, we will simply provide an overview of definitions and clarifications of culture and its role in human behaviour in order to explore the possibilities of utilizing the dynamic of cultural transformation for the promotion of human rights in contemporary African societies. While so limiting the scope of this discussion for our purposes here, we wish to emphasize the fundamental and far-reaching role of culture in all human societies, regardless of their level of development, religious or ideological orientation, and forms of political and social organization. To be human is to have been enculturated to some specific culture whose characteristics have been internalized (Pearce and Kang 1988: 29). As Clifford Geertz has explained, without culture,

> [h]uman beings would be unworkable monstrosities with very few useful instincts, fewer recognizable sentiments, and no intellect; mental basket cases. As our central nervous system ... grew up in great part in interaction with culture, it is incapable of directing our behavior or organizing our experience without the guidance provided by systems of significant symbols ... Such symbols are thus not mere expressions, instrumentalities, or correlates of our biological, psychological, and social existence, they are prerequisites of it. (Geertz 1973: 49)

Geertz has defined culture as 'historically transmitted patterns of meanings embodied in symbols, a system of inherited conceptions expressed in symbolic forms by means of which men [and women] communicate, perpetuate, and develop their knowledge about and attitudes towards life' (Geertz 1973: 89). Another oft-cited definition takes culture to be all the 'historically created designs for living, explicit and implicit, rational, irrational, and nonrational, which exist at any given time as potential guides for human behavior' (Longva 1991: 12).

Ali Mazrui suggests seven functions for culture. First, it helps to provide lenses of perception and cognition. How people view the world is greatly conditioned by one or more cultural paradigms to which they have been exposed. Second, it motivates human behaviour, whereby people tend to respond behaviourally in a particular manner. Third, culture provides criteria of evaluation of what is deemed better or worse, ugly or beautiful, moral or immoral, attractive or repulsive. Fourth, it is a basis of people's identity, as can be seen from how religion and race are often a basis for solidarity or a cause of hostility. Fifth, culture is a mode of communication, through language as well as many other forms of communication of ideas. Sixth, it also provides a basis of stratification, since class, rank and status are profoundly conditioned by cultural variables. For example, the fact that a university education has become a major factor in redefining status and gradation in modern African societies indicates that the cultural criteria for stratification have changed. Seventh, culture regulates the system of production and consumption, as patterns of consumption sometimes affect production as profoundly as production helps to shape consumption (Mazrui 1990: 7).

Glenn Fisher has explored the relationship between culture and what is popularly called 'mindsets', in discussing how contrasts in habits of perception and patterns of reasoning affect give-and-take on the international scene. He defined culture as a pre-tested design, a store of knowledge and an entire system of coping skills that has been crafted by preceding generations, a design that has been socially created, tested and shared, and one that can be transmitted to the next generation. In other words, culture is learned and shared behaviour, which is important because it systematizes the way people do things (Fisher 1988: 45, 46). It takes considerable effort to override our habitual ways of perceiving and reasoning, to break out of established mindsets (Fisher 1988: 25). The function of culture is to establish a more or less homogenous set of beliefs and assumptions by means of which everyone can project their perceptions and expectations on to other people without thinking about it. This provides the sense of security that comes with predictability; it is the cement that holds societies together by vastly simplifying interaction and cooperation. Deep culture is internalized and does not ordinarily need to be examined or questioned; it is the foundation for basic beliefs, for common sense and conventional wisdom (Fisher 1988: 67). In most systems, law is more a codification of what the society already believes and values, a codification of the mindsets that are at work as related to commercial dealings, marriage, settling conflicts and so forth. Conformity with the law can therefore be based more on sharing the mindset than on fearing the sanction (Fisher 1988: 106).

A similar analysis would apply to the notion of 'tradition', which is often applied to non-Western people who seek to live up to norms unfamiliar to the West or are perceived as resistant to Western (or westernized) practices and values. But the terms culture and tradition are often used interchangeably in anthropological literature, whereby 'tradition is not taken in the sense of the dead weight of an ossified past but as something that people inherit, employ, transmute, add to, and transmit' (Barth 1982: 80). As Tore Lindholm explains, in any societal collectivity, there are certain repertories of practice (skills, competencies, the exercise of rules or frameworks, opinions, aspirations, sensibilities, roles or institutions) that are taken for granted, and shared, as a matter of course. Newcomers to the collectivity have no viable alternative but to acquire those repertories if they are to have access to the activities and experiences that define social practice. As historical social structures, traditions are shared and unquestioned repertories which are reproduced by the in-dividuals in a given generation, passed on to newcomers who are included in the collectivity when they receive and continue the practice, while passing it on to other newcomers, as they arrive (Lindholm 1985: 109, 110). Therefore, traditions are reproduced, and transformed, only through the activities of individuals, and are suspended or discontinued when the upholders of a given tradition entertain viable alternatives to it (Lindholm 1985: 108). His main point in this regard is that traditions are reproduced only through intentional human agency, as an outcome of an ongoing exercise of unquestioned and shared repertories for whatever agents do or make or suffer, though not neces-sarily as the product or object intended by those agents (Lindholm 1985: 111). Traditions cannot exist independently of the activities they govern, but by existing only in continuing practices they constitute people's spontaneously given and immediately shared anticipations of the future (Lindholm 1985: 114).

A particularly helpful approach to our subject here is that presented by Ann Swidler who has criticized confining the role of culture to shaping ultimate action by supplying ultimate ends or values towards which action is directed, thus making values the central causal element of culture. The analysis of culture she proposes is based on an image of culture as a 'tool kit' of symbols, stories, rituals and world-views, which people may use in varying configurations to solve different kinds of problems. According to Swidler, culture has an independent causal role because it shapes the capacities from which such strategies of action are constructed:

People do not build lines of action from scratch, choosing actions one at a time as efficient means to given ends. Instead, they construct chains of action beginning with at least some pre-fabricated links. Culture influences action through the shape and organization of those links, not by determining the ends to which they are put ... A culture is not a unified system that pushes action in a consistent direction. Rather, it is more like a 'tool kit' from which actors select different pieces for constructing lines of action ... if culture provides the tools with which persons construct lines of action, then styles or strategies of action will be more persistent than the ends people seek to attain. Indeed, people will come to value ends for which their cultural equipment is well suited. (Swidler 1986: 277)

Other authors have also underscored the ability of human beings to change their culture. For Diane Austin-Broos, culture is the condition of humankind, our very mode of existence, but the fact that human beings make, indeed create, the various cultures in which we live means that we 'constantly carry with us the capacity to transform society and create new human environments' (Austin-Broos [ed.] 1987: xix).

To analyse culture's causal effects, Swidler suggests, one should focus on 'strategies of action', that is to say, persistent ways of ordering action through time. Therefore, one should see culture's causal significance not in defining ends of action, but in providing cultural components that are used to construct strategies of action (Swidler 1986: 273). She notes that, according to Max Weber, human beings are motivated by ideal and material interests. Ideal interests, such as the desire to be saved from the torments of hell, are also ends-oriented, except that these ends are derived from symbolic realities. Interests are the engines of action, pushing it along, but ideas define the destinations human beings seek to reach (inner-worldly versus outer-worldly possibilities of salvation, for example) and the means for getting there (mystical versus ascetic techniques of salvation). But the question she suggests is: how does this view affect the selection of the strategies of action people tend to make and implement? (Swidler 1986: 274).

More recent 'cultural studies' scholarship would emphasize material and political factors over ideal interests and ends-orientation, but one can also see dynamic mutual influence between the two, instead of seeing these competing explanations as independent or mutually exclusive. This synergy between ideal interests and material conditions is better reflected, in my view, in Swidler's inquiry about the selection of strategies of action people tend to make and implement, whatever their reasons may be.

Taking this emphasis on human agency in selecting among alternative strategies of action in an organic relationship between ends and means as our point of departure, we suggest that the increasing availability of human rights norms and institutions as part of the present tool kits of African societies can enhance the possibilities of building strategies of action to promote and protect these rights as a culturally sanctioned objective. But to emphasize human agency also means that one should not take any particular direction of change as inevitable or automatic, whether in favour of or against the protection of human rights. People have to make certain choices, and engage in particular forms of sustained action, if one outcome or another is to be realistically expected. As Mahmood Mamdani suggests, culture does not explain the choices people make because it is full of tension, diversity and differentiation, rather than compact and singular as it is sometimes made out to be (Mamdani 1996: 226). From this perspective, one can see the possibilities of strategies of action in support of human rights in any culture, but the question becomes how to promote those possibilities into the actual direction of cultural transformation in a specific society. ·

Since individuals and groups tend selectively to call upon diverse cultural resources from which they can construct strategies of action, it is important to understand the circumstances under which those choices are made, by whom and for which purposes. For example, as Swidler explains, while in all situations people select certain elements from their cultural tool kit, the influence of culture in settled lives is especially strong in structuring those un-institu-tionalized but recurrent situations in which people act in concert. Settled cultures constrain action over time because of the high costs of cultural retooling to adopt new patterns of action (Swidler 1986: 284). In what she calls 'cultural lag', people 'do not readily take advantage of new structural opportunities which would require them to abandon established ways of life. This reticence is not because people cling to cultural values, but because they are reluctant to abandon familiar strategies of action for which they have the cultural equipment' (Swidler 1986: 281). It is true that a distinction between 'settled' and 'unsettled' cultures is problematic in principle for implying that any culture is too settled for change, in addition to the practical difficulty of deciding who is to characterize a culture as settled or not, and by what criteria. Nevertheless, one can see clear indications of 'unsettledness' in some aspects of a culture at certain times, in comparison to other aspects of the same culture at a different time. In other words, an appreciation of cycles of en-trenchment and openness to change may be useful in understanding the conditions and process of cultural transformation. By understanding these processes, one can assess the relative degree to which some aspects of culture are more open to change at one time rather than at another time.

Applying this analysis to the African context, one can argue that the various forms of political instability, economic uncertainty, social upheaval and demographic dislocation which affect most parts of the continent mean that there are stronger possibilities of cultural transformation in these societies. It is clear, for example, that civil war in countries like Liberia, Rwanda, Somalia and Sudan, or drastic political change as in post-apartheid South Africa, are more conducive to significant change in the cultures of those societies than times of peace and greater political and social stability in the same societies. But to expect relatively rapid and significant transformation in unsettled African cultures is not to suggest a particular direction of change because that will depend on the choices people make for themselves and the context within which they have to act in furtherance of their own existential objectives.

The point we draw from this analysis for our purposes here is that cultural transformation has to be mediated between the pull of continuity and the push of the existence of viable competing alternatives, as these two operate on and through human agency. Since culture is a tool kit from which actors select different pieces for constructing lines of action, in so doing people are making choices between continuity and its alternative. But because culture is the medium of people's basic solidarity and the vehicle of their spontaneity, a rivalling alternative to any aspect of culture can be a viable choice only to the extent that it is sufficiently consistent with the basic qualities of the culture in question as to become part of the shared and unquestioned repertory of practice. In other words, people are unlikely to opt for a proposed alternative in an arbitrary and capricious manner because the new course of action would normally appear to be counter-intuitive, and probably threatening, to those who are supposed to select it over the established ways of their culture. However, the role of human agency would also lead one to expect the perception of what is counter-intuitive and threatening to change over time, as people come to accept different directions of change to which their new cultural equipment is well suited. This is more likely to happen in unsettled cultures than in settled ones, but, as emphasized earlier, no culture is settled enough to avoid change.

To underscore the role of human agency in the process of cultural transformation does not mean that adherents of a culture or tradition are in complete control of all the elements or conditions under which selections from the cultural tool kit are made at any given time. A living tradition or culture (one that is maintained in force) is to its adherents something obvious, unproblematic and taken for granted. As such, the contents of a tradition may remain unnoticed among its bearers until it is attacked, broken or breaks down (Lindholm 1985: 108). In other words, since the way of doing things within a culture is the basis of people's sense of solidarity, spontaneity and basis of shared expectations, the introduction of new elements to the cultural kit is usually resisted as foreign or alien. Moreover, the scope and intensity of resistance are probably correlated to the degree to which the new elements are seen as a deliberate attack on the integrity of the culture and the security of the social order. Nevertheless, 'breaks with tradition' are constantly happening in all cultures, though not necessarily as intended consequences that are immediately observed or acknowledged. As Giddens says, 'all action consists of social practices, situated in time-space, and organized in skilled and knowledge-able fashion by human agents. But such knowledgeability is always "bounded" by unacknowledged conditions of action on the one side, and unintended consequences on the other' (Giddens 1981: 19).

In concluding this section, we emphasize that human agency is always present on all sides of the issue, namely, on the part of proponents as well as opponents of change, and certainly in the case of those who are asked to change or modify their strategies of action or behaviour. As Mineke Schipper observes, one should always focus on the subject – not only on who is speaking, seeing and acting, but also who is not speaking, or does not have the right to speak in the context. One should note whose perspective is, or is not, repres-ented (Schipper 1993: 46, 47). Accordingly, one must take into account the history and present context of power relations within a society in order to understand the role of human agency in cultural transformation. How certain voices or positions get to be privileged or disregarded in the selection of specific strategies of action from the cultural tool kit is not a mysterious, unknowable or arbitrary process. Unmasking the factors that determine these and other conditions of internal discourse is essential for understanding how cultural transformation works, it is hoped with a view to using that to promote stronger and more sustainable commitment to the implementation of human rights.

Cultural Transformation and Human Rights in Post-colonial Africa

There is very little understanding of the actual process of cultural change or transformation. 'We do not know why something that has often been said before will suddenly catch on, or why both events and opinions seem to remain static for a long time, and suddenly begin to move, and keep on moving. Most mysterious of all is how a consensus of opinion forms, and why it takes the shape it does' (Daniel 1975: 88). In our view, however, better understanding of the inner working of the formation and transformation of cultural norms or practices can be achieved by examining the synergy of context and process. For our purposes here, the focus should be on how the context, and the terms of the interaction of actors and factors, influence transformation, whether in favour of, or opposition to, the domestic protection of human rights.

With regard to context, we are concerned with the role of the post-colonial state in Africa in its broader regional and global setting. While each state should be understood in its own specific pre-colonial history, type of colonial experience, and political and economic conditions at independence, it would be useful to consider such factors in the light of the broader processes of interaction between the local and the global. As briefly explained below, there are political, social and cultural, as well as economic, dimensions to what is commonly referred to as 'globalization'. For our purposes here, we focus on the dynamic of the pull of self-determination and domestic jurisdiction, on the one hand, and the push of diminishing sovereignty under conditions of multifaceted globalization, on the other. By 'process' we are referring to the relationship between what we call internal discourse within each culture, and cross-cultural dialogue between cultures (An-Na'im [ed.] 1992: 4–5).

In our view, understanding the operation of process in context is important for mediating the dichotomy between the so-called internal and external actors and factors who participate in cultural transformation, and the likely outcome of their interaction. However, this duality of context and process is used here merely for the purposes of analysis, without suggesting a dichotomy between the two. In fact, many of the factors indicated below under the rubric of context can also be seen as part of process, and vice versa. The impact of such factors on each aspect is also contingent and ambivalent. Globalization, for example, is a vehicle of economic liberalization and consequent political penetration through such processes as the decentralization of production, mobility of capital and labour and international trade regimes. At the same time, and by its very nature, globalization can also facilitate mobilization and collaboration between global social movements and non-governmental organizations working on the local protection of human rights, or of the environment.

Moreover, African cultures and their transformations should be understood in historical perspective. This will be difficult and problematic not only because of the lack or inadequacy of written documentation for the pre-colonial period, but also because all phases of the history of any society are often contested for the purposes of the present. But that is hardly a good reason for rejecting the historical component in culture. So, such factors as the nature and dynamics of political organization, social institutions and economic relations during the pre-colonial and colonial periods should be taken into account in understanding the nature of the post-colonial state and its role in cultural transformation today. In probing the past so as to understand the present, however, one should note that such historical reconstructions can only be statements of probability rather than established historical fact (Bascom and Herskovits [eds] 1959: 8).

The state, with its juridical sovereignty, extensive powers and relatively much larger resources, is a key element in the context of cultural transformation everywhere, both as an object of contestation among the competing perspectives, as well as a proponent of the policy priorities of those who control it. At the local level, many actors seek directly or indirectly to capture the state in order to implement, or at least influence its behaviour in favour of, their own concerns. Moreover, its presumed monopoly over the legitimate use of force induces all other actors to look to it as the arbiter of disputes. It is therefore clear that the nature and functioning of the state are particularly important for the prospects and orientation of cultural transformation. The exclusive or hegemonic control of the state by one religious or ethnic faction of the population is bound to provoke severe strife and probably civil war, as can be seen in the tragic conflicts in Liberia, Rwanda, Somalia and Sudan and many other countries. In these cases, cultural transformation is likely to be manipulated to support the militant or confrontational objectives of each side to the conflict, rather than enhance peaceful coexistence and cooperation.

The post-colonial state in Africa has been cogently characterized by Patrick Chabal as 'with few exceptions, both overdeveloped and soft. It was overdeveloped because it was erected, artificially, on the foundations of the colonial state. It did not grow organically from within civil society. It was soft because, although in theory all-powerful, it scarcely had the administrative and political means of its dominance. Neither did it have an economic basis on which to rest political power' (Chabal [ed.] 1986: 13). Another study of the colonial/post-colonial state finds it hardly surprising that the post-colonial state followed so closely its parent, the colonial state. The legitimacy of the state is derived from international agreements, earlier among European colonial states, and through the UN Charter and the Organization of African Unity (OAU) since 1963, rather than the consent of their African populations. The colonial system of government organized according to European colonial theory and practice (tempered by expediency) was simply continued after independence, but only as a poor copy. Colonial economic relations, legal systems and administrative policies were largely continued by the post-colonial state. Even the lack of constitutional standing for the majority of African populations under colonial rule was continued after independence through the effective exclusion of major segments of citizens from the political process, despite the explicit terms of the constitutions of the newly independent African states (Jackson and Rosberg 1986: 5–6).

To almost all African societies, independence usually signified the transfer of control over authoritarian power structures and processes of government from colonial masters to local elites (Ayoade 1988: 104). Lacking an effective presence in most of the state's territory, ruling elites tend to focus on controlling the government apparatus and patronage system. Instead of seeking popular legitimacy and accountability to the people at large, ruling elites strive to retain the support of key traditional leaders (Ayoade 1988: 107–15). State security became the security of the regime in power, with no possibility of transparency in the functioning of security forces, or of their political and legal accountability for their actions. Constitutional instruments, where they were allowed to exist, have repeatedly failed to hold governments legally or politically accountable to their own citizens (Okoth-Ogendo 1991). Moreover, the majority of constitutions were either suspended or radically altered by military usurpers or single-party states within a few years of independence. It is not surprising, therefore, that African societies tend to regard the post-colonial state with profound mistrust, instead of with a sense of ownership, expectation of protection and service, and a general belief in their ability to influence its functioning. They tolerate its existence as an unavoidable evil, but prefer to have the least interaction with its institutions and processes (Young 1994: 5).[5]

Of particular importance for our purposes here is the continuation of colonial attitudes to rights. Organized differently in rural areas from urban ones, the colonial state contained a duality of two forms of power under a single hegemonic authority. 'Urban power spoke the language of civil society and civil rights, rural power of community and culture. Civil power claimed to protect rights, customary power pledged to enforce tradition. The former was organized on the principle of differentiation to check the concentration of power, the latter around the principle of fusion to ensure a unitary authority' (Mamdani 1996: 16). Once more, these attitudes continue for decades under both civilian or military governments.

To emphasize such strong continuities from the colonial to the post-colonial state does not mean that there is no tension between the two worlds. In fact, suspicion of the motives and intentions of the former colonial powers and their allies remains a strong factor in all cultural interchange between African and Western societies today. There is a genuine sense of moral indignation felt by millions of people all over the world about colonial rule and post-colonial Western exploitation and African dependencies. To many opposition groups and community leaders, the knowledge that such exploitation continues is grounds for suspecting ulterior motives beneath whatever Western powers tend to support in international relations, especially their advocacy of human rights (Daniel 1975: 22, 23).

Another key element of the context of cultural transformation is civil society, which is supposed to be the partner/protagonist of the state, whereby their relationship is often described from one of two perspectives. For the state-centrists, the question would be whether the state has failed to penetrate society sufficiently and is therefore hostage to it. For the society-centrists, it is whether society has failed to hold the state accountable and is therefore prey to it (Mamdani 1996: 11). For example, Ali Mazrui cautions 'that whoever captures the state is in mortal danger of being captured by it … The survival of the state becomes the paramount aim, even if this means repressing fellow workers or fellow nationals' (Mazrui 1990: 55). Upon capturing the state, leaders of liberation and grassroots movements become converted to the state system itself.

As a historical construct, civil society is said to be the result of an all-embracing process of differentiation: of power in the state and division of labour in the economy, giving rise to an autonomous legal sphere to govern civil life (Mamdani 1996: 14). The realm of civil society is not the market but public opinion and culture. Its agents are intellectuals, and its hallmarks are voluntary association and free publicity, the basis of an autonomous organizational and expressive life. Although autonomous of the state, this life cannot be independent of it, for the guarantor of the autonomy of civil society can be none other than the state, presumably in interaction with civil society itself. A specific constellation of social forces organized in and through civil society may be the guarantor of the autonomy of civil society, but they can do so only by ensuring a form of the state and a corresponding legal regime to undergird the autonomy of civil society (Mamdani 1996:15).

Whatever role civil society may have is also conditioned by the nature of the state in its global context. In addition to the global system of sovereign states, social movements are also constrained by the global capitalist system and its implications. 'The underprivileged races, classes and groups like women or ethnic/religious minorities, have not as yet made a difference to the fate of the two global systems' (Mazrui 1990: 58). Generally speaking, men dominate both the state system and the capitalist global economy. In West Africa, for example, women have been conspicuous in trade and marketing, but this is only in relation to small-scale economic activities. The ratio of men to women changes dramatically upon considering the growing internationalization of local economies, with 'more men taking decisions on boards of directors or assuming control in factories, overshadowing the "market ladies" of yesteryear … Similarly, greater mechanization of African economies has resulted in a diminishing feminine share in them' (Mazrui 1990: 60).

Another integral component of the context of cultural transformation is the nature of interaction between different levels of so-called internal and external actors or factors. With regard to this aspect of the context, it can be argued that human rights can be an instrument of mutual cooperation between European powers and African nationalist leaders in a new form of 're-colonialization' of Africa that allows colonial power relations to continue without direct colonialism (Hargreaves 1996; Bach 1993). Instead of the dependency of former African colonies on their colonial powers diminishing, there are now multiple and complex dependencies, ranging from daily reliance on colonial ties in economic activities, political processes and security arrangements, to technological, legal, administrative and educational matters (Mamdani: 145, 146). Even the internal security of the ruling elites against political challenge is sometimes 'delegated' to former colonial powers, as shown by the continued French military presence in several west and central African countries to 'keep the peace' (Gambari 1995). These complex dependencies continue to intensify under the growing globalization of the post-colonial world.

Globalization is normally taken to mean such phenomena as the transformation of relations between states, institutions, groups and individuals; the universalization of certain practices, identities and structures; and the expression of the global restructuring that has occurred in recent decades within the framework of modern capitalist relations. But what many popular definitions fail to appreciate is 'the importance of notions such as coercion, conflict, polarization, domination, inequality, exploitation and injustice … there is little or nothing about monopolies, disruptions and dislocations of the labor and other markets, the emergence of a global regulatory chaos and possible anomie and how these are being exploited for gains' (Aina 1997: 11). To the extent that globalization is the expression of existing power relations, it will become the means by which developed countries sustain their economic and political hegemony over developing countries. Should those power relations be transformed to reflect partnership in development and more equitable distribution of wealth and power around the world, globalization will become the instrument of justice and liberation for all human societies.

As suggested earlier, the process of cultural transformation can be seen in terms of internal discourse and cross-cultural dialogue, but this distinction is only for the purposes of analysis, as the two processes constantly overlap and interact. There are many aspects to cross-cultural dialogue, including inter-state economic, political and other relations. Regarding human rights in particular, the governments of some developed countries, mainly in Europe and North America, claim to seek to influence the governments of developing countries through what is known as political conditionality, whereby the provision of foreign aid and assistance is linked to the 'human rights record' of African or Asian governments. But the nature, size and scope and other features of such aid are determined by considerations of the domestic politics of Western countries, rather than the needs and conditions of developing countries. Moreover, there is also the strong role of the principle of exchange in the capitalist ethos. 'Much of the transfer of capital to developing countries ends up by profiting the giver more than the receiver. Conditions are imposed on the receiver, designed to "maximize returns" for the donor countries' (Mazrui 1990: 202).

Cross-cultural dialogue is also exceedingly difficult because of universally deeply engrained ethnocentrism. 'It is common to all cultures to dislike what is not common to them ... xenophobia is a basic condition of humanity. Unfamiliarity creates misunderstanding, and misunderstanding, suspicion, and hatred and suspicion grow rapidly from small beginnings' (Daniel 1975: 7–10). As Mineke Schipper has explained:

[P]eople tend to reject differentness, and the definition of what is human often extends no further than the borders of one's own group, country, race, or sex, to the borders of one's own language, continent and culture. The 'barbarians' are always the others ... During the twentieth century, a Western multinational 'Otherness' industry has developed, allowing a relatively small but powerful group to decide the fate, content, form, presence, and absence of its Others – to decide whether, where, and how these Others are supposed to exist, to be seen, or to be ignored ... The Other has been studied and classified in terms of appearance, gender, language, behavior and customs. When the results of these investigations are presented, one is told that this is what 'they' look like, that this is their reality, or that this is how our ancestors or learned predecessors characterized 'them' ... the assumption that only the representatives of a single group are qualified to interpret the world ... prevents dialogue and perpetuates a stereotype that is exploited to label Others and to justify their exclusion from a mutually beneficial partnership. (Schipper 1993: 39–40)

Mike Featherstone has suggested that by trying to employ a broader definition of culture and to think more in terms of processes, it might be possible to talk of the globalization of culture. Processes of cultural integration and cultural disintegration are taking place not only on an inter-state level, but also at a trans-national level. 'It therefore may be possible to point to trans-societal cultural processes which take a variety of forms, some of which have preceded the inter-state relations' (Featherstone 1990: 1). Instead of the binary logic of seeing culture in mutually exclusive terms of homogeneity/heterogeneity, integration/disintegration, or unity/diversity, there should be an inquiry into the grounds and generative processes of the formation of cultural images, as well as the inter-group struggles and interdependencies (Featherstone 1990: 2). Increasing cultural interrelatedness is generating a series of processes which produce both cultural homogeneity and cultural disorder, in linking together previously isolated pockets of relatively homogenous culture which in turn produces more complex images of the other as well as generating identity-reinforcing reactions. This global interrelatedness is also producing trans-national cultures, as genuine 'third cultures' oriented beyond national boundaries (Featherstone 1990: 6). This is not to suggest that there is or will be a unified global culture, but rather to indicate the growing possibility of global cultures in the plural. 'The world is a singular place which entails the proliferation of new cultural forms for encounters' (Featherstone 1990: 11).

Conclusion

To recall the basic tension underlying the human rights paradigm, as discussed above, human beings cannot help starting from their own moral perspective, which contains both moral principles about justice that people tend to believe should apply to the actions of others outside their own society or community, as well as moral principles about respecting the autonomy of others, thereby indicating the limitation of one's ability to judge how others live their lives, individually and collectively (Carrens 1992: 591). It is true, we believe, that the requirements of justice set moral limits to the pursuit of cultural preservation, but the question is whose conception of justice should apply. Since different cultures embody varied moral views, would it not be a form of cultural imperialism to use the standards of one culture to judge another (Carrens 1992: 589)? The only way to avoid that charge, we suggest, is by developing and applying a collaboratively constructed set of standards that are at least not peculiar to a specific culture, if not equally valid for all cultures. This is what the human rights paradigm should seek to achieve, and is capable of achieving.

The basic point we have tried to argue for in this chapter is that the tension inherent to the notion of the universality of human rights should be acknowledged and mediated, rather than overlooked or suppressed. Successful mediation is possible, we suggest, provided it is appreciated that cultures evolve and change over time; their different, sometimes conflicting, features are subject to many different interpretations by both members and outsiders; and that the extent to which a particular culture provides value and meaning to the lives of the people who participate in it may vary among the members of the culture and may itself be the subject of different interpretations. It is also important to acknowledge that all cultures are influenced, directly and indirectly, by other cultures; and that members of one culture may be exposed or have access to other cultures, and even participate as members in one or more other cultures (Carrens 1992: 551, 552). This is particularly true under the present conditions of growing intensive globalization, as emphasized earlier in this chapter.

In the final analysis, the main purpose of this chapter is to emphasize that a clear understanding of the processes of cultural transformation is always important for those concerned with international human rights norms, whether as active advocates, scholars, policy-makers or the public at large. The thesis presented in this chapter is that one needs to appreciate how perceptions of difference are constructed by human agency before one can seek to change them, also through human agency. Whether through this and/or some other approaches, we believe that the issues raised in this chapter, and in the Introduction to this book, have to be addressed if the human rights paradigm is to play its role in the protection of human dignity and promotion of social justice within and among societies and communities throughout the world.

Notes

1. For extensive materials on, and discussion of, a wide range of issues in this field see, generally, Steiner and Alston (eds) (1996); and Martin et al. (1997).

2. See Rawls (1987). This idea is applied to the justification of universal human rights in different cultures by several authors from different perspectives in An-Na'im and Deng (eds) (1990) and An-Na'im (ed.) (1992: 1–15).

3. Article 2(7) of the Charter of the United Nations, 1945, and Declaration on Principles of International Law Concerning Friendly Relations and Cooperation among States (GA Res. 2625, Annex UN GAOR, 25th Sess. [Supp. No. 28 at 122], UN Doc. A/8028; ILM 1292 [1970]). In relation to African states see, for example, Young (1994: 27–30). See, generally, Keller and Rothchild (eds) (1996).

4. It should be noted that despite the Western origins of present human rights formulations, there is also strong philosophical and ideological opposition to at least some of these rights. On these two currents in the West, see V. Leary, 'The Effect of Western Perspectives

on International Human Rights', in An-Na'im and Deng (eds) (1990: 15–30); V. Leary 'Postliberal Strands in Western Human Rights Theory: Personalist-communitarian Perspectives', in An-Na'im (ed.) (1992: 105–32).

5. Young (1994: 2–12) discusses the crisis of the post-colonial state and the search for explanation. He also examines 'the integral state' which he defines as 'a design of perfected hegemony, whereby the state seeks to achieve unrestricted domination over civil society' (pp. 287–90).

References

Aina, T. A. (1997) *Globalization and Social Policy in Africa: Issues and Research Directions*, Dakar, Senegal: CODESRIA Working Paper Series 6/96.

An-Na'im, A. A. (1990) 'Problems of Universal Cultural Legitimacy for Human Rights', in A. A. An-Na'im and F. M. Deng (eds), *Human Rights in Africa: Cross-Cultural Perspectives*, Washington, DC: Brookings Institution, pp. 331–67.

— (2001) 'The Legal Protection of Human Rights in Africa: How to Do More with Less', in A. Sarat and T. R. Kearns (eds), *Human Rights: Concepts, Contests, Contingencies*, Ann Arbor, MI: Michigan University Press, pp. 89–115.

— (ed.) (1992) *Human Rights in Cross-Cultural Perspectives: Quest for Consensus*, Philadelphia, PA: University of Pennsylvania Press.

An-Na'im, A. A. and F. M. Deng (eds) (1990) *Human Rights in Africa: Cross-Cultural Perspectives*, Washington, DC: Brookings Institution.

Austin-Broos, D. J. (ed.) (1987) *Creating Culture: Profiles in the Study of Culture*, Boston, MA: Allen and Unwin.

Ayoade, J. A. A. (1988) 'States without Citizens: An Emerging African Phenomenon', in D. Rothchild and N. Chazan (eds), *The Precarious Balance: State and Society in Africa*, Boulder, CO: Westview Press, pp. 100–18.

Bach, D. C. (1993) 'Reappraising Postcolonial Geopolitics: Europe, Africa and the End of the Cold War', in T. Ranger and O. Vaughan (eds), *Legitimacy and the State in Twentieth-Century Africa: Essays in Honour of A. H. Kirk-Greene*, London: Macmillan, pp. 247–57.

Barth, F. (1982) 'Problems in Conceptualizing Cultural Pluralism with Illustrations from Sohar, Oman', in D. Maybury-Lewis (ed.), *The Prospects for Plural Societies*, Washington, DC: American Ethnological Society, pp. 77–87.

Bascom, W. R. and M. J. Herskovits (eds) (1959) *Continuity and Change in African Cultures*, Chicago, IL: University of Chicago Press.

Carrens, J. H (1992) 'Democracy and Respect for Difference: The Case of Fiji', *University of Michigan Journal of Law Reform*, 25: 547–631.

Chabal, P. (ed.) (1986) *Political Domination in Africa: Reflections on the Limits of Power*, Cambridge: Cambridge University Press.

Daniel, N. (1975) *The Cultural Barrier: Problems in the Exchange of Ideas*, Edinburgh: Edinburgh University Press.

Featherstone, M. (ed.) (1990) *Global Culture: Nationalism, Globalization and Modernity*, Newbury Park, CA: Sage.

Fisher, G. (1988) *Mindsets: The Role of Culture and Perception in International Relations*, Yarmouth, ME: Intercultural Press.

Gambari, I. A. (1995) 'The Role of Foreign Intervention in African Reconstruction', in I. W. Zartman (ed.), *Collapsed States: The Disintegration and Restoration of Legitimate Authority*, Boulder, CO: Lynne Rienner, pp. 221–33.

Geertz, C. (1973) *The Interpretation of Cultures*, New York: Basic Books.

Giddens, A. (1981) *Contemporary Critique of Historical Materialism*, Berkeley, CA: University of California Press.

Hargreaves, J. D. (1996) *Decolonization in Africa*, 2nd edn, New York: Longman.

Jackson, R. H. and C. G. Rosberg (1986) 'Sovereignty and Underdevelopment: Juridicial Statehood in the African Crisis', *Journal of Modern African Studies*, 24: 1–32.

Keller, E. J. and D. Rothchild (eds) (1996) *Africa in the New International Order: Rethinking State Sovereignty and Regional Security*, Boulder, CO: Lynne Rienner.

Lindholm, T. (1985) 'Coming to Terms with Tradition', in H. Hoibraaten and I. Gullvag (eds), *Essays in Pragmatic Philosophy I*, Oslo: Norwegian University Press, pp. 103–17.

Longva, A. N. (1991) 'Anthropology and the Challenge of Tradition', unpublished paper, Department of Anthropology, University of Oslo.

Mamdani, M. (1990) 'The Social Basis of Constitutionalism in Africa', *Journal of Modern African Studies*, 28: 359–74.

— (1996) *Citizen and Subject: Contemporary Africa and the Legacy of Late Colonialism*, Princeton, NJ: Princeton University Press.

Martin, F. F. et al. (1997) *International Human Rights Law and Practice*, The Hague: Kluwer Law International.

Mazrui, A. A. (1990) *Cultural Forces in World Politics*, Portsmouth, NH: Heinemann.

Okoth-Ogendo, H.W. (1991) 'Constitutions without Constitutionalism: Reflections on an African Political Paradox', in I. G. Shivji (ed.), *State and Constitutionalism: An African Debate on Democracy*, Harare, Zimbabwe: Southern African Political Economy Series (SAPES) Trust, pp. 3–25.

Pearce, W. B. and K. Kang (1988) 'Conceptual Migrations: Understanding "Travelers'" Tales for Cross-Cultural Adaptation', in Y. Y. Kim and W. B. Gudykunst (eds), *Cross-Cultural Adaptation: Current Approaches*, Newbury Park, CA: Sage, pp. 20–41.

Rawls, J. (1987) 'The Idea of Overlapping Consensus', *Oxford Journal of Legal Studies*, 7 (1): 1–25.

Schiper, M. (1993) 'Culture, Identity and Interdiscursivity', *Research in African Literature*, 24: 39–48.

Steiner, H. and P. Alston (eds) (1996) *International Human Rights in Context: Law, Politics, Morals: Text and Materials*, Oxford: Clarendon Press.

Swidler, A. (1986) 'Culture in Action: Symbols and Strategies', *American Sociological Review*, 51: 273–86.

Young, C. (1994) *The African Colonial State in Comparative Perspective*, New Haven, CT: Yale University Press.

TWO

Human Rights and Cultural Branding: Who Speaks and How

Martin Chanock

Rights and Culture

This chapter is an effort to unravel the discourses around the question of 'culture' and the connections between current modes of explaining the world after the end of the Cold War and the current distribution of power. A number of new narrative paradigms – the New World Order, the End of History, the Clash of Civilizations – have recently appeared as we try to come to grips with explaining the present to ourselves and working out new narratives to project into the future. The collapse of Marxism as theory and state communism as practice, and the development of theorizing about an era of globalization have naturalized 'culture' as a vital node of explanation. It is always hard to contextualize our own ways of thinking, but we should be clear at least that there is a close association between power and explanation. In this context it would be apt to recall the long coexistence of Empire with race as the node around which many social scientific explanations of human differences, intelligence, social organization and the capacity for self-government revolved. For a long time, race and theories of racial difference held a central place in 'realistic' explanations in the West,[1] and political and scientific analysis turned around race. It is almost too easy to contextualize such thinking and its connection with Empire now, but harder to come to grips accurately with the connections in the present between the ways in which power is distributed in the world and the growing centrality of culture as an explanatory tool.

In essence the suggestion in this chapter is that those rights discourses in which culture is invoked as an argument against universalism now largely belong to rulers, not to those who may need their rights protected, those who talk in terms of wrongs and needs, not rights and culture. There is typically a wide gap between those who speak for cultures and those who live the culture spoken about. While cultures are complex and multi-vocal, in the representation of cultures the voices of the elites overwhelm others. Assertions about culture tend to be totalizing and simplifying, privileging some voices and patterns of acts, and ignoring and marginalizing others. I consider below the resemblances between the processes of cultural representation and those of the discourses of advertising, the most prominent form of persuasive communication in the globalizing world.

Rights, Culture and Religion

This section will remind us of some basic elements of the history of rights in the West that were overshadowed during the Cold War, during which Western propaganda presented rights as inherent to a particular path of historical evolution and progress. The section points to certain features of the history of rights: that the entrenching of rights in politics and law typically has its origins not in processes of cultural evolution, but has come about as the result of major conflicts and sharp breaks with the past; that conceptualizations of rights have necessarily been universalist in nature; and that they have been inextricably linked to the triumph of secularism in the state and the breaking of the hold of religious orthodoxy on public institutions.

The major foundational rights declarations have had what Preuss has called 'catastrophic origins' (Rosenfeld [ed.] 1994: 150). The British Bill of Rights, the American Bill of Rights, and the French Declaration of the Rights of Man all arose from civil war, or wars for independence, or revolution. Each reflects a revolt against specific oppressions, specific wrongs.[2] The Universal Declaration of the Rights of Man followed the worst of global wars. More recently the new rights-based constitutional orders, first ushered in by the West German constitution, and later for the post-communist regimes of Eastern Europe, depended on a dramatic break with the practices, and the legal and political cultures, of the prior homicidal and dictatorial regimes – a repudiation of the immediate political and legal past and not an evolution. Indeed, it was the sharpness of the break which established the legitimacy of the new rights-based legal order, which was based on imported political and legal models. The same was the case with the new South African constitution. Disjunction, in other words, rather than continuity has given birth to rights. It is not easy to combine with this a cultural view of rights which implies that a consensus about rights is deeply embedded in, and reflective of, cultures. Rights would seem to belong to the disputed realm of politics rather than a deeper expressive realm of culture. Human rights have depended on the deliberate (bitterly opposed) active remaking of a new order, on a denial of the past, on a reinvention of political mythologies, not simply on an evolution of what had been historically and culturally acceptable. In doing this, the rights makers have specifically reached out towards universalism, and very often explicitly away from 'culture' in a more specific sense. Rights may be claimed by their proponents as an inherent immanent virtue but they do not simply emerge and they do not proclaim compatibility with what 'is' in a culture. They come from the fiercest of political contestation, from revolution, and from war, and if constitutionalized, depend thereafter very much on artificial legal formulations with almost infinitely variable wordings and meanings. (The protracted debates about how to word particular rights in Bills of Rights, and the endless and convoluted legal debates as to how they should be interpreted, should make this clear.)[3]

It is with this notion of catastrophic origins that we should be approaching the history of rights in the contemporary world. The past five decades have seen the end of European empires and the intense political struggles between those who wished to establish alternative regimes of power over much of the globe. These struggles have taken place first in the context of the Cold War, and now in the context of the new and disruptive processes known as globalization. War, internal violence and political repression, and not an immanent progress towards rights, have dominated recent political history.

It is also very clear from the history of rights in Western political cultures that they were established as a part of the struggle between political rights and religion, and that they have been a part of the conquest of the power of institutionalized religion in the state. In both the French and American cases the rights-based state came with (and has continued to be associated with) the firm separation of church and state. Rights, then, are a product of a continuing secularizing of political institutions, not a product of accommodation with religious power as part of state power. While they have clearly coexisted with the continuation of strong religious cultures, they have been established as a part of law and politics when state and church have been separated by political struggle. It is notable that Western political theorizing on the basis of state and society boils down to what Preuss has termed 'blood or contract' – a shared racial and ethnic kinship, or a social contract, as the basis of citizenship and community. Absent from the theorizing of the modern state has been 'belief' as an organizing basis of society. Western political, legal and constitutional thought became fundamentally secular. The absence for so long of 'belief' as part of what is discursively legitimate in Western constitutional traditions is, therefore, more than fashion or oversight but is built into the nature of constitutionalism (and concomitantly of rights discourses) itself. Current post-communist political discourses turn around the polarities of state and market and the identification of the former with coercion and the latter with consent. Within these polarities, as within the realms of public and private, Western institutions, law, theorizing and practices have now placed religion within the realm of the private and the consensual. Neither the discourses nor the institutions of Western constitutionalism appear to permit a relocation of religion into the public and coercive realm.

International Rights Standards and the African Case: The Nature of Culture

The primary problem is to identify what is meant by culture, the times at which the notion of culture is invoked, and the uses to which this invocation is put. Many of the problems posed by these questions result from a tendency to posit a concept of cultures as unities, and therefore easily distinguishable from and opposable to each other. After centuries of imperialism, and in the current period of high-velocity cultural globalization, both of which have created a complex world of fragmented ways of life and symbolic disorder, this is a fantasy. The idea of culture derived from anthropology, a discipline which studied the encapsulated exotic, is no longer appropriate. There are no longer (if ever there were) single cultures in any country, polity or legal system, but many. Cultures are complex conversations within any social formation. These conversations have many voices. Yet, as I remarked above, the concept of culture has become a prime way of describing groups and is displacing other primary labels like race, class or nationality at a particular time and in particular circumstances. This process has involved essentializing cultures and quieting the diversity of voices so that only the dominant are heard. How and when culture assumed this importance in describing group difference and political affiliation should therefore be our framing question. We may note that it is a departure from the universalism implicit in class analysis in which the worker had no country. And it is also a departure from the differentiating idea of nation. The cultural rejection of universal rights is now not based on *national* differences but assumes that above and beyond national distinctiveness (based on language, place, historical association and narrative etc.) there is something larger – European, Asian, African, or Christian, Muslim, Confucian – which distinguishes people from each other. The first of these looks suspiciously like a different way of talking about racial differences, while the second invokes not just broad differences in 'civilizations' but links them to the possession of religious truths. Why our discourses have passed from class and nation to this kind of analysis is a question of some importance. It could be said that it is a part of the development of a global narrative in a post-nation-state, post-Cold War world – as evidenced by the 'clash of civilizations' thesis. But culture has also developed, not just as a way of substituting larger aggregations for nation and class, but also as a way of distinguishing very small groups from each other. While 'nation' and 'class' seem to be dying as explanatory categories for conflict and difference, larger 'civilizations' and smaller ethnic groups have come to life as legitimate aggregations. Both find culture to be a usable discursive weapon in a world of globalized symbolization.

The African case illustrates specifically how the evolving relationship between using race as the way to describe difference, and using culture to perform the same task, is a part of the intellectual history of Empire. Even while the earlier social sciences were freeing themselves from racially determined explanations of difference, they remained within a broad narrative of cultural evolution in which there were backward cultures (which could, if guided, move forward). Cultural difference, like racial difference, was a marker of inferiority and condemnation. The practical experiences of colonial rule, and the development of the anthropology of African societies, produced changes in this paradigm. African cultures were subject to a variety of portrayals: from exotic to different but functionally equal, or functionally necessary to prevent social disintegration. For a variety of reasons, both Western governors and social scientists came to defend cultural differences. Likewise, African intellectuals abandoned an early acceptance of cultural assimilation, and celebrated, elaborated and defended difference. (A notable early example was Kenyatta 1938.) The point being laboured is simple: that discursive deployment of culture takes place within particular histories of political and intellectual power and in each has had its particular usages and meanings. Therefore, if we are now using culture as an important variable we must seriously analyse the context, reasons and meanings of its deployment. Clearly also, this is not just a matter of intellectual discourses but also of popular experiences. How and when do people experience having a cultural identity, rather than a class or national one? What can the defence of cultural authenticity mean in a world in which the conditions of symbolic production and exchange are being so dramatically altered?

The leaders (and their defenders) of those states in Africa and Asia which do not meet the standards laid down in the various international declarations of rights frequently make the claim that the rights enumerated are cultural, and are part of alien formerly dominant cultures, rather than universal. It is important to recall that this 'cultural' rejection of universal human rights is the second phase of the rejection of rights by powerful Third World elites. During the Cold War, the hostility towards civil and political rights was expressed in the rejection of their primacy in favour of social and economic rights and the right to development, upon which political rights were to wait. Now that social and economic rights have been subsumed into global rights discourses and international legal instruments, a new defence against universal rights has been raised.[4] The rejection of rights on 'cultural' grounds is clearly correct if the claim is seen as a recognition that these rights, and the ways in which they are described (and institutionalized), arise out of particular historical experiences in Western Europe and America and that they are part of a constantly worked-over narrative of the legal and political cultures of some of these countries. They were also originally 'universal' only rhetorically, and they could coexist without much discomfort not only with both Empire and slavery, but with the effective denial of the universal rights to an 'internal' majority by the exclusion of women, as well as, in varying times and places, racial minorities and a disenfranchised working class. But the claim that 'rights' are cultural does not dispose of the question of the desirability of 'rights' being universal. There is little reason why the currently dominant versions of 'culture' in parts of Africa or Asia should remain unchanged and unchallenged. They could as well be subjected to precisely the kind of cultural work that transformed a rhetoric of rights in the West applicable only to property-owning white men to one which eventually spread to encompass in form, and slowly in practice, all persons regardless of colour or gender. The achievement of both colour and gender equality in the West required and still requires a transformation of the cultures of many institutions – workplaces, trade unions, the church, professions, families, political parties, schools etc. – all at a different rate and in different ways. Gender equality, for example, could just as well have been described as alien to Western cultures as to non-Western ones. It was (and continues in important aspects to be) for example, rejected by the major Christian churches. It is the product of intense political struggle and cultural work, not immanence. This single most obvious 'gap' between Western and some other cultures is a gap that has opened very recently. Some of the intellectual difficulty in approaching this appears to lie partly in differing views about the place of history in Western and non-Western life. For some, the non-Western world appears to have cultures so deeply rooted that change would do radical harm, or at least call into question the dignity and identity of its members. Thus gender equality would threaten culture. In the 'West', a revolution in white

male attitudes towards women is absorbed into a narrative of historical progress, not as a threat to the culture, but as a strengthening of it.

One might wonder also just how much the current state of lack of rights
in Africa and Asia has anything to do with African and Asian cultures at all.
The major abuses of political rights at the state level are the products of the
political institutions bequeathed by the colonial powers. The failures of the
multi-ethnic states created by colonialism, and their powerlessness in relation
to the goals of development because of the structure and workings of the
world economy, arise from premises given to Africa, not originating in it. Why
anyone outside of the small elite which has benefited from this state of affairs
would want to defend it as culturally 'African' is not clear. On the other hand,
there are features of post-colonial African 'cultures' which do not conform
with the universalized version of rights rhetoric, particularly in relation to
gender discrimination in property ownership and marriage. Should these be
protected, on the grounds of cultural inviolability, from the kind of political
and cultural struggle over property and gender which has been, and is, a
feature of politics elsewhere?

Much of the international debate about 'culture' and rights concerns gender,
a field in which mutual occidentalizing and orientalizing has been long
established (Nader 1989). As I have said, it is essentially only in the last few
decades that a wide gap has opened between the 'West' and 'non-West' on the
issue of gender equality. What need to be explored are the reasons for the
rapidity of changes in one part of the world and not in others, but this is not
an exploration which is either useful or necessary for those engaged in cultural
representations, either as defence or offence. This issue might usefully be
considered in our context in relation to sexual behaviour, and the rules governing the permissible and impermissible, and the long history of inter-cultural
representations of sexuality. Judgements about the sexual behaviour of the
people colonized by Europe played a core part in cultural othering and were
central to the representation of the 'horror', to use Kurtz's term, that was
seen. In the early judgements of the West on matters like harems, *lobola* and
Hindu art, promiscuity was perceived to be at the core of other cultures. Now
this same judgement is being made in the other direction. This should at least
alert us towards its role in cultural othering. Gender equality is linked, by the
spokesmen of, for example, Islamic cultures, to promiscuity in the West, as a
twinned pair of horrors in an othered sexual culture. The power of this cultural
imagery stands in the way of movement on each specific legal instance of
gender inequality. Culturalist discourses, and the power of cultural imagery
can also simply obscure reality. Rwezaura has written movingly of the epidemic

of violence against children, and of the abuse, neglect and abandonment now existent in Tanzanian society in which children are no longer an asset, as in an agricultural economy, but a severe, and under current harsh conditions, a sometimes unbearable, burden. But, as he says, this has been invisible to a society in which the overwhelmingly powerful cultural values and assumptions are that children are welcomed and cared for (Rwezaura 2000).

Much of the essentializing of the notion of culture, in the past few decades of rapid change in Africa, has been done in the context of the confronting dialogues between generations and genders. These confrontations became particularly acute in times of change associated not simply with acculturation to 'foreign' ideas, but with fundamental economic and social changes which accompanied the introduction of the money economy, migrant labour, urbanization and pressures on forms of land tenure. The entrenchment of the 'cultural' response to change in Africa owes much as well to the attitude of both colonial and successor governments towards economic and social change. Colonial governments wanted to minimize the 'cultural' effects of economic changes because of an overriding fear of social and political instability that might threaten their rule. A similar stance, the view of change as disintegration, has been evident in successor independent governments. Culture was therefore employed both as a defence for, justification of, and positioning for advantage in a field of conflict over resources, as well as a metaphor for handling and resisting huge changes in ways of living. It has also been employed as a metaphor around which generations and genders, otherwise sharply divided, could be encouraged to unite in opposition to outsiders.

It is relatively easy to trace these processes in the history of Africa in the twentieth century. The challenge in the present is to realize that it is processes of this sort that continue to be what gives rise to invocations of culture, and not the 'existence' of unified 'cultures'. *It is internal conflict about ways of doing things far more than any conflict with outsiders that has led to the essentializing of cultures.* Pragmatic practices become 'customs' to be insisted on; styles of religious practice become beliefs and orthodoxies. The intensity of some of the feelings of cultural belonging, and strength in attachment to custom, are testimony to the seriousness of the conflicts and the pace of displacement and change. The language of culture and identity resonates strongly in these circumstances.[5] The elite controllers of institutions (perhaps most importantly state education systems) and of symbols can resist internal generational, gender and other challenges by the deployment of images of an essentialized culture under external challenge. 'Authenticity', and a consequent cultural patriotism, become a routinized response to globalization. Such essentializing responses to change are ways of exerting authority, and they display partial immunity to discursive challenge, especially if it comes from an external source, as such challenge frequently serves to strengthen convictions.

Cultural differences are not simply given. The experience of difference depends on the power to create culture, on the labour of elites in essentializing, displaying and institutionalizing elements of the myriad of practices in any community. Our focus should therefore be on the current processes of cultural creation instead of treating cultures as historical givens which weigh upon presents and futures. The processes of creation and representation of cultures in the post-colonial and post-Cold War world is one of mutual and multiple intersections between the elites of West and non-West.[6] While the continuing process of 'orientalizing' has been much complained of by the orientalized, the elites of the 'orientalized' cultures of the world have been actively complicit both in their own self-representation as 'other' and the reverse process of occidentalizing. In this process the 'West', and especially individuality in Western cultures, is symbolized and portrayed as an opposing essence to the communality of the cultures that non-Western intellectuals (religious and secular) represent and control. Indeed the establishment of this difference between the individualism and communalism is crucial to the non-Western elites' claim to constitute and to lead their 'cultures'. This claim has become increasingly vociferous precisely because globalized communications, public cultures, rights and constitutionalism have all meant that the claims of local elites are more fiercely resisted and contested within their own 'homes'.

There has been far less interest in the intellectual process of occidentalizing than there has been in orientalizing.[7] The former has taken two basic forms. One is the habit of scholars of non-Western societies in having resort to unexamined clichés concerning an undifferentiated 'West'. As Carrier notes of this imagined entity: 'The occidentalised West is an imagined entity that, in its memorable clarity, obscures the vast areas of Western life that conflict with its vision' (Carrier 1995: 28). The second is the process by which the intellectuals in non-Western societies construct identities in opposition to imagined features of the 'West'. Both draw consciously on the major dichotomy of the grand narrative of Western history – that of *gemeinschaft* and *gesellschaft* – but allocate cohesive community to the non-West, and atomized society to the West. An historical transition from agricultural to industrial societies is thereby transmuted into an ahistorical cultural divide. New value judgements have become a part of this essentializing. Carrier observes how non-Western societies are typified by 'generosity, peace and dignity', inhabited by 'wise ecologist(s) attuned to a fragile nature', while the West is 'violent, rapacious and heedless' (Carrier 1995: 10). There is a search, writes Spencer, for essences, cores or central cultural symbols where differences between cultures seem to 'hover on the edge of absolute incommensurability' (Spencer 1995: 242).

Just as orientalizing was a part of imperialism and colonialism, so occidentalizing is a part of the emergence from colonial rule and cultural power. The West is used, Spencer writes, as a 'rhetorical counter'; occidentalism is a 'mnemonic for the cultural contradictions engendered by colonial domination' (Spencer 1995: 236). Images of the West are deployed as a part of a 'rhetoric of authenticity' (ibid.), which opposes itself to Western modes of thought and cultural institutions and practices. This is frequently a positive process. Spencer writes: 'Other people's essentialisms are … often crucial components in attempts to re-imagine or re-build forms of community and solidarity which they feel are needed to deal with the West' (Spencer 1995: 250). Historical dichotomies, as he points out, can be used to illustrate widely differing political positions, 'the village community of the East was once used as a kind of political Rorschach from which all observers could draw their own conclusions' (Spencer 1995: 246).

The deploying of the dichotomy between those cultures which emphasize individuals or individualism and those cultures which emphasize the 'group' (so common a part of the 'dialogue' about rights between the West and some Asian countries) has a long history. The critique of so-called individualism had particular strength in socialist attacks on capitalism in the late nineteenth century. These European debates spilled over into analyses of other cultures which became one of the terrains on which the European ideological battles were waged. As Kidd's book *Kafir Socialism* (1908) shows, in reverse mode, description of the communal aspects of African life could be used as a condemnation and marker of cultural inferiority, and the suggestion that Africans were communal was used as an argument that this was a mode of social organization of primitives, and obviously not meant for progressive Europeans.[8] The terms, and the drawing in of non-European cultures, were deployed in this one sense in the struggle between Right and Left at the end of the nineteenth century, and in the opposite sense during the Cold War. In the 1960s African socialism was linked by its protagonists to all that was progressive in universal history, ahead of the outdated individualism of the West. It is this critical approach to individualism that remains in the non-Western world even though its erstwhile universalist partner, socialism, has lost contemporary credibility. Reflections on the nature of these discursive deployments should at least make us aware that when the terms are used, they are not only for purposes of description or analysis. There is a complex history of the opposition of the representations, and it has been as much about marking difference as about substance.

The long tradition of liberal philosophies of rights, as well as Western-inspired rights declarations *are* very clearly about groups. They are about the nature of group life, and how it should ideally work. They endeavour to prescribe the rules for associating in groups. The differences, therefore, are about the ground rules for associating in groups, not about individuals as opposed to groups, nor even about which has priority. Classical liberalism, from which rights doctrines flow, does not subordinate group to individual, but is concerned with the kind of group to which individuals belong. Furthermore, the attempt to depict Western societies as individualistic misses the point that these very societies, with their powerful cohesive ideologies of nationalism, patriotism, collective action and welfarism, have been and are far more 'successful' groups on a larger scale over long periods of time, with better working consensual traditions of government than the often fragmented, authoritarian, familistic, localistically-based societies which invoke their cultural attachment to groupness.[9]

Culture/Rights and Brands: Twinned Discourses?
An Excursus into Advertising

My recourse to literature on advertising came about first from an interest in the more conventional socio-legal questions regarding the regulation of political advertising and the notion of commercial free speech. A passing acquaintance has led me to explore the issues raised in writing about advertising in relation to human rights discourses. Like human rights discourse, advertising discourse is deeply involved in questions of culture and cultural essences. The cultural branding that is involved in orientalizing and occidentalizing involves similar discursive strategies to those which are central to globalized advertising. The issues of universalism as opposed to cultural particularism are a feature of international advertising analysis, and the notion of the 'brand' with its emphasis on creating an attachment may well be a way into an analysis of the processes of creating cultures in the post-colonial world. Like human rights discourses, advertising is now a fundamental feature of globalized communications and the analysis of advertising, the primary globalized discourse, seems to offer possibilities for thinking about globalized rights discourses, because globalized advertising confronts, penetrates and uses national and regional cultures as do discourses about rights. Finally, it is becoming harder to continue to separate the issues surrounding the discourses in the public sphere – those relating to law and government – from those in the commercial sphere. It is clear that these are becoming increasingly alike: with the growth of advertising as a primary means by which government communicates, and political persuasion of all sorts is conducted, as well as the claims that commercial speech (in the form of advertisements) is entitled to the same protections accorded to 'political' and 'cultural' speech.

Analysis of the methods of advertising, in particular the core process of creating brands, may well yield insights into the selling of cultures by intellectual entrepreneurs in the post-colonial world. The long-standing analyses of culture relate it to social structure, to behaviours predicated upon that structure, to the world of materiality and action from which are derived the intellectual constructs which explain and interpret the society to itself and others. In a world of globalized communications and representations, these links between structure, behaviour and cultural representation can no longer be taken for granted. As Daniel Boorstin has asked: 'How do the expressions of our peculiar folk culture come to us? They no longer spring from the earth, from the village, from the farm, or even from the neighbourhood or the city.' They come, he says, from centralized sources, 'from advertising agencies, from networks of newspapers, from radio and television' (Mattelart 1991: 32). These different ingredients, if now taken into account, should suggest to us that culture may be analysed without giving primacy to social structure. Compare Fredric Jameson's formulation:

> a profound modification of the public sphere needs to be theorised, the emergence of a new realm of image reality which is both fictional (narrative) and factual ... and which now – like the former classical 'sphere of culture' – becomes semi-autonomous and floats above reality, with this fundamental historical difference that in the classical period reality persists independently of that sentimental and romantic 'cultural sphere' whereas today it seems to have lost that separate mode of existence, culture impacting back on it in ways that make any independent and as it were non- or extra-cultural form of reality problematical. (Mattelart 1991: 210, 211)

The disjunction of representation from reality, and the power of unreal representations to create behaviours give a different chicken-and-egg sequence to the explanation of cultures. Another basic feature of analyses of culture is that they are based on the assumption that the realm of culture is one of relative permanence and stability and temporal depth. Cultures are seen as being developed over long periods in relatively closed and stable communities that generate shared patterns of behaviour and belief which are comprehensible, communicable and legitimate to members of a group over prolonged periods of time. While not static they retain sufficient 'core' to remain recognizably differentiated from other cultures. But this form of analysis, while it may once have been appropriate to explain the long-term development of nationalism and national cultures, or the practices and beliefs of isolated communities, may no longer be appropriate to a world of globalized communications in which the circulation of knowledge and images has been dramatically increased in volume and speed, as has the circulation of people. In Mattelart's words, there is a contest between 'globalised industrial cultural production and individual cultures', in a world in which, through advertising, a permanent, daily and generalized connection is developed between particular societies and cultures, local, regional and national (Mattelart 1991: 216, 231). This is not an argument which necessarily leads towards global homogeneity of cultures (for the existence of new stimuli may accelerate the production of differences), simply one which suggests that the circumstances of cultural formation are now significantly different, and that temporal depth and relative continuities of practice and belief may no longer be at the heart of a concept of culture. All of this is well known to students of media, communications and popular culture, but is curiously absent from the notions of 'culture' used in the human rights debates in which a sacralized idea of culture still dominates. Another related issue is that of lifestyle. Year after year my students have wondered why I have objected so strongly to the use of the phrase 'the peasant lifestyle', for today's students do not differentiate between culture, economics and consumer choice. Yet, to an extent there is a blurring of the lines between culture and custom and chosen style. '"The social classes are dead. Long live lifestyles" is the motto of the lifestyle professionals' (Mattelart 1991: 167). This is still not to suggest that such choices are universally available (or even that they are really choices), but to indicate that there are other ways of making identities. Mattelart quotes Wolfgang Haug: 'Commodity aesthetics organises imaginary spaces around the commodity ... [which] offer the addressee the promise that after purchase, they will reflect in his new self-representation, and ... will solve the problem of identity. The imaginary spaces around the product are intended to become spaces in our imagination that will be filled through aesthetic-symbolic activity ... consumption induces an imagination of identity' (Mattelart 1991: 202).

In inducing this imagination of identity, successful advertising campaigns draw upon deep 'cultural' motifs. As has been frequently pointed out, the 'Marlboro Man' depended on the significance of the '(American) West' in popular culture, as much as he exploited it (Mattelart 1991: 50). Mattelart writes of the techniques used to develop (and sell) popular fiction and TV series by legitimating pleasure through the use of 'indicators of authenticity', and through the 'promotion of verisimilitude' by the use of historical references and historical culture (Mattelart 1991: 136). One can see a parallel in which the promoters of all cultural versions of rights 'use' the past as a way of lending verisimilitude to their versions.

While most public discourses, which are controlled by national elites, emphasize continuing differences, the discourses of the international marketplace tend towards universalizing patterns of consumption and behaviour. But while certain images (like the Nike logo) are easily universalized, marketers have found that different cultures require that brands be promoted in different ways. The international market, then, does not make cultures disappear, but it manipulates them in particular ways, using cultural essences to create loyalty to the universal brand. The cultural element is important because it is the manipulation of identity which creates the attachment, which is not based on utility. As advertising agency Saatchi and Saatchi says: 'The relationship that consumers enjoy with a brand is ... a complex mixture of rational and emotional factors ... There are many categories where the emotional relationship ... is ... more important than the functional relationship' (Mattelart 1991: 163).

Cook describes the advertising for Bacardi, which features slim young men and women swimming in blue water and lying on a tropical sunlit beach. He comments on what he calls the 'extraordinary reversal': 'Drinking spirits makes people fatter, less fit, less sexually potent and poorer; in direct sunlight it gives people headaches; it is not typically the activity of muscular young men or slim young women in cutaway swimwear, but rather of fat, stressed, middle aged men in suits' (Cook 1992: 18). Yet these 'reversed' fantasy advertisements were hugely successful in establishing the brand. Fantasies work where reality fails. We must transfer this thought to the way in which we think about cultures. In spite of the retreat of materialism and structuralism, the assumption remains that cultural representations reflect actual social practices. We might try and see if our understanding is enhanced by a consideration of cultures as sustained social imagination, fed in part by imagined versions of other 'cultures' – i.e. by the process of orientalization/occidentalization. These fantasies, like the Bacardi fantasy, depend on establishing links between aspirations and a brand. The process of branding may, therefore, be full of clues to the understanding of how allegiances to cultures are made. Cultures, like brands, must essentialize, and successful and sustainable cultures are those which brand best.[10] In this context, it is essential to take note of the ways in which cultures increasingly brand themselves for sale in the international tourist market. Part of this process involves the emphasis and display of the exotic; part the assertion of intellectual property rights over forms of cultural production, and the subsidizing and increased production of art and artefacts. 'Heritage' – stories, song, design, art, landscape, buildings and artefacts – and brand are now hard to distinguish, especially as the promotion of cultural heritage is so closely linked to the cultural tourism market. Cultural 'authenticity' is the commodity.

How far are the usual forms of public communication essentially different from those of advertising? If we assume that they once were different, are they now converging? And, if they are, why now? And what can rights/culture discourses tell us about this convergence? It is becoming harder to continue to accept the view that a clear distinction can ultimately be made between reason and manipulation in public discourses. In particular, in relation to 'culture', 'commoditised space has become so pervasive that it becomes impossible to continue thinking of culture as a reserved and uncontaminated terrain' (Mattelart 1991: 216). George Orwell's *Nineteen Eighty-Four* is based on the absolute premise that behind corrupted political discourses and language use lay a real truth and a clear way of expressing it. Whether we can meaningfully work with this paradigm in the area of rights discourses seems to me to be increasingly doubtful. For these discourses appear to have more in common with the language and techniques of advertising behind which no truths lie. Design, logo, symbol and packaging (see Mattelart 1991: 210) are a part of the world of rights and cultures as they are a part of the basic techniques of advertisements. Indeed, bills of rights often appear to be like the huge hoardings in Third World cities which advertise luxury products to people who will never be able to purchase them, as part of the creation of the illusion that they are in some way a part of the life of everyone. We can at least wonder whether the rights that are proclaimed in universal declarations and bills of rights are a luxury product, a product at all, or an advertisement? We know that the media can be mixed: a cigarette can be 'the taste of freedom' (*The Australian*, 28 April 1998). What can freedom be the taste of?

Cultures, of course, have always branded themselves through art and ritual, but verbal discourses internal to a culture have, in the past, not tended to perform a branding function. However, as cultures increasingly are thrown together and inter-leaved in globalized symbolic exchanges, verbal branding of cultural essences tends towards the nature of visual branding – towards art or image. But even bearing these things in mind, can it possibly be correct to situate the ways in which we talk and write about people's greatest needs, most severe oppressions and most vital aspirations – which is what rights discourses are nominally about – in these terms? It is, particularly, formerly oppressed and colonized cultures that demand that their own historical experiences and cultural differences be respected, and it is this demand for parity of respect which underpins the stress on the preservation of cultural differentiation, the 'invention of tradition' and the 'imagining of communities'. The need to fight for recognition of different historical experiences as 'reflected' in different 'cultures' is even greater for the most vulnerable of indigenous communities, as well as for established non-Western societies, in a world in which English is the global language, and in which Western images dominate global commerce. If one suggests that what is happening is to be likened to the process of 'branding', the danger is that one is contributing to a weakening of just claims for recognition, respect and resources. Should we not rather acknowledge Bourdieu's view of culture as a kind of 'self-defence' against 'ideological pressure ... against abuses of symbolic power directed against them, be they advertising, political propaganda or religious fanaticism?' (Mattelart 1991: 216).

These questions have a long discursive history through the colonial period in which issues of 'authenticity' were often canvassed. There is a long history of colonial hostility to social and cultural change. The dominant model, as Indians, Africans and others came into contact with 'the West', was that those people who were partly 'Westernized' were rather ridiculous, essentially culturally other, yet assuming a comic and inappropriate veneer of Western civilization. This model of acculturation had a political purpose, but analytically it failed completely as a means of understanding the nature of the negotiation between different social and symbolic worlds. However, the fallacious notion of 'authenticity' around which this explanation was built survives, indeed it is now embraced by, the culturalist discourses of the present. It is equally useless in explanation. What this section might suggest is that in contrast to the notion that a veneer of civilization lay over the essentially primitive colonized peoples, for many now a veneer of symbolic cultural 'authenticity' lies over people who are becoming part of an increasingly universalized economy of labour, consumption and imagination. This is not to suggest that this world is uniform at all, but that it is here, rather than cultural authenticity, where analysis must start.

Africa: State, Market, Rights and Culture

In the years when colonialism was coming to an end, and nation-states were being established, much of Western scholarship concerned with Africa looked at Africa's prospects (and practices) with a markedly sympathetic eye. Freedom, modernization and development were all goals and processes which were promised in the new era and there was little doubt displayed that the state was to be the main vector of all of these desirable developments. Now Western scholarship sees the African states through a miasma of failed promises, disappointments and disasters, and the result is suspicion and condemnation. In the later post-Cold War view, the model of the African state had changed. No longer the vector of economic change, it is now seen as a guarantor of the 'rule of law', a holder of the ring, while a private economy delivers development. In both periods, the model of the state is seen as essentially politically neutral in a process in which *all* would benefit. Whitaker describes the expectation in the early years of independence of a culturally African yet Keynesian polity, a specifically African democracy with Keynesian (or African socialist) management of the development process, in which the elites were to be midwives of development (Sklar and Whitaker 1991: 333). Analysts constructed a picture of an African state innocent of class conflict, though bedevilled by ethnic conflict ('tribalism' – which was Bad Culture) which development would supersede. It took time for the view of the state as violent, dominant and predatory to be routine in analyses of African political development. The veil of nation-building was pierced to reveal countries in the hands of what has been described as a 'state bourgeoisie' or 'bureaucratic bourgeoisie' (Sklar and Whitaker 1991: 215), a class whose economic base and power depended on control of the state. It is in the existence of this class, in Africa and elsewhere, that analysis of the differences in rhetoric about human rights can be located. The scorn poured on the Western version of individualism and civil rights by the class which depends on the complete authoritarian control of state power and resources is so easily explicable without resorting to 'culture'. The Asian version of this has been frequently described. Asian governments such as those of China, Singapore, Indonesia and Malaysia have been the most scornfully explicit in their rejection of Western versions of rights. In doing so they have laid particular stress on culture – claiming a culture for Asia based on authority, religion, duty, community and family – while depicting the West as individualist, and in a state of moral and social decay because of the decline of the authority vested in state and family. (This latter critique is, of course, also widely deployed in the Islamic world.) The eerie echoings between the ruling elites of anti-democratic states in Asia, Africa and the Middle East have more to do with shared political insecurities than with cultures (see Carrier 1995; Ghai 1994).

Some analysts have presented the current phase of African politics, in which the statist economies of Africa have been subjected to the structural adjustment requirements of the World Bank, as one which poses a particular crisis for the development of a rights paradigm in Africa on the grounds that such a paradigm depends on a lively (and culturally based) conception of economic and social rights. It *was* the case that many pre-structural adjustment states paid lip service to such concepts of rights, often elevating them for politically oppressive reasons to a priority over civil and political rights. The interests of the idealogues of the 'bureaucratic bourgeoisie' in emphasizing so-called 'second generation' collective rights, and thereby in sanctifying the increasing sphere of state activity, seem plain. It is probable, however, that few rights of any kind can be achieved without radical changes to the existing degraded polities. It follows that whatever was hoped for during the decade of decolonization, the successor states can no longer be seen as the vehicles of African self-determination, and, therefore, as the basis on which to build rights in Africa.[11] Inasmuch as structural adjustment contributes to fundamental changes in the post-colonial state (and it may not), it can be said to be laying the ground work for the development of a rights culture. Perhaps the most important lessons to learn are to renew doubt about the oft-repeated mantra that economic, social and cultural rights must be achieved before civil and political ones, and, more urgently, that we should not continue to mistake states for peoples.

A number of features contributed to the view of the state as culprit in Africa – growing violence and oppression, the failure of development, the end of the Cold War, the triumph of the market, the emerging dominance of the World Bank – all put the predatory state and the bureaucratic bourgeoisie in the dock. Structural adjustment, as Whitaker says, challenged the class basis, and the patronage politics, of the African ruling class (Sklar and Whitaker 1991: 215). Externally, in place of statist development strategies, the demand was now for a better quality of governance to preserve, protect and enhance the market. This implied a level of stability which could, in the World Bank's model, be achieved best through political democracy and fairer and more effective administration. The demand for 'rights' comes now, therefore, in the case of most of Africa, not as the ideological driving force of an internal political revolution, but as a measure of quality control for the governance of the kind of state approved of by dominant outside economic powers and institutions. (Even in the South African rights revolution this has been an important ingredient.) The dominant elites of Africa are threatened by this kind of state and by this model of rights and prefer to mobilize support for their position by invoking versions of collective rights based on state action (and therefore on their own political power). As the foreign-inspired structural adjustment programmes cut into popular areas of patronage it is easier for elites to organize support for their own version of rights against a 'foreign' version which had little basis of internal support to begin with. It was not difficult for the challenged elites to present the different versions of rights in terms of a cultural struggle because in the first place the demand for first-generation civil rights was 'foreign'-supported, and, in the second, second-generation collective rights, which could be portrayed in culturally collective terms, were compatible with and, indeed, strengthened the elites' control of the state.

The Cold War, in the context of which the African successor states to colonialism were constructed, and in which they developed, explains simultaneously the heightened rhetoric about rights, and the lack of concern with securing their effectiveness. States which were economically dependent on, and politically a part of, the West, were not subjected to rights audits, the primary requirement of governments being that they maintained themselves in power and did not deliver their populations to any form of communism. Only in the post-Cold War period, when the huge costs of maintaining these structures – in terms of military expenditures, debts and aid – have become evident, has a demand for better government become a Western requirement. One of the languages in which this demand is made is the language of rights, and there is concomitant pressure for the development of constitutional states. Yet while one may (as many Africans do) place the utilization of rights language in the context of the power which others seek to exercise over African polities, the question of what alternative languages, or methods, there are for achieving a greater measure of justice for the subjects of African states remains. Large numbers of states in the modern world were established on the basis of the right of national self-determination, which was the foundational political right of the international state system over a period from the French Revolution to the end of European colonialism. Yet in the post-colonial and post-communist years, self-determination has become the claim of smaller and smaller fragments, undermining the claims of the existing nation-states. In Africa, while the rhetoric of national self-determination accompanied the end of colonialism, the successor states were not based on cultural or linguistic nations, and provided neither a shared democracy based on citizenship, nor a linguistic, cultural or ethnic self-determination. A basic political community, membership of which gave access to rights of all kinds, was thus absent.

Some further basic thought needs to be given to the nature of Empire's successor states in Africa. The very use of the word 'state' obscures the very real distinctiveness of the political structures which succeeded colonialism, and which were based on its political forms. Colonial state structures were notoriously small, capable of random violence, but not of governing in the comprehensive contemporary sense. The efforts which the successor states undertook, to build more comprehensive states, to overcome local powers, often through the utilization of the mass political party, have failed. As Migdal has written: 'Ambitious goals for states – aims of actually penetrating throughout the society, regulating the nitty gritty of social relations, extracting revenues, appropriating resources that determine the nature of economic life, and controlling the most dearly held symbols – have seldom been achieved, certainly not in most of the new or renewed state organisations in the Third World' (Migdal 1994: 14). What has been witnessed in the past decade is the disintegration and diminishing of the capacity of these efforts. Introducing a rights-based governance into functioning state structures is therefore not the task which faces those who would transform Africa's political institutions. Rebuilding collapsing structures, or, perhaps, building states where none had really been built before, seems to be the first step towards rights-based governance. It is in this context that we should look briefly at the role of the World Bank because its intervention has been so important in the recent history of the remaking of African states. The Bank's claim is that its primary emphasis has been on the 'efficiency' of government as a *sine qua non* of sustainable economic growth (World Bank 1989: viii). Its use of the term governance came to the fore in its 1989 report, *Sub-Saharan Africa: From Crisis to Sustainable Growth*. The intervention of the Bank in Africa was based on the perception of 'the collapse of public sector capacity' in many countries (World Bank 1989: 8). The claim has been that the efficiency of the management of the country's resources is vital for the promotion of sustainable economic development. While the aim was not the promotion of rights as such (the Bank's remit purportedly specifically excluded the form of political regime), the Bank was none the less concerned with the political capacity of the state to formulate and carry out policies. While the African Development Bank also laid little emphasis on the political nature of regimes, donors like the United Kingdom, and the OECD specifically linked the World Bank's definition of governance to human rights, accountable government and the rule of law (World Bank 1989: xiv).

Thus, while there was a difference between the Bank and the OECD in relation to the overt agenda on rights and politics, the Bank's thrust nevertheless had vital political impact. The World Bank developed its concept to require a move from 'a highly interventionist paradigm of government' towards a smaller state with an accountable bureaucracy which would create the 'enabling environment' for private-sector-led growth (World Bank 1989: xvi, 2). Effectiveness, credibility and accountability of state institutions were linked to privatization, decentralization and reduction of government: 'The trend towards *decentralisation of government* ... has become one of the principal ways in which this demand for accountability is being expressed' (World Bank 1989: 13). To those accustomed to thinking about the protection of rights in terms of a state-centred model which emphasizes the role of the state as the agency which effectively secures rights throughout the territory over which it claims sovereignty, smaller and decentralized government implies a weaker state which would find it harder to 'deliver' rights protection. On the other hand, where the state itself has been the main threat to rights, reduction in its capacity may well be the first necessary step to rights protection.

The Bank did emphasize the need for the strengthening of the legal framework of states in receipt of aid. In line with what has been described above, the starting point was not human rights. In its view, market economies:

> [r]equire a framework of clear laws and efficient institutions ... Creating wealth through the cumulative commitment of human, technological and capital resources depends on a set of rules securing property rights, governing civil and commercial behaviour, and limiting the power of the state ... this set of rules must be clearly defined and known in advance ... In many countries the inappropriateness of laws, uncertainty in their application, weak enforcement, arbitrariness of discretionary power, inefficient court administration, slow procedures, and the subservience of judges toward the executive branch greatly hinder development, discourage and distort trade and investment, raise transaction costs, and foster corruption. (World Bank 1989: 27)

Thus the Bank was involved in projects in Africa to strengthen legal institutions 'relating to property rights and contracts in the context of private sector development loans and credits' (World Bank 1989). While it was the effect of an inadequate legal system on the business sector that was uppermost, the Bank acknowledged that the '[l]egal framework also affects the lives of the poor and, as such, has become an important dimension of strategies for poverty alleviation ... Inherent in the concept of the rule of law is the notion of fairness and social justice' (World Bank 1989: 23). It noted also that the wholesale transfer of Western institutions was to be avoided and that the 'effectiveness of legal reforms depends greatly on how reforms take into account the social, religious, customary, and historical factors in a society' (World Bank 1989: 27).

The Bank has always claimed that its Articles of Agreement prohibited it from taking 'political' considerations into account (World Bank 1989: 53). Its position has been, therefore, that, 'the focus of the Bank's efforts in the area of human rights is on those rights that are economic and social in nature' (World Bank 1989). There is an irony in the linking of the Bank's aggressively capitalist agenda with the second- and third-generation rights that were once the ideological preserve of communist and socialist rhetoric on rights, especially as it has destroyed the state-based programmes which were supposed to deliver these rights. The Bank's 'contribution to economic and social human rights is embedded in its strategy on poverty reduction'. Consequently, lending for 'human resource development' had increased (World Bank 1989: 54). My purpose in canvassing the World Bank's interventions into restructuring the state in Africa in the course of a discussion on human rights and culture is, however, really to suggest that what is to be seen are the limits of claims of rights and cultures. The market, and the legal regime to support the market, are not subject to 'culture' in the Bank's eyes. History and 'culture' are nodded to as afterthoughts only, an icing on the analysis of a culture-free market regime.

In the struggles associated with the collapse of the communist states of Eastern Europe, a revived notion of 'civil society' was deployed against the state (Migdal et al. [eds] 1994: Ch. 1; see also Ch. 10). Understanding of the deployments and meanings of the concept of culture may well be assisted if it is related to the analyses of civil society. Indeed, it is of some interest that 'culture' is rarely invoked in political analyses of Eastern Europe while 'civil society' is rarely deployed in the Third World. One fundamental difference relevant to the African context appears to be that culture is often presented as a unified field of practice at a level 'above' and beyond that of individual states, while civil society as a political concept has been related to a plurality of local-level agencies and communities 'below' each state. Situating rights practices in cultures rather than civil society is clearly a very different intellectual and political strategy, and one which is directly suited to the interests of those who favour authoritarian and uniform politics. A 'civil society' as a freely interactive realm outside the state is a more subversive concept to those who control authoritarian states than that of an overarching culture, especially if the latter can be said to be sustained by a divinely ordained, or a deeply historically embedded, moral and legal order. Yet it has clearly been the case that 'civil society' in much of Africa has been alive and well in both the colonial and post-colonial periods (Chazan 1994), and it is to some extent surprising that civil society as the locus of rights has received relatively little attention from African rights scholars. Chazan observes that, 'both statism (which invites populism) and state decay (which evokes localism) stymie the growth of civil society' (Chazan 1994: 278). The weakness of the state, she suggests, is a factor in slowing the growth of organizations committed to its reform, as the state is not seen as the source of advantage. Current circumstances have led, instead, to the growth of religious organizations 'antithetical' to the concept of civil society (Chazan 1994: 273). However, there are signs of new developments. We should think here about the important and growing role not only of international, but of local, non-governmental organizations, and of associated social movements, in struggling for rights, and in producing a rights culture outside the state. It is from these locations, rather than from governments, that the formulations which express the struggles for social justice and rights in terms compatible with local cultures may come.[12]

Constitutions and Rights

The inter-cultural debates about human rights have been sharpened by a dual process of legalization, both in the recent rapid growth of international human rights law and in the accompanying constitutionalism of rights discourses inside countries. International political rhetoric about rights drove the proliferation of international and regional rights instruments, and declarations and covenants assumed the legalized status of treaties. Regional treaties (for example in Europe and the Americas) moved beyond rhetoric to regional courts which could hold signatory states to account for their behaviour towards their citizens. It is worth underlining, given the theme of rights and culture, the rapidity with which the culturally very different peoples and states of Europe – with different histories, languages, religions and legal and political systems – have accommodated to a single rights convention, and to a court which enforces it. And, as discussed above, states in Africa, in Eastern Europe and elsewhere have, in the post-Cold War era, been expected not only to conform to international rights law, but to remake their internal political processes to display both democratic and rights-based constitutional government in order to achieve international legitimacy. The scale of this global constitutionalist revolution deserves emphasis. Klug tells us that 104 countries underwent fundamental constitutional reform, with eighty-one of them adopting completely new constitutions (Klug 2000: 597; see also Ackerman 1997 on the emergence of 'world constitutionalism'). In this remarkable and recent process, human rights have become constitutionalized, increasingly to be construed by judiciaries which draw upon a common bank of interpretative techniques and legal concepts (see Alston 2000). In place of rights declarations which were brief and inspirational, and drawn in the language of political aspiration, the new bills of rights are drafted like statutes, detailing ever lengthening lists of claims on the courts.

This process takes the discourse of rights further away from those who experience wrongs. The irony is that the current strength of rights jurisprudence in the Western world has been contemporaneous with the weakening of the welfare state model. In place of a politics in which rights of substance were supposed to be delivered through the political process, now rights jurisprudence is premised on the possibility of resituating important allocatory decisions into judicial hands. No longer a part of the constant bargaining and struggle of the political arena, decisions about who is entitled to what are, in the rights-governed future, conceived of as depoliticized and rendered according to a set of legal principles. Most significantly, however, the twin processes of legalization are having the effect of displacing other ways of talking about rights as their authority and effectiveness are seriously compromised.

The processes of legalization and judicialization of rights have been ones which have been entered by culturalist as well as universalist discourses. Constitutions sometimes constitutionalize culturalist as well as universalist discourses. Constitutions, like South Africa's, constitutionalize persons' 'right to enjoy their culture' (Section 31[1]) and the UN Draft Declaration of the Rights of Indigenous Peoples which acknowledges 'rights to practise and revitalise traditions and customs' (Article 12) are part of a process of drawing cultural identities into the discourses of human rights law. This process will produce severe tensions for both discourses as it is already doing in South Africa where there is serious scholarly dispute in relation to whether the constitution has provided protection for gender discrimination in customary family law by the provisions on the right to culture (see Nhlapo 2000; and Bennett 1995). It is clear, too, that it is part of the process of situating rights and cultural discourses in elite and professional locations. That we 'need a language other than that of law to express difference' (Mamdani 2000: 4) is clear, but we appear to be moving in the opposite direction.[13]

Rights and Law: Land and Family

As we near the conclusion of this chapter, we need to pursue the rights and culture questions into the realms of law 'beneath' those of constitutions and rights declarations. The areas of family law and land law are most often invoked as falling within the realm of the cultural, and are both often linked also to religion. In industrialized societies this kind of classificatory tie has virtually been broken, and why it should still be made by and for non-Western societies deserves a brief questioning, for it is by no means obvious why some areas of law have retained seemingly secure places in the realm of culture while others relating to basic matters of rights, entitlements, powers and duties (say contract, labour law or torts) do not. Both family law and land law regulate the structural building blocks of rural societies. Land, and the reciprocal duties of labour and support among kin, provided and provide the necessary means of subsistence for the subordinated peasantries of colonial and post-colonial countries. It is precisely when the security of access to land, and family support, come under threat and strain that the need to claim them as absolutely fundamental to cultures is strongest. It was and is the threatened loss of land that produces the most vigorous claims about its cultural embeddedness and inalienability. And it was and is the strains on family organization produced by the cash economy, migration and urbanization, and the feared collapse of reciprocal obligations between generations, that make emphasis on the cultural nature of family authority and duties so necessary (Chanock 1998).

Yet enshrining rights in universalized rhetorical form at the highest levels of law can do little to redress the fears and needs of those trapped within these necessary cultural assertions about the customary and traditional forms of family and land law. The complex legal questions about the enduring nature of marriage and disputes over separation; of rights and duties in relation to children; about division of property and access to inheritance; about the duties between generations and kin in regard to mutual support – are not soluble by the invocation of a rights paradigm. Assertions at the level of rights about access to and use of land likewise will not address the questions of population growth, food scarcity, market pressures and responses in relation to rural produce, and the interplay between urbanization, the desire for security on land, and the market. Rapid urbanization under the severest conditions of social and economic dislocation and struggle for existence could be flagged as the major African experience of recent years. People in this process are highly vulnerable to culturalist discourses. Partly this is, as diasporas worldwide have shown, because of the idealization of essences of 'home' and 'past': absence makes the heart grow fonder of symbols. But it is also because identity enacted and maintained is the key to claims to rural resources at home. The resonance of culturalist discourses is also enhanced because it appears to be an expression of local autonomy against the harsh oppressions of the globalizing economy.[14]

Some Concluding Rhetoric

In conclusion, I would emphasize three points. The first concerns my remarks about culture made above. All that we say about 'culture' comes from a history of imperialism, and from the current dual framework of 'orientalizing' and 'occidentalizing' in a world of globalized symbolic exchange. If we are to treat 'culture' as a fundamental factor in our analyses of rights, and of government and institutions, we need a very high degree of self-awareness of the history and current circumstances of the deployment of the concept. The rulers of many of the states of Africa and Asia have tried to push rights issues out of the realm of both state and society and into that of 'culture'. And it is into a macro-realm of culture, which overarches particular states and societies, that it is placed, rather than in the micro-realm of the daily practices of particular and local communities. The macro-realm is, clearly, representable as both more legitimate, and more resistant to change. This brings me to the second point. We should ask what narratives are being replaced by the focus on 'culture'. Post-everythingism has not changed everything.[15] In the post-communist world material explanations have dropped suddenly from social analysis. Yet one does not have to be clinging to the wreckage of Marxism, or conspiracy theory, to insist on the need for an adequate account of the material world in which concepts of rights are deployed. The relationships between the rights debates and African poverty, lopsided Asian 'miracles' and collapses, world trade and international debt, must be a part of the analysis of cultural transformation. Third, we should consider carefully the relationship between analyses on the micro- and the macro-level. Within the framework of the recent African past – the terrible civil wars in Angola and Mozambique, the long-running oppression of the Southern Sudan, the collapse of states in Sierra Leone, Somalia and Liberia, the wars and oppressions in Ethiopia, the implosion of Zaire, the genocide in Rwanda – at what level do we pitch analysis? Where, in the material, international, institutional and local fields do questions about rights and culture become important? So much of the discussion of 'rights' and 'cultures' is on the meta-levels of the rights declarations in international law and state constitutions, and on whether these are compatible with meta-cultures. Yet local communities have fundamental ideas of justice and know when these have been transgressed, as the often violent resistance to imposed change shows. It is to the content of these local reactions that we should look when thinking about cultures and rights.

A focus on rights and culture continues to produce a sacralized discourse which tends to push us beyond the world of known oppressions, and empirical political demands and interests. I have attempted to historicize the moment in which this sacralized discourse has become to appear so cogent, and also to suggest that it involves a process of creating 'brands' – both of politics and cultures – in ways similar to the methods of international advertising. I think that there are better ways to approach these questions, and the clearest is through an attention to the detailed articulation by those affected, of wrongs, and of needs.

Notes

1. The use of the term 'the West' is almost automatically used to indicate an un-examined conglomerate of the USA and Europe and like offshoots. This usage, which lumps together so many very different histories, cultures and state practices, is analysed below. I use it here partly to draw attention to the fact that no one would now contemplate using the term 'the East' in such a manner. Occidentalizing is discussed further in the chapter which was originally written for a conference on Human Rights and Cultural Transformation in Africa, held in Cape Town in 1997. An earlier version was published in Mamdani (ed.) (2000).

2. To understand American rights we should first look at the wrongs recited in the Preamble to the Declaration of Independence, and, in the case of France, to the grievances presented to the Estates General.

3. A certain (deliberate) innocence pervades some of the disputes about the wording of rights instruments. Both lawyers and their opponents tend to pretend that Bills of Rights have plain meanings, as opposed to meanings and applications which are highly contextual, more so than any other part of formal law. It is this tendency towards exaggerated neo-formalism that contributes much to the idea that Rights and Cultures conflict

4. The right to development itself, once a primary Third World claim, is now also sometimes rejected as culturally destructive, involving as it does the incorporation of peoples into a globalized capitalist economy, with a concomitant loss of control over their resources, and destruction of their way of life.

5. Without wishing to trivialize the issue, stylistic self-enrichment as well as resentment of foreign influences contribute. And, it should be noted, very deeply felt identifications need not be wholly serious. Consider, for example, the strength of the lifetime attachment of a football supporter to his team. Readers of the literature on cultural identity could benefit by reading the account of such a supporter in Hornby (1998). We should be aware of the dimensions of pleasure in the creation of attachments and selves. Identity is not simply a matter of tragic destiny.

6. We should note, however, that one of the most important struggles over the repres-entations of culture in recent times was fought between France and the USA in the recent GATT negotiations. And, in this dispute, the defence of French culture was really being waged by the French elite against the preference of French mass audiences for American over French films.

7. I use the verb form rather than the nouns – orientalism and occidentalism – in order to emphasize that I am describing a constant, active (and necessary) process in trans-cultural studies, and not something that can be noted, analysed or put aside.

8. Kidd wrote: 'Dawn is breaking on the Dark Continent, and the Kafirs are stirring in their sleep. Democratic Individualism is disturbing the Socialism that has reigned un-disputed for ages' (Kidd 1908: 285). For the Right a century ago, communalism was in the past; for the Left, it was in the future. Now, it has been shunted sideways to neither past nor future, but to a timeless realm of culture. Kidd's interest was in contributing to the politically central debate in the West over the struggle between collectivity and individuality. While much that is written now appears to take for granted the triumph of a form of individualism in the West, we might note that A.V. Dicey's classic *Lectures on the Relation*

between Law and Public Opinion in England during the 19th Century, first published in 1905, which was about the struggle between individualism and collectivism in England, assumed, gloomily, that collectivism had won irrevocably.

9. Most notoriously they have been able to demonstrate their aptitude for group solidarity by their ability to organize for war. To take the case of Britain, an allegedly most 'individualistic' Anglo-Saxon society, national sentiment and group cohesion were such that millions joined the armed forces *voluntarily* in World War One. On a more positive note, one might point to the long and (sometimes) successful history of solidarity in the trade union movement. Of course the issue is not really about the differences in relation to individualism and communalism, but about the differences between the types of groups that are important at different times in history and in different state and social structures. Currently in many societies 'communal' groups provide what the state does not in vital areas like physical security and social welfare.

10. Issue after issue of *National Geographic* are superb sources of examples of cultural branding.

11. These states also manipulated cultural concepts in oppressive ways. The example of the invocation of the concept of *Ujamaa* by the Nyerere regime in Tanzania in its oppressive and destructive villagization campaign is instructive (Nyerere 1968; Scott 1998). For a less dramatic example, but one which encapsulates other forms of the capture of cultural ideas by the state, one might consider the South African Communal Property Associations Act of 1996 by which African 'cultural' concepts of property rights are rendered an instrument of state law and policy.

12. This may be too idealistic a hope. Chidi Odinkalu's formulation of the rights discourses in these locations mirrors my portrayal of those in the realm of the state. 'Instead of being the currency of a social justice or conscience-driven movement, "human rights" has increasingly become the specialised language of a select professional cadre ... human rights activism is ... increasingly a certificate of privilege' (extract from C. Odinkalu, 'Why More Africans Don't Use Human Rights Language', *Human Rights Dialogue*, Winter 2000, in Steiner and Alston 2000: 946–7). Those who study advertising are concerned with the gap between the intended message about the product, and the ways in which it can be received by consumers. A similar focus on the reasons for the gap between message and reception may help rights scholars explain the lack of acceptance in ways other than cultural difference. While those who speak the language of rights see themselves as being concerned with social justice, those who hear it hear a language of privilege.

13. Something of the difference between legal and other formulations may be illustrated, in keeping with my theme, from advertising. The function of advertising, it was said at Coca-Cola, 'is to perpetuate and develop a specialness about the brands we sell, which take the product above and beyond what is in the bottle itself' (quoted in Averill 1996: 206). This is what culturalist discourses do to social practices. But legal formulations tie us specifically to what must be in the bottle itself. This can be at the same time more specific a claim than a member of the culture might ever make, while being far less than the total felt content of cultural belonging.

14. Avery uses the concept of 'asserted difference' for the 'heightened or exaggerated sense of locality, local identity and local cultural distinctiveness' resulting from globalization.

15. I thought leaders of nations used to dream of vast land empires – expansion, annexation, troop movements, armoured units driving in dusty juggernauts over the plains, the forced march of language and appetite, the digging of mass graves. They wanted to extend their shadows across the territories ...

Brian says, 'Now they want computer chips.'

'Exactly.'

And Victor Maltsev says, 'Yes, it's true that geography has moved inward and smallward. But we still have mass graves, I think.' (DeLillo 1997: 788)

References

Ackerman, B. (1997) 'The Rise of World Constitutionalism', *Virginia Law Review*, 83: 771.

Alston, P. (2000) *Promoting Human Rights Through Bills of Rights*, Oxford: Oxford University Press.

An-Na'im, A. A. (1992) *Human Rights in Cross-Cultural Perspectives: A Quest for Consensus*, Philadelphia: University of Pennsylvania Press.

Averill G. (1996) 'Global Imaginings', in R. Ohmann (ed.) with G. Averill et al., *Making and Selling Culture*, Hanover and London, Wesleyan University Press, pp. 203–23.

Bennett, T. (1995) *Human Rights and African Customary Law*, Cape Town: Juta.

Carrier, J. G. (ed.) (1995) *Occidentalism: Images of the West*, Oxford: Clarendon Press.

Chanock, M. (1991) 'Law, Nation and Culture: Black Law in a Post-apartheid South Africa', *Acta Juridica*: 52–70.

— (1998) 'Globalisation: Culture: Property' in G. Couvalis et al. (eds), *Cultural Heritage: Values and Rights*, Adelaide: Flinders University Press, pp. 47–60.

— (2000) 'A Post-Calvinist Catechism or a Post-communist Manifesto? Intersecting Narratives in the South African Bill of Rights Debate', in P. Alston (ed.), *Promoting Human Rights Through Bills of Rights*, Oxford: Oxford University Press, pp. 392–428.

Chazan, N. (1994) 'Engaging the State: Associational Life in Sub-Saharan Africa', in J. S. Migdal, A. Kohli and V. Shue (eds), *State Power and Social Forces: Domination and Transformation in the Third World*, Cambridge: Cambridge University Press, pp. 255–89.

Cook, G. W. D. (1992) *The Discourse of Advertising*, London: Routledge.

DeLillo, D. (1997) *Underworld*, New York: Scribner.

Dicey, A.V. (1905) *Lectures on the Relation between Law and Public Opinion in England during the 19th Century*, London: Macmillan.

Ghai, Y. (1994) *Human Rights and Governance: The Asia Debate*, occasional paper, Asia Foundation.

Hornby, N. (1998) *Fever Pitch*, London: Penguin Books.

Howard, R. E. (1986) *Human Rights in Commonwealth Africa*. Totowa, NJ: Rowman and Littlefield.

Hyden, G. and M. Bratton (eds) (1986) *Governance and Politics in Africa*, Boulder, CO: Lynne Rienner.

International Bank for Reconstruction and Development (1994) *Governance. The World Bank's Experience*, Washington, DC: World Bank.

Kenyatta, J. (1938) *Facing Mount Kenya: The Traditional Life of the Gikuyu*, London: Secker and Warburg.

Kidd, D. (1908) *Kafir Socialism and the Dawn of Individualism*, London: A. and C. Black.

Klug, H. (2000) 'Model and Anti-model: The United States Constitution and the "Rise of World Constitutionalism"', *Wisconsin Law Review*, 597: 597–616.

Mamdami, M. (1990) 'The Social Basis of Constitutionalism in Africa', *Journal of Modern African Studies*, 28: 359–74.

— (ed.) (2000) *Beyond Rights Talk and Culture Talk*, Cape Town: David Philip.

Mattelart, A. (1991) *Advertising International. The Privatisation of Public Space*, trans. M. Chanan, London and New York: Routledge.

Migdal, J. S. (1988) *Strong Societies and Weak States. State–Society Relations and State Capabilities in the Third World*, Princeton, NJ: Princeton University Press.

— (1994) 'The State in Society: An Approach to Struggles for Domination', in J. S. Migdal, A. Kohli and V. Shue (eds), *State Power and Social Forces: Domination and Transformation in the Third World*, Cambridge: Cambridge University Press, pp. 7–36.

Migdal, J. S., A. Kohli and V. Shue (eds) (1994) *State Power and Social Forces: Domination and Transformation in the Third World*, Cambridge: Cambridge University Press.

Nader, L. (1989) 'Orientalism, Occidentalism and the Control of Women', *Cultural Dynamics*, 2: 323–55.

Nhlapo, T. (2000) 'The African Customary Law of Marriage and the Rights Conundrum', in M. Mamdani (ed.), *Beyond Rights Talk and Culture Talk*, Cape Town: David Philip, pp. 136–48.

Nyerere, J. (1968) *Ujamaa: Essays on Socialism*, Dar es Salaam: Oxford University Press.

Ohmann, R. (ed.) with G. Averill et al. (1996) *Making and Selling Culture*, Hanover and London: Wesleyan University Press.

Orwell, G. (1949) *Nineteen Eighty-Four*, New York: Harcourt Brace.

Rosenfeld, M. (ed.) (1994) *Constitutionalism, Identity, Difference, and Legitimacy: Theoretical Perspectives*, Durham, NC: Duke University Press.

Rwezaura, B. (2000) 'The Value of a Child: Marginal Children and the Law in Contemporary Tanzania', *International Journal of Law and Family*, 14: 326–64.

Scott, J.C. (1998) *Seeing Like a State*, New Haven, CT: Yale University Press.

Sklar, R. L. and C. S. Whitaker (1991) *African Politics and Problems in Development*, Boulder, CO, and London: Lynne Rienner.

Spencer, J. (1995) 'Occidentalism in the East: The Uses of the West in the Politics and Anthropology of South Asia', in J. G. Carrier (ed.), *Occidentalism: Images of the West*, Oxford: Clarendon Press, pp. 234–59.

Steiner, H. J. and P. Alston (2000) *International Human Rights in Context*, Oxford: Oxford University Press.

World Bank (1989) *Sub-Saharan Africa: From Crisis to Sustainable Growth: A Long-term Perspective Study*, Washington, DC: World Bank.

THREE

The Banjul Charter: The Case for an African Cultural Fingerprint

Makau Mutua

§ THE African Charter on Human and Peoples' Rights (the African Charter),[1] the basis of Africa's continental human rights system, entered into force on 21 October 1986, upon ratification by a simple majority of member states of the Organization of African Unity (OAU).[2] The African Charter has attracted criticism because it departs from the narrow formulations of other regional and international human rights instruments.[3] Apart from the African Charter, the other major regional human rights instruments include (i) the American Convention on Human Rights, 22 November 1969, the document that anchors the inter-American human rights system; (ii) the (European) Convention for the Protection of Human Rights and Fundamental Freedoms, 4 November 1950; and (iii) the European Social Charter, 18 October 1961, which forms the basis for the European human rights system (Buergenthal 1988; see also Hannum 1992 [hereafter Human Rights Practice Guide] and United Nations 1993). In particular, the African Charter codifies the three generations of rights, including the controversial concept of peoples' rights, and imposes duties on individual members of African societies.[4] While a number of scholars have focused attention on apparent tensions between human and peoples' rights, there has been little discussion of the notion of individual duties in the context of the African Charter.[5] Yet a thorough understanding of the meaning of human rights, and the complicated processes through which they are protected and realized, would seem to link inextricably the concepts of human rights, peoples' rights and duties of individuals. Individual rights cannot make sense in a social and political vacuum, devoid of the duties assumed by individuals.[6] This appears to be more true of Africa than of any other place. The individualist, narrow formulation of human rights is ill-suited to the African political and cultural universe.[7]

The argument by current reformers that Africa merely needs a liberal democratic, rule-of-law state to be freed from despotism is mistaken. The transplantation of the narrow formulation of Western liberalism cannot adequately respond to the historical reality and the political and social needs of Africa. The sacralization of the individual and the supremacy of the jurisprudence of individual rights in organized political and social society is not a natural, 'trans-historical' or universal phenomenon, applicable to all societies, without regard to time and place. The ascendancy of the language of individual rights has a specific historical context in the Western world. The rise of the modern nation-state in Europe and its monopoly of violence and instruments of coercion gave birth to a culture of rights to counterbalance the invasive and abusive state (Cover 1987).[8] John Locke reduced this thinking to a philosophy in his *Two Treatises of Government* (Laslett 1988). He argued that each individual, together with his compatriots, contractually transfers to a public authority his individual right to implement the law of nature. But this power is conditional and limited to the state's duty to 'protect individual rights and freedoms from invasion and to secure their more effective guarantee' (Donnelly 1990: 34). According to Locke, a government that systematically breaches these duties becomes illegitimate. While Locke's conception is the floor – the modern state is more intrusive and pervasive than he imagined – it remains the basic justification for the existence of the state in the West.

The development of the state in Africa is so radically different from its European equivalent that the traditional liberal concept of the relationship between the state and the individual is of limited utility in imagining a viable regime of human rights. The modern African state was imposed on ethno-political communities by European imperialists and did not result from the natural progression or evolution of those societies.[9] Only a handful of modern African states bear any territorial resemblance to the political formations which existed prior to penetration and subjugation by European states.[10] The majority of states were contrived overnight, often dismantling existing ethno-political communities and their organizational structures. Communities that lived independently of each other were coerced to live together under the newly created colonial state. Most of these new citizens lacked any instinctual or nationalistic bond to the colonial state. The failure of the successor post-colonial state points to the continued inability of the 'unnatural' and forced state to inspire loyalty and distinct national identities.[11] This disconnection, between the people and the modern African state, is not merely a function of the loss of independence or self-governance over pre-colonial political and social structures and the radical imposition of new territorial bounds with unfamiliar citizenry. It is above all a crisis of cultural and philosophical identity: the delegitimation of values, notions and philosophies about the individual, society, politics and nature developed over centuries. Severe as these problems are, the crisis of the African state is not insoluble. The purpose of this chapter is to imagine and reconfigure a rights regime that could achieve legitimacy in Africa, especially among the majority rural populace, and become the basis for social and political reconstruction. The reconstruction proposed here is not merely that of human rights norms. In order for the proposal to make sense, a reconfiguration of the African state must also be simultaneously attempted. The imposed colonial state, and its successor, the post-colonial state, stand as moral and legal nullities, entities whose salvation partially lies in new constitutionalism and map-making in the context of self-determination for Africa's many nationalities, democratization, and, most importantly, historical reconnection with certain pre-colonial ideals. However, the purpose of this chapter is not to explore the creation of a new political map, but rather to reconstruct the human rights corpus. This choice does not imply a hierarchy or ranking. In practice, both paradigms must be simultaneously addressed for the formulation to bear fruit.

For the present purposes, the current human rights movement must be understood as only a piece of the whole. Its roots in Western liberal thought and tradition necessarily deny it completeness, though not the universality of many of its ideals and norms. To paraphrase the famous metaphor, the gourd is only partially filled by the Western tradition; it falls on other traditions fully to fill it. On this premise, this chapter makes several interrelated arguments. Part II stresses the African notions of human rights which existed prior to colonization and how those notions differed from the contemporary Eurocentric articulation of human rights. In particular, these notions saw the individual social being as the bearer of both rights and duties. Accordingly, Part III asserts that the pre-colonial concept of duty remains a valid means of conceptualizing human rights and, thus, should be the basis for the construction of a unitary, integrated rights regime capable of achieving legitimacy in Africa. Finally, Part IV of this chapter presents a vision that strikes a balance between duties and rights. Not only does this vision restrain the runaway individualism of the West, but it also has strong roots in the continent and indeed may be Africa's last hope for reversing societal collapse. The present attempt is not meant to deny the validity of the Western liberal tradition to the human rights corpus, but only to inform it with an African contribution that entwines duties and rights in a society consumed by the socialization of the individual, a concept articulated by the African Charter.

The purpose of this chapter is not to find parallel rights in African conceptions of human rights in order to show the equality of African cultures to European ones. Although that is one incidental by-product, this chapter does not set out to clothe these parallel rights in the language of rights. In fact, the vindication of rights in Africa had a very different dimension. In the West, the language of rights primarily developed along the trajectory of claims against the state; entitlements which imply the right to seek an individual remedy for a wrong. The African language of duty, however, offers a different meaning for individual/state–society relations: while people had rights, they also bore duties. The resolution of a claim was not necessarily directed at satisfying or remedying an individual wrong. It was an opportunity for society to contemplate the complex web of individual and community duties and rights to seek a balance between the competing claims of the individual and society.

This view is not relativist. It does not advance or advocate the concept of apartheid in human rights or the notion that each cultural tradition has generated its own distinctive and irreconcilable concept of human rights.[12] It proceeds from the position that, although extreme 'cultural relativism' in human rights as an anti-imperial device is admirable, it is a misunderstanding inspired by cultural nationalism. What its proponents see as radically distinctive, irreconcilable traditions also possess ideals which are universal. But this author also takes issue with the term 'cultural relativism' itself, which he sees as a form of name-calling promoted by those who resist the construction of a multi-cultural human rights corpus. Most critiques of 'cultural relativism' are ethnocentric and symptomatic of the moral imperialism of the West.[13] Both extremes serve only to detain the development of a universal jurisprudence of human rights.[14]

In reality, the construction and definition of human rights norms are dynamic and continuous processes. Human rights are not the monopoly or the sole prerogative of any one culture or people, although claims to that end are not in short supply.[15] In one culture, the individual may be venerated as the primary bearer of rights, while, in another, individual rights may be more harmonized with the corporate body. Rather than assert the primacy of one over the other, or argue that only one cultural expression and historical experience constitutes human rights, this author views each experience as a contributor to the whole. The process of the construction of universal human rights is analogous to the proverbial description of the elephant by blind people: each, based on their sense of feeling, offers a differing account. However, all the accounts paint a complete picture when put together. As a dynamic process, the creation of a valid concept of human rights must be universal. That is, the cultures and traditions of the world must, in effect, compare notes, negotiate positions and come to an agreement over what constitutes human rights. Even after agreement, the doors must remain open for further inquiry, reformulation or revision.

Human Rights in Pre-colonial Africa: Content and Context

This segment of the chapter will explore the validity of both the argument made often by Africans, and the controversy it engenders, that the concept of human rights was not alien to pre-colonial societies and that such notions were the foundation of social and political society. Recent debates, which are primarily interpretive, have focused attention on this divisive theme. They agree on basic behavioural, political and social characteristics but disagree as to their meaning (Fernyhough 1993: 39).[16] There are no easy answers for a number of reasons. In particular, methodological pitfalls exist for any analysis that attempts to address the length and width of sub-Saharan Africa. The sheer size of the continent, and the diversity of African peoples and their societies, defy easy categorization or generalization. Second, with regard to human rights, there are very few extant sources of pre-colonial societies. The oral tradition common to most of Africa had its own imprecision even before its interruption by the forces of colonialism.

Nevertheless, several broad themes are discernible from the past. It is now generally accepted that the African pre-colonial past was neither idyllic nor free of the abuses of power and authority common to all human societies. However, the despotic and far-reaching control of the individual by the omnipotent state, first perfected in Europe, was unknown.[17] Instead, pre-colonial Africa consisted of two categories of societies: those with centralized authority, administrative machinery and standing judicial institutions, such as the Zulu and the Ashanti, and those with more communal and less intrusive governmental paraphernalia, such as the Akamba and Kikuyu of Kenya.[18] But a feature common to almost all pre-colonial African societies was their ethnic, cultural and linguistic homogeneity – a trait that gave them fundamental cohesion.[19]

Had these political societies developed the concept of human rights? Proponents of the concept of human rights in pre-colonial African societies are accused by their opponents of confusing human dignity with human rights (Howard 1990: 165). This view holds that the 'African concept of justice', unlike human rights, 'is rooted not in individual claims against the state, but in the physical and psychic security of group membership' (Howard 1990: 166).[20] While it is probably correct to argue that African societies did not emphasize individual rights in the same way that European societies did, it is not a correct presumption to claim that they did not know the concept of individual rights at all.

According to Ronald Cohen, a right is an entitlement:

> At its most basic level, a human right is a safeguarded prerogative granted because a person is alive. This means that any human being granted person-hood has rights by virtue of species membership. And a right is a claim to something (by the right-holder) that can be exercised and enforced under a set of grounds or justifications without interference from others. The subject of the right can be an individual or a group and the object is that which is being laid claim to as a right. (Cohen 1993: 3, 4)[21]

Moreover, a brief examination of the norms governing legal, political and social structures in pre-colonial societies demonstrates that the concept of rights, like that articulated by Cohen, informed the notion of justice and supported a measure of individualism. Two societies which are representative of the two basic organizational paradigms prevalent in pre-colonial Africa illustrate the point. The Akamba of east Africa were symptomatic of the less rigidly organized societies, whereas the Akans of west Africa were character-istic of the more centralized state systems. In Akan thought, the individual had both descriptive and normative characteristics (Wiredu 1990: 243).[22] Both endowed the person with individual rights as well as obligations. Similarly, the Akamba believed that 'all members were born equal and were supposed to be treated as such beyond sex and age' (Muthiani 1973: 84).[23] The belief prevailed in both societies that, as an inherently valuable being, the individual was naturally endowed with certain basic rights.

Akan political society was organized according to the principle of kinships. A lineage of those who were descended from the same ancestress formed the basic political unit. Adults in each lineage elected an elder. All lineage heads, in turn, formed the town council which was chaired by a chief who, though chosen according to descent, was in part elected (Wiredu 1990: 248–9).[24] The chief, however, could not rule by fiat, because decisions of the council were taken by consensus. Moreover, council decisions could be criticized publicly by constituents who found them unacceptable. As Wiredu explains, there was no 'doubt about the right of the people, including the elders, to dismiss a chief who tried to be oppressive'.[25]

Among the Akamba, individuals joined the elders council, the most senior rank in Akamba society, after demonstrating commitment to the community and responsibility in personal matters. Maintaining a stable household, which included a spouse or spouses and children, was a necessary precondition. The council was a public forum which made decisions by consensus. Although the Akamba resented any social organization with a central authority, the council's services included the legislation of public norms and customs (Muthiani 1973: 83). These two examples demonstrate that individuals in pre-colonial society had a right to political participation in determining by whom and through what policies to be ruled.

Much of the discussion about whether pre-colonial societies knew of and enforced individual human rights has taken place in the absence of considered studies of, and references to, judicial processes in those societies. A preliminary examination of both the Akan and Akamba societies strongly indicates individual-conscious systems of justice. With respect to the Akamba, a party to a complaint appeared before the council of elders in the company of his jury, a selection of individuals who enjoyed the party's confidence. Unlike Western-style jurors, the Akamba did not hand down a verdict, but advised the party on how to plead and what arguments to put forth to win the case. They had to be steeped in Kamba law, customs and traditions. The threat of the administration of Kithitu, the Kamba oath, which was believed to bring harm to those who lied, encouraged truthfulness (Muthiani 1973: 85; Hobley 1971: 78). After presentations by parties, the elders would render judgment or give counsel on the appropriate settlement. Each offence carried a punishment: murder was compensated by the payment of over ten head of cattle; rapists were charged goats; assaults, depending on their seriousness, could cost over ten head of cattle; adultery was punishable by the payment of at least a goat and bull; and an arsonist was required to build his victim a new house or replace the lost property. Individual rights to cultivated land were also recognized and protected (Hobley 1971: 78–9).[26] These elaborate punishments present just one indication of the seriousness with which Kamba society took individual rights to personal security, property, marriage, and the dignity and integrity of the family.

In Akan society, the presumption of innocence was deeply embedded in social consciousness. According to Wiredu, 'it was an absolute principle of Akan justice that no human being could be punished without trial' (Wiredu 1990: 252).[27] The Akans, like the Akamba, also recognized a wide range of individual rights: murder, assault and theft were punished as violations of the person (Ayisi 1979: 64–70).

For those who deny the recognition of human rights in pre-colonial societies, it must come as a strange irony that the human rights corpus shares with pre-colonial Africa the importance of personal security rights. The right to life, for example, was so valued that the power over life and death was reserved for a few elders and was exercised 'only after elaborate judicial procedure, with appeals from one court to another, and often only in cases of murder and manslaughter' (Fernyhough 1993: 56). This respect for human life was not an aberration. Fernyhough notes that much of Africa is characterized by a 'preoccupation with law, customary and written, and with legal procedure' (Fernyhough 1993: 61; Gluckman 1969). He adds that the Amhara of Ethiopia, for example, have historically relished litigation and the lengthy cross-examination of witnesses. Whether a society was highly centralized or not, 'there existed elaborate rules of procedure intended to protect the accused and provide fair trials' (Fernyhough 1993: 62).[28] The protection of individual rights was of pre-eminent importance to pre-colonial societies.

Many of the Akamba and Akan socio-political norms and structures were common to other pre-colonial ethno-political entities or cultural-nations. This chapter refers to these shared basic values as the index of the African cultural fingerprint, that is, a set of institutional and normative values governing the relationship between individuals, the society and nature. To be sure, the fingerprint belongs to Africa although it is also human and, thus, aspects of it reveal universal characteristics. In the search for the definition of the continent, for what sets it apart from Asia and Europe or the Americas, some writers have labelled the cultural and social patterns distinctive to the continent as the 'African personality' (Ki-Zerbo 1964: 46–59). Leopold Sedar Senghor, for one, called it negritude or 'the manner of self-expression of the black character, the black world, black civilization', while Aimé Cesaire described it simply as 'recognition of the fact of being black, and the acceptance of that fact, of our destiny of black, of our history and our culture' (Senghor 1977: 269–70; Vaillant 1990: 244).[29] Julius Nyerere named it *Ujamaa*, the Kiswahili term for African socialism.[30] The principles and ideals common to all these conceptions are, according to the author's own observations of various African societies, respect for, and protection of, the individual and individuality within the family and the greater socio-political unit; deference to age because a long life is generally wise and knowledgeable; commitment and responsibility to other individuals, family and community; solidarity with fellow human beings, especially in times of need; tolerance for difference in political views and personal ability; reciprocity in labour issues and for generosity; and consultation in matters of governance (Ki-Zerbo 1964).[31] As aptly put by Cohen:

[m]any African cultures value the group – one should never die alone, live alone, remain outside social networks unless one is a pariah, insane, or the carrier of a feared contagious disease. Corporate kinship in which individuals are responsible for the behavior of their group members is a widespread tradition. But in addition, the individual person and his or her dignity and autonomy are carefully protected in African traditions, as are individual rights to land, individual competition for public office, and personal success. (Cohen 1993: 14)[32]

Both Nyerere and Wai have argued, separately, that pre-colonial societies supported individual welfare and dignity and did not allow gross inequalities between members (Wai 1979: 115–44; Nyerere 1968). To buttress his claim that African societies 'supported and practiced human rights', Wai argues that the rulers were bound by traditional checks and balances to limit their power and guarantee a 'modicum of social justice and values concerned with individual and collective rights' (Wai 1979: 116).[33] Legesse emphasizes the importance of distributive justice in 'formally egalitarian', as well as hierarchical, societies to ensure that 'individuals do not deviate so far from the norm that they overwhelm society' (Legesse 1980: 125). Wiredu likewise tabulates a list of rights and responsibilities borne by the Akans in the pre-colonial era. These included rights to political participation, land and religion, as well as the duty to defend the nation (Wiredu 1990). Fernyhough, though not subscribing to a unique African concept of human rights, has outlined many of the rights protected in pre-colonial societies, including the rights to life, personal freedom, welfare, limited government, free speech, conscience and association (Fernyhough 1993; Marasinghe 1984: 32). Many of these rights were protected in complex processes of interaction between the individual and the community.

Thus far, this chapter has identified and elaborated human rights ideals which existed in pre-colonial societies. However, as in other cultures, notions or practices that contradict concepts of human dignity and human rights also existed, some particularly severe. Among the Akamba, for example, a suspect in a serious crime could be tried by a fire or water ordeal if he did not admit guilt.[34] When a chief died in Akan society, a common citizen's life would be taken so that he could 'accompany' the chief and 'attend' to him on his 'journey to the land of the dead' (Wiredu 1990: 258). This practice of human sacrifice was a clear abrogation of the right to life, even by Akan norms which attached an intrinsic value to every individual. Speech and dissent rights of non-adults or minors were also severely restricted (Wiredu 1990: 259). The discriminatory treatment of women – by exclusion from decision-making processes and the imposition of certain forms of labour based on gender – in the home and outside it flew in the face of the concept of gender equality.[35] However, these practices which were inimical to human rights are not peculiar to Africa; all cultures suffer from this duality of the good and the bad.

A number of Western academics have attacked the index of the African cultural fingerprint and the concept it represents – the African contribution to the human rights corpus – as false and erroneous. In an impassioned critique of scholars she regards as African cultural relativists, Howard notes that although 'relatively homogeneous, undifferentiated simple societies of pre-colonial Africa' had 'effective means for guaranteeing what is now known as human rights' (Howard 1984: 176), there was nothing specifically African about them. Such a model, which she calls the communitarian ideal, 'represents typical agrarian, precapitalist social relations in nonstate societies'.[36] Elsewhere, Howard argues that industrialization has dismantled what she refers to as the peasant world-view, or communitarian ideal, and replaced it with 'values of secularism, personal privacy, and individualism' (Howard 1990: 170).[37]

Donnelly, in many respects Howard's ideological soulmate, concedes that while societies based on the communitarian ideal existed at one point in Africa, they are now the exception. He dismisses the notion that pre-colonial societies knew the concept of human rights; an argument he thinks moot because the communitarian ideal has been destroyed and corrupted by the 'teeming slums' of non-Western states, the money economy and 'Western' values, products, and practices (Donnelly 1989: 119).[38] In effect, both Donnelly and Howard believe that human rights are possible only in a post-feudal state, and that the concept was alien to specific pre-capitalist traditions and ideals such as Buddhism, Islam or pre-colonial African societies. In other words, these traditions can make no normative contribution to the human rights corpus. But the other implausible suggestion derived from these positions is that societies – governed under a centralized modern state – necessarily Westernize through industrialization and urbanization. Moreover, such societies become fertile ground for the germination of human rights.

Donnelly and Howard dismiss with too much haste the argument that many Africans are still influenced by pre-colonial norms and notions. They assume, apparently without adequate research, that the old ways have been eroded by modernization. The examples that Howard gives, those of Kenya and Nigeria, two of the 'more developed' economies on the continent, in fact point in the opposite direction: that in spite of the ubiquity of the centralized modernizing state, kinship ties and group-centred forms of consciousness still influence growing urban populations. Matters concerning marriage, birth and death are still supported by extensive family and kinship networks. This is evident even among the peoples of South Africa and Zambia, Africa's most urbanized countries. Fernyhough correctly finds 'Howard's assessment of the new culture of modernity, like her new "modern" African, strangely unsophisticated and lacking in sensitivity' (Fernyhough 1993: 49). It is difficult, if not impossible, he adds, to 'measure individuation or judge changing worldviews by counting radios and cinemas'. Without a doubt, pre-colonial values have been undermined and deeply affected by the forces of change. But it is difficult to believe that this process will completely invalidate them, just as it is unlikely that the modernization of Japan, China and Saudi Arabia will completely destroy the cultural norms and forms of consciousness evolved through Buddhism and Islam.

Donnelly and Howard face other problems as well. The first difficulty, and perhaps the most troublesome, is the implication in their works that only European liberalism – a philosophy they seem to think inevitable under modernization – can be the foundation for the concept of human rights. Although Donnelly and Howard would deny it, this argument in effect destroys any claim of universality because it places the concept of human rights exclusively within a specific culture. Unless they believe that the ideals of liberalism are inherently universal, it is impossible to reconcile their assertion that the concept of human rights is universal, while at the same time assigning to it uniqueness and cultural specificity.

The second difficulty, which is an extension of the first, is the implied duty on Westerners to impose the concept of human rights on non-European cultures and societies because it is a universal concept that all societies must accept for their own good. Seen from other cultural perspectives, such a view barely masks the historical pattern by the West – first realized through colonialism – to dominate the world by remaking it for the benefit and in the image of Europe.

This conflict between Howard and Donnelly, on the one hand, and their opponents, on the other, is summed up beautifully by Fernyhough who illustrates how politicized the debate about the origin of the concept and content of human rights has become:

> From one perspective the human rights tradition was quite foreign to Africa until Western, 'modernizing' intrusions dislocated community and denied newly isolated individuals access to customary ways of protecting their lives and human dignity. Human rights were alien to Africa precisely because it was precapitalist, preindustrial, decentralized, and characterized by communal

forms of social organization. From the opposing viewpoint there is a fundamental rejection of this as a new, if rather subtle, imperialism, an explicit
denial that human rights evolved only in Western political theory and practice,
especially during the American and French revolutions, and not in Africa.
(Fernyhough 1993: 40)

Fernyhough adds, and this author agrees, that the protest of those who reject
the chauvinistic view of the West articulates the 'very plausible claim that
human rights are not founded in Western values alone but may also have
emerged from very different and distinctive African cultural milieus' (Fernyhough 1993: 40–1).[39] It is impossible to sustain the argument made by Donnelly
and Howard because of its internal inconsistency and ethnocentric, moral
arrogance. Conversely, African writers who claim a distinctively African concept of human rights exaggerate its uniqueness. By implication they make the
point that such a concept could not have any universal application, a position
which fails to recognize that concepts of human dignity – the basis of a concept
of human rights – are inherent in all human societies. As Fernyhough notes:

> Thus Donnelly and Howard contend that in pre-colonial Africa, as in most
> non-Western and preindustrial societies, forms of social and political organ-
> ization rendered the means to attain human dignity primarily through duties
> and obligations, often expressed in a communally oriented social idiom and
> realized within a redistributive economy. Yet both reject with unwarranted
> emphasis the notion that in the search for guarantees to uphold human life
> and dignity precolonial Africans formulated or correlated such claims to pro-
> tection in terms of human rights. (Fernyhough 1993: 39)

It is indeed the notion, common to all societies, that human beings are
special and worthy of protection that distinguishes humans from animals. The
dogged insistence, even in the face of evidence to the contrary, on the exclusive
or distinctive 'possession' of human rights has no real place in serious scholarship; the only purpose of such a claim could lie either in the desire to assert
cultural superiority or to deny it. It would be more fruitful to study other
cultures and seek to understand how they protect, and also abuse, human
rights.

Above all else, the view of the ethnocentric universalist is at best counterproductive. It serves only to alienate state authorities who would purposefully
manipulate concepts in order to continue their repressive practices. How are
human rights to be realized universally if cultural chauvinists insist that only
their version is valid? Through coercion of other societies or modern civilizing

crusades? The only hope for those who care about the adherence by all communities to human rights is the painstaking study of each culture to identify norms and ideals that are in consonance with universal standards. Only by locating the basis for the cultural legitimacy of certain human rights and mobilizing social forces on that score can respect for universal standards be forged. It would be ridiculous, for example, for an African state to claim that, on the basis of African culture, it could detain its own citizens without trial. As An-Na'im succinctly explains:

> Enhancing the cultural legitimacy for a given human right should mobilize political forces within a community, inducing those in power to accept accountability for the implementation or enforcement of that right. With internal cultural legitimacy, those in power could no longer argue that national sovereignty is demeaned through compliance with standards set for the particular human right as an external value. Compliance with human rights standards would be seen as a legitimate exercise of national sovereignty and not as an external limitation. (An-Na'im 1990: 332)

No Rights Without Duties: An African Dialectic

Except for the African Charter's clawback clauses[40] and provisions concerning peoples' rights, much of the criticism of the Charter has been directed at its inclusion of duties on individuals (Flinterman and Ankumah 1992: 166–7; wa Mutua 1993: 33; Amnesty International 1993). This criticism, which this author shared at one point, appears to be driven primarily by the gross and persistent violations of human rights in post-colonial African states and the fear that vesting more power in the states can only result in more abuses (wa Mutua 1993: 32).[41] This fear aside, this chapter will examine the concept of duty in pre-colonial African societies and demonstrate its validity in conceptualizing a unitary, integrated conception of human rights in which the extreme individualism of current human rights norms is tempered by the individual's obligation to the society.

Capturing the view of many Africans, Okere has written that the 'African conception of man is not that of an isolated and abstract individual, but an integral member of a group animated by a spirit of solidarity' (Okere 1984: 148). Keba Mbaye, the renowned African jurist, has stated that in Africa 'laws and duties are regarded as being two facets of the same reality: two inseparable realities'.[42] This philosophy has been summed up by Mbiti as well: 'I am because we are, and because we are therefore I am' (Mbiti 1970: 141).[43]

According to this view, individuals are not atomistic units 'locked in a constant struggle against society for the redemption of their rights' (Kiwanuka 1988: 82). The Dinka concept of *cieng*, for example, 'places emphasis on such human values as dignity, integrity, honor, and respect for self and others, loyalty and piety, compassion and generosity, and unity and harmony' (Deng 1990: 266). But *cieng* not only attunes 'individual interests to the interests of others; it requires positive assistance to one's fellow human beings' (Deng 1990). Among the Bantu peoples of east and southern Africa, the concept of a person, *mundu* in Kikamba or *mtu* in Kiswahili, is not merely descriptive; it is also normative and refers to an individual who lives in peace and is helpful to his community.[44] In practical terms, this philosophy of the group-centred individual evolves through a series of carefully taught rights and responsibilities. At the root were structures of social and political organization, informed by gender and age, which served to enhance solidarity and ensure the existence of the community into perpetuity. The Kikuyu of Kenya, for example, achieved a two-tiered form of community organization: at the base was the family group composed of blood relatives, namely a husband and his wife or wives, their children and grandchildren, and often great-grandchildren; the second tier consisted of the clan, a combination of several family groups bearing the same name and believed to have descended from one ancestor (Kenyatta 1953: 1–2; Lambert 1965). Social status and prestige were based on the execution of duties within a third tier: the age-group. Marriage conferred eligibility for the elders council, the governing body (Kenyatta 1953: 200). Like the Kikuyu, the Akamba were organized in similar lineages and age-groups, culminating in the elders council, the supreme community organ (Muthiani 1973: 80–5). The Akan organizational chart also was similar (Wiredu 1990).

Relationships, rights and obligations flowed from these organizational structures, giving the community cohesion and viability. Certain obligations, such as the duty to defend the community and its territory, attached by virtue of birth and group membership. In the age-grading system of the Akamba, for example, each able-bodied male had to join the *anake* grade which defended the community and made war (Muthiani 1973: 82). In return for their services, the warriors were allowed to graduate into a more prestigious bracket, whereby others would defend them and their property thereafter. The expectations were similar among the Akans:

> But if every Akan was thus obligated by birth to contribute to defense in one way or another, there was also the complementary fact that he had a right to the protection of his person, property, and dignity, not only in his own state

but also outside it. And states were known to go to war to secure the freedom of their citizens abroad or avenge their mistreatment. (Wiredu 1990: 249)

Defence of the community, a state-type right exacted on those who came under its protection, was probably the most serious positive public obligation borne by young men. The commission of certain offences, such as murder, treason and cowardice, were also regarded as public offences or crimes against the public dimension of the community or state, imposing negative public duties on the individual. But most individual duties attached at the family and kinship levels and were usually identifiable through naming: an aunt was expected to act like a mother, an uncle like a father.[45] This is the basis of the saying, found in many African cultures, that it takes a whole village to raise a child.[46] As Cobbah correctly explains, the naming of individuals within the kinship structure 'defines and institutionalizes' the family member's required social role. These roles, which to the Western outsider may appear to be only of morally persuasive value, are 'essentially rights which each kinship member customarily possesses, and duties which each kinship member has toward his kin' (Cobbah 1987: 321). Expressed differently, 'the right of one kinship member is the duty of the other and the duty of the other kinship member is the right of another'. Sudarkasa and Cobbah thematically group the principles tying the kinship system together around respect, restraint, responsibility and reciprocity.[47] In a very real sense, 'entitlements and obligations form the very basis of the kinship system' (Cobbah 1987: 322).

The consciousness of rights and correlative duties is ingrained in community members from birth. Through every age-grade, the harmonization of individual interests with those of the grade is instilled unremittingly. As Kenyatta has remarked, the age-group is a 'powerful instrument for securing conformity' with the community's values; the 'selfish or reckless youth is taught by the opinion of his gang that it does not pay to incur displeasure' (Kenyatta 1953: 115).[48]

Through age-groups and the 'strength and numbers of the social ties' (Kenyatta 1953: 116–17), community solidarity is easily transmitted and becomes the basis for cohesion and stability. Furthermore, initiation ceremonies – for both girls and boys – taught gender roles and sexual morality (Kenyatta 1953: 130–54). Among the Kikuyu, a series of ceremonies, culminating in clitoridectomy for girls and circumcision for boys, marked passage into adulthood. Clitoridectomy, which was brought under sharp attack first by Christian missionaries and now by Western or Western-inspired human rights advocates, was a critical departure point in socialization.

This concept, that of the individual as a moral being endowed with rights but also bounded by duties, proactively uniting his needs with the needs of others, was the quintessence of the formulation of rights in pre-colonial societies. It radically differs from the liberal concept of the individual as the state's primary antagonist. Moreover, it provides those concerned with the universal conception of human rights with a basis for imagining another dialectic: the harmonization of duties and rights. Many of those who dismiss the relevance of the African concept of man by pejoratively referring to it as a 'peasant' and 'pre-industrial' notion fail to recognize that all major cultures and traditions – the Chinese, European, African, and the Arab, to mention a few – have a basic character distinctive to them. While it is true that no culture is static, and that normative cultural values are forever evolving, it is naive to think that a world-view can be eroded in a matter of decades, even centuries. Why should the concession be made that the individualist rights perspective is 'superior' to more community-oriented notions? As Cobbah has noted, 'in the same way that people in other cultures are brought up to assert their independence from their community, the average African's worldview is one that places the individual within his community' (Cobbah 1987: 323). This African world-view, he writes, 'is for all intents and purposes as valid as the European theories of individualism and the social contract'. Any concept of human rights with pretensions of universality cannot avoid mediating between these two seemingly contradictory notions.

Problems and Prospects for the Duty/Rights Conception

The idea of combining individual rights and duties in a human rights document is not completely without precedent. No less a document than the Universal Declaration of Human Rights (UDHR) blazed the trail in this regard when it provided, in a rare departure from its individualist focus, that '[e]veryone has the duties to the community in which alone the free and full development of his personality is possible' (UDHR, Art. 29).[49] However, the African Charter is the first human rights document to articulate the concept in any meaningful way. It is assumed, with undue haste, by human rights advocates and scholars that the inclusion of duties in the African Charter is nothing but 'an invitation to the imposition of unlimited restrictions on the enjoyment of rights' (Buergenthal 1988: 178).[50] This view is simplistic because it is not based on a careful assessment of the difficulties experienced by African countries in their miserable attempts to mimic wholesale Western notions of government and the role of the state. Such critics are transfixed by the allure of models of democracy prevalent in the industrial democracies of the West, models which promise an opportunity for the redemption of a troubled continent.

Unfortunately, such a view is shortsighted. Perhaps at no other time in the history of the continent have Africans needed each other more than they do today. Although there is halting progress towards democratization in some African countries, the continent is generally on a fast track to political and economic collapse. Now in the fourth decade of post-colonialism, African states have largely failed to forge viable, free and prosperous countries. The persistence of this problem highlights the dismal failures of the post-colonial states on several accounts. The new African states have failed to inspire loyalty in the citizenry; to produce a political class with integrity and a national interest; to inculcate in the military, the police and the security forces their proper roles in society; to build a nation from different linguistic and cultural groups; and to fashion economically viable policies. These realities are driving a dagger into the heart of the continent. There are many causes of the problem, and, while it is beyond the scope of this chapter to address them all, it will discuss one: namely, the human rights dimensions of the relationship between the individual, the community and the state.

Colonialism profoundly transformed and mangled the political landscape of the continent through the imposition of the modern state.[51] Each pre-colonial African 'nation', and there were thousands of them to be sure, had several characteristics: one ethnic community inhabited a 'common territory; its members shared a tradition, real or fictitious, of common descent; and they were held together by a common language and a common culture' (Busia: 1967: 31).[52] Few African nations were also states in the modern or European sense, although they were certainly political societies. In contrast, the states created by European imperialists, comprising the overwhelming majority of the continent, ordinarily contained more than one nation: 'Each one of the new states contains more than one nation. In their border areas, many new states contain parts of nations because the European-inspired borders cut across existing national territories' (Hansen 1993: 161).

The new state contained a population from many cultural groups coerced to live together. It did not reflect a 'nation', a people with the consciousness of a common destiny and shared history and culture.[53] The colonialists were concerned with the exploitation of Africa's human and natural resources, and not with the maintenance of the integrity of African societies. For the purposes of this expediency, grouping many nations in one territory was the only feasible administrative option. To compound the problem, the new rulers employed divide-and-conquer strategies, pitting nations against each other, further polarizing inter-ethnic tensions and creating a climate of mutual fear, suspicion and hatred. In many cases, the Europeans would openly favour one group or cluster of nations over others, a practice that served only to intensify tensions. For example, in Rwanda, a country rife with some of the worst inter-communal violence since decolonization, the Belgians heightened Hutu–Tutsi rivalry through preferential treatment towards the Tutsi.[54]

Ironically, colonialism, though a divisive factor, created a sense of brotherhood or unity among different African nations within the same colonial state, because they saw themselves as common victims of an alien, racist and oppressive structure.[55] Nevertheless, as the fissures of the modern African state amply demonstrate, the unity born out of anti-colonialism has not sufficed to create an enduring identity of nationhood in the context of the post-colonial state. Since in the pre-colonial era the primary allegiances were centred on lineage and the community (Busia 1967: 30), one of the most difficult challenges facing the post-colonial political class was the creation of new nations. This challenge, referred to as 'creating a national consciousness … was misleading', as there was 'no nation to become conscious of; the nation had to be created concurrently with a consciousness' (Hansen 1993: 161–2).

This difficult social and political transformation from self-governing ethno-cultural units to the multi-lingual, multi-cultural modern state – the disconnection between the two Africas: one pre-colonial, the other post-colonial – lies at the root of the current crisis. The post-colonial state has not altered the imposed European forms of social and political organization even though there is mounting evidence that they have failed to work in Africa (Hansen 1993: 161–2).[56] Part of the problem lies in the domination of the continent's political and social processes by Eurocentric norms and values. As correctly put by Hansen:

> African leaders have adopted and continued to use political forms and precedents that grew from, and were organically related to, the European experience. Formal declarations of independence from direct European rule do not mean actual independence from European conceptual dominance. African leaders and peoples have gone through tremendous political changes in the past hundred years. These profound changes have included the transformation of African societies and polities. They are still composed of indigenous African units, such as the lineage, village, tribe, and chieftainship, but they have been transformed around European units, such as the colony, district, political party, and state. (Hansen 1993: 161–2)

This serious and uniquely African crisis lacks the benefit of any historical guide or formula for its resolution. While acknowledging that it is impossible to recapture and reinstitute pre-colonial forms of social and political organization, this chapter asserts none the less that Africa must partially look inwards, to its pre-colonial past, for possible solutions. Certain ideals in pre-colonial African philosophy, particularly the conception of humanity, and the interface of rights and duties in a communal context as provided for in the African Charter, should form part of that process of reconstruction. The European domination of Africa has wrought social changes which have disabled old institutions by complicating social and political processes. Pre-colonial and post-colonial societies now differ fundamentally. In particular, there are differences of scale; states now have large and varied populations. Moreover, states possess enormous instruments of control and coercion, and their tasks are now without number. While this is true, Africa cannot move forward by completely abandoning its past.

The duty/rights concept of the African Charter could provide a new basis for individual identification with compatriots, the community and the state. It could forge and instil a national consciousness and act as the glue to reunite individuals and different nations within the modern state, and at the same time set the proper limits of conduct by state officials. The motivation and purpose behind the concept of duty in pre-colonial societies was to strengthen community ties and social cohesiveness, creating a shared fate and common destiny. This is the consciousness that the impersonal modern state has been unable to foster.[57] It has failed to shift loyalties from the lineage and the community to the modern state, with its mixture of different nations.

The series of explicit duties spelled out in Articles 27, 28 and 29 of the African Charter could be read as intended to re-create the bonds of the pre-colonial era among individuals and between individuals and the state (African Charter, Art. 45). They represent a rejection of the individual 'who is utterly free and utterly irresponsible and opposed to society'.[58] In a proper reflection of the nuanced nature of societal obligations in the pre-colonial era, the African Charter explicitly provides for two types of duties: direct and indirect. A direct duty is contained, for example, in Article 29(4) of the Charter which requires the individual to 'preserve and strengthen social and national solidarity, particularly when the latter is threatened'. There is nothing inherently sinister about this provision; it merely repeats a duty formerly imposed on members of pre-colonial communities. If anything, there exists a heightened need today, more than at any other time in recent history, to fortify communal relations and defend national solidarity. The threat of the collapse of the post-colonial state, as has been the case in Liberia, Somalia and Rwanda, is only too real. Political elites as well as the common citizenry, each in equal measure, bear the primary responsibility for avoiding societal collapse and its devastating consequences.

The African Charter provides an example of an indirect duty in Article 27(2), which states that '[t]he rights and freedoms of each individual shall be exercised with due regard to the rights of others, collective security, morality and common interest'. This duty is in fact a limitation on the enjoyment of certain individual rights. It merely recognizes the practical reality that in African societies, as elsewhere in the world, individual rights are not absolute. Individuals are asked to reflect on how the exercise of their rights in certain circumstances might adversely affect other individuals or the community. The duty is based on the presumption that the full development of the individual is possible only where individuals care about how their actions would impact on others. By rejecting the egotistical individual whose only concern is fulfilling self, Article 27(2) raises the level of care owed to neighbours and the community.

Duties are also grouped according to whether they are owed to individuals or to larger units such as the family, society or the state. Parents, for example, are owed a duty of respect and maintenance by their children.[59] Crippling economic problems do not allow African states to contemplate some of the programmes of the welfare state. The care of the aged and needy falls squarely on family and community members. This requirement – a necessity today – has its roots in the past; it was unthinkable to abandon a parent or relative in need.[60] The family guilty of such an omission would be held in disgrace and contempt pending the intervention of lineage or clan members. Such problems explain why the family is considered sacred and why it would be simply impracticable and suicidal for Africans to adopt wholesale the individualist conception of rights. Duty to the family is emphasized elsewhere in the Charter because of its crucial and indispensable economic utility.[61] Economic difficulties and the dislocations created by the transformation of rural life by the cash economy make the homestead a place of refuge.

Some duties are owed by the individual to the state. These are not restricted to African states; many of them are standard obligations that any modern state places on its citizens. In the African context, however, these obligations have a basis in the past, and many seem relevant because of the fragility and the domination of Africa by external agents. Such duties are rights that the community or the state, defined as all persons within it, holds against the individual. They include the duties to 'preserve and strengthen social and national solidarity' (African Charter, Art. 29, para. 4), not to 'compromise the security of the State' (Art. 29, para. 3), to serve the 'national community by placing his physical and intellectual abilities at its service' (Art. 29, para. 2), to 'pay taxes imposed by law in the interest of the society' (Art. 29, para. 6), and to 'preserve and strengthen the national independence and the territorial integrity of his country and to contribute to its defence in accordance with the law' (Art. 29, para. 5).

The duties that require the individual to strengthen and defend national independence, security, and the territorial integrity of the state are inspired by the continent's history of domination and occupation by outside powers over the centuries.[62] The duties represent an extension of the principle of self-determination, used in the external sense, as a shield against foreign occupation. Even in countries where this history is lacking, the right of the state to be defended by its citizens can trump certain individual rights, such as the draft of younger people for a war effort. Likewise, the duty to place one's intellectual abilities at the service of the state is a legitimate state interest, for the 'brain drain' has robbed Africa of massive intellect.[63] In recognition of the need for the strength of diversity, rather than its power to divide, the Charter asks individuals to promote African unity, an especially critical role given arbitrary Balkanization by the colonial powers and the ethnic animosities fostered within and between the imposed states.[64]

In addition to the duties placed on the state to secure for the people within its borders economic, social and cultural rights, the Charter also requires the state to protect the family, which it terms 'the natural unit and basis of society' (Art. 18, para. 1) and the 'custodian of morals and traditional values' (Art. 18, para. 2). There is an enormous potential for advocates of equality rights to be concerned that these provisions could be used to support the patriarchy and other repressive practices of pre-colonial social ordering. It is now generally accepted that one of the strikes against the pre-colonial regime was its strict separation of gender roles and, in many cases, the limitation on, or exclusion of, women from political participation. The discriminatory treatment of women on the basis of gender in marriage, property ownership and inheritance, and the disproportionately heavy labour and reproduction burdens were violations of their rights.

However, these are not the practices that the Charter condones when it requires states to assist families as the 'custodians of morals and traditional values'. Such an interpretation would be a cynical misreading of the Charter.[65] The reference is to those traditional values which enhanced the dignity of the individual and emphasized the dignity of motherhood and the importance of the female as the central link in the reproductive chain; women were highly valued as equals in the process of the regeneration of life. The Charter guarantees, unambiguously and without equivocation, the equal rights of women in its gender equality provision by requiring states to 'eliminate every discrimination against women' and to protect women's rights in international human rights instruments.[66] Read in conjunction with other provisions, the Charter leaves no room for discriminatory treatment against women.

The articulation of the duty concept in the Charter has been subjected to severe criticism. Some of the criticism, however, has confused the African concept of duty with socialist or Marxist formulations.[67] Such confusion is unfortunate. In socialist ideology, states, not individuals, are subjects of international law (Kartashkin 1982: 645). Thus the state assumes obligations under international law, through the International Covenant on Civil and Political Rights (ICCPR) for example, to provide human rights (Kartashkin 1982: 644–5). Under socialism, the state secures economic, cultural and social benefits for the individual. Hence, the state, as the guardian of public interest, retains primacy in the event of conflict with the individual (Wieruszewski 1990: 270). Human rights, therefore, are conditioned on the interest of the state and the goals of communist development.[68] There is an organic unity between rights and duties to the state.[69] In this collectivist concept, duties are owed only to the state. In contrast, in the pre-colonial era, and in the African Charter, duties are primarily owed to the family – nuclear and extended – and to the community, not to the state.[70] In effect, the primacy attached to the family in the Charter places the family above the state, which is not the case under communism.[71] In pre-colonial Africa, unlike the former Soviet Union or Eastern Europe, duties owed to the family or community were rarely misused or cynically manipulated to derogate from human rights obligations.[72]

The most damaging criticism of the language of duties in Africa sees them as 'little more than the formulation, entrenchment and legitimation of state rights and privileges against individuals and peoples' (Okoth-Ogendo 1993: 78–9).[73] However, critics who question the value of including duties in the Charter point only to the theoretical danger that states might capitalize on the duty concept to violate other guaranteed rights (Okoth-Ogendo 1993: 79).[74] The fear is frequently expressed that emphasis on duties may lead to the 'trumping' of individual rights if the two are in opposition (Cohen 1993: 15). It is argued that: 'If the state has a collective right and obligation to develop the society, economy, and polity (Article 29), then as an instrument it can be used to defend coercive state actions against both individuals and constituent groups to achieve state policies rationalized as social and economic improvement' (Okoth-Ogendo 1993).[75]

While the human rights records of African states are distressingly appalling, facts do not indicate that the zeal to promote certain economic and political programmes is the root cause of human rights abuses. Since 1978, the regime of Daniel Arap Moi in Kenya, for example, has not engaged in the widespread suppression of civil and political rights because of adherence to policies it deems in the national interest; instead, abuses have been triggered by an insecure and narrow political class which will stop at nothing, including political murder, to retain power.[76] Similarly, Mobutu Sese Seko of Zaire (now the Democratic Republic of the Congo) drove the country into the ground because he could not contemplate relinquishing power.[77] Alienated and corrupt elites, quite often devoid of a national consciousness, plunder the state and brutalize society to maintain their personal privileges and retain power.[78] The use of the state to implement particular state policies is almost never the reason, although such a rationale is frequently used as the pretext. Okoth-Ogendo persuasively argues that the attack on the duty conception is not meritorious because the 'state is the villain against which human rights law is the effective weapon' and towards which 'individuals should not be called upon to discharge any duties' (Okoth-Ogendo 1993: 79).[79] Valid criticism would question the 'precise boundaries, content, and conditions of compliance' contemplated by the Charter (ibid.). It should be the duty of the African Commission in its jurisprudence to clarify which, if any, of these duties are moral or legal obligations, and what the scope of their application ought to be.[80] The Commission could lead the way in suggesting how some of the duties – of the individual as well as the state – might be implemented. The concept of national service (African Charter, Art. 29), for example, could utilize traditional notions in addressing famine, public works, and community self-help projects. The care of parents and the needy (ibid.) could be formalized in family/state burden-sharing. The Commission should also indicate how, and in what forum, the state would respond to the breach of individual duties. It might suggest the establishment of community arbitration centres to work out certain types of disputes. As suggested by Umozurike, a former chairman to the Commission, state responsibility for these duties implies a 'minimum obligation to inculcate the underlying principles and ideals in their subjects' (Umozurike 1983: 907).[81]

The duty/rights formulation is also inextricably tied to the concept, articulated in the African Charter, of peoples' rights. Although a long discussion about the concept itself and the controversy it has attracted will not be made here, this chapter will outline its necessity to the duty concept. Like the duty concept, the idea of peoples' rights is embodied in the African philosophy which sees men and women primarily as social beings embraced in the body of the community.[82] It was pointed out during the drafting of the African Charter that individual rights could be justified only in the context of the rights of the community; consequently the drafters made room in the Charter for peoples' rights.[83]

The concept was not new in a human rights document. For example, Common Article 1 of the two basic international human rights covenants makes peoples the subject of rights, a departure from Western notions that human rights attach only to individuals.[84] There is recognition of the fact that individual rights cannot be realized unless groups hold collective rights. As clearly noted by Sohn:

> One of the main characteristics of humanity is that human beings are social creatures. Consequently, most individuals belong to various units, groups, and communities; they are simultaneously members of such units as a family, religious community, social club, trade union, professional association, racial group, people, nation, and state. It is not surprising, therefore, that international law not only recognizes inalienable rights of individuals, but also recognizes certain collective rights that are exercised jointly by individuals grouped into larger communities, including peoples and nations. These rights are still human rights; the effective exercise of collective rights is a precondition to the exercise of other rights, political or economic or both. If a community is not free, most of its members are also deprived of many important rights. (Sohn 1982: 48; Kiwanuka 1988)

The African Charter distinguishes human rights from peoples' or collective rights, but sees them in cooperation, not competition or conflict. The Charter's preambular paragraph notes this relationship and recognizes 'on the one hand, that fundamental human rights stem from the attributes of human beings, which justifies their national and international protection and on the other hand, that the reality and respect for peoples' rights should necessarily guarantee human rights'. This unambiguous statement, notes van Boven, is conclusive proof of the Charter's view: human rights are inalienable and intrinsic to individuals and are not in conflict with peoples' rights, which they complement (van Boven 1986: 188–9).[85]

The exercise of sovereignty rights by a 'people' or 'peoples' as contemplated by the Charter is a necessary precondition for the enjoyment of individual rights.[86] This dialectic between individual and peoples' rights is one of the bases for the Charter's imposition of duties on individuals. Solidarity between the individual and the greater society safeguards collective rights, without which individual rights would be unattainable.

Conclusions

Today Africa is at a crossroads. Since colonization, when Europe restructured its political map, Africa has lunged from one crisis to another. Whether it was famine consuming millions, Idi Amin dispatching political opponents and innocents with impunity, senseless coups by soldiers who could barely read, the Rwandese and Burundian catastrophes, the wars in Sierra Leone, the Democratic Republic of the Congo and Angola, ethnic tensions turned deadly, or corrupt political elites, the list of abominations is simply unbearable. The failure of the post-colonial state is so pervasive that it has become the rule, not the exception. Needless to say, there are numerous causes for this crisis, perhaps the most important of which is the disfiguration of the continent's political identity by the imposition of European forms and values of government and society. Narrow political elites who barely comprehend the Western notions they eagerly mimic – and who have lost the anchor in their past – remain in power, but without a rudder (Chege 1995: 45).[87] This crisis of cultural identity is Africa's most serious enemy. But with the end of colonization and the Cold War – the two driving reasons for past European and American interest in Africa – Africans should re-examine the assumptions underlying the role and purpose of the state and its organization. It must be conceded, however, that the negative forces of globalization may not provide the continent with relief from this past of unthinkable tragedies.

This chapter is not intended to dismiss concerns about the potential for the misuse of the duty/rights concept by political elites to achieve narrow, personal ends. However, any notions are subject to abuse by power-hungry elites. There is no basis for concluding that the duty/rights concept is unique in this respect. While it is true that the pre-colonial context in which the concept originally worked was small in scale and relatively uncomplicated, the argument made here is not about magnitude. Instead, the ideals that can be distilled from the past are the central thrust of this argument. Is it possible to introduce in the modern African state grassroots democracy, deepening it in neighbourhood communities and villages in the tradition of the pre-colonial council of elders? Can the family reclaim its status as the basic organizational political unit in this re-democratization process? Is it possible to create a state of laws, where elected officials are bound by checks and balances, as in the days when chiefs were held accountable, at times through destooling? Can the state and the family devise a 'social security' system in which the burden of caring for the aged and the needy can be shared? Is it possible to require individuals to take responsibility for their actions in matters relating to sexuality, community security and self-help projects in the construction of community schools and health centres, utilizing concepts such as *harambee*,[88] the Kenyan slogan for pulling together? Childcare and -rearing, including lighter forms of discipline such as a reprimand, for example, have always been community affairs in Africa (Cobbah 1987: 322). Could community-based programmes be devised and encouraged to promote the 'village-raising' of children? These are the typical questions that the new formulation of human rights must ask in the context of re-creating the African state to legitimize human rights on the continent.

This chapter represents a preliminary attempt to begin rethinking Africa's pre-colonial articulation of human rights and propose how some of the ideals imbedded in the past could be woven into conceptions of man, society and the state in a way that would make the human rights corpus more relevant to Africa today. Senghor has stressed the need for an Afrocentric document which would 'assimilate without being assimilated', but he has also cautioned against a charter for the 'African Man' only; he has emphasized that '[m]ankind is one and indivisible and the basic needs of man are similar everywhere' (Kunig 1985: 124). Part of the reason for the failure of the post-colonial state to respect human rights lies in the seemingly alien character of that corpus. The African Charter's duty/rights concept is an excellent point of departure in the reconstruction of a new ethos and the restoration of confidence in the continent's cultural identity. It reintroduces values that Africa needs most at this time: commitment, solidarity, respect and responsibility. Moreover, it also represents a recognition of another reality. Individual rights are collective in their dimension. '[T]heir recognition, their mode of exercise and their means of protection' is a collective process requiring the intervention of other individuals, groups and communities (Marie 1986: 199). The past, as the Africans of old used to say, is part of the living. It ought to be used to construct a better tomorrow.

Notes

1. The African Charter on Human and Peoples' Rights, 27 June 1981, OAU Doc. CAB/LEG/67/3/Rev.5 (1981), reprinted in 21 ILM 59 (1982) (hereinafter African Charter).

2. The African Charter, also referred to as the Banjul Charter, was adopted in 1981 by the 18th Assembly of Heads of State and Government of the Organization of African Unity (OAU), the official body of African states. It is known as the Banjul Charter because the final draft was produced in Banjul, the capital of The Gambia. One of the Charter's implementing organs, the African Commission on Human and Peoples' Rights (the African Commission), was established in 1987. The African Commission's eleven members, known as commissioners, are elected by the OAU by secret ballot for a six-year term and serve in

their own personal capacities. See African Charter (supra note 1), Arts 31, 33, 36, 45, 21 ILM at 64–5. In June 1998, the OAU adopted the Protocol to the African Charter on Human and Peoples' Rights, on the Establishment of an African Court on Human and Peoples' Rights, OAU/LEG/MIN/AFCHPR/PROT./(1)Rev.2 (1997). The African Human Rights Court is expected to complement the African Commission in implementing the African Charter.

3. The major human rights instruments include the trilogy of documents commonly referred to as the International Bill of Rights: (i) the 1948 Universal Declaration of Human Rights, GA Res. 217 A(III), UN Doc. A/810, at 71 (1948) (hereinafter UDHR); (ii) the 1966 International Covenant on Civil and Political Rights, GA Res. 2200 A(XXI), UN GAOR, 21st Sess., Supp. No. 16, at 52, UN Doc. A/6316 (1966) (hereinafter ICCPR), what many call the Bible of the human rights movement; and (iii) the 1966 International Covenant on Economic, Social and Cultural Rights, GA Res. 2200 A(XXI), UN GAOR, 21st Sess., Supp. No. 16, at 49, UN Doc. A/6316 (1966) (hereinafter ICESCR). The last two instruments entered into force in 1976.

4. Civil and political rights, the staple of the human rights movement, have been commonly referred to as 'first-generation' rights, while economic cultural, and social rights are called 'second-generation' rights. In addition to these, the African Charter provides for 'peoples' rights', known also as collective or group rights, which include the right of peoples to self-determination, political sovereignty over their natural resources and the right to development (Buergenthal 1988: 176–7). One group right, the right to self-determination, is widely recognized and enshrined in Article 1 common to both the ICCPR (Art. 1, para. 1) and the ICESCR (Art. 1, para. 1). Chapter II of the African Charter, which imposes various duties on individuals, is that document's most radical contribution to human rights law. See African Charter, Arts 27–29, 21 ILM at 63.

5. For detailed discussions and analyses of the relationships between peoples' and human rights in the African Charter, see generally Gittleman 1982; Umozurike 1983; van Boven 1986; Marie 1986; Weston et al. 1987; and Kiwanuka 1988.

6. There seems little doubt that private duties, implied and direct, are contemplated by most human rights instruments. Examples abound. Article 5 of the ICCPR provides, in part, that nothing contained therein can imply 'for any state, group or person' any right to limit the rights of others. Moreover, individuals can be punished for violations of human rights, as was the case in Nuremburg, given that the Geneva Conventions impose duties on private individuals (Paust 1992: 51–63).

7. The human rights movement is based on the Western liberal tradition which conceives of the individual as atomistic and alienated from society and the state. Although Jack Donnelly makes a case for other trajectories within the liberal tradition, he concedes that '[t]he "Western" or "liberal" conception of human rights is conventionally characterized as resting on a social vision of largely isolated individuals holding (only) property rights and "negative" civil and political liberties' (Donnelly 1990: 31). This formulation, which this author terms Eurocentric because it grows out of European history and philosophy, sees the human rights corpus merely as an instrument for individual claims against the state. Donnelly argues that this 'conventional, or minimalist, conception of liberalism … is only one strand of the liberal tradition of political theory and practice' (Donnelly 1990: 32). In fact, Donnelly posits that there is an 'alternative strand that rests on a broader, more subtle – and … more coherent and defensible – social vision'. In this more radical liberal tradition, Donnelly argues, 'individualism is moderated by social values, private property rights are limited rather than absolute, and civil and political rights are coupled with economic and social rights' (Donnelly 1990: 33). It is this strand of liberalism that is

the source of the social democratic regimes and the welfare states of the Western industrial democracies.

Notwithstanding Donnelly's alternative insight, it is primarily the conventional strand of liberalism that has dominated the theory and practice of the human rights movement. Scholars and activists in the West, the main authors of the discourse, have articulated a vision that places civil and political rights above other categories of rights. In effect, the human rights movement has become an anti-catastrophe crusade, under the captive leadership of Amnesty International and Human Rights Watch, to contain and control state action against the individual. The practice of human rights by inter-governmental organizations (IGOs), non-governmental organizations (NGOs) and national human rights institutions has been primarily focused on civil and political rights. Economic, social and cultural rights, while part of the rhetoric of rights, remain severely underdeveloped.

8. Cover argues that the myth, the jurisprudence of rights, is essential to counterbalance the omnipotent state. This myth 'a) establishes the State as legitimate only in so far as it can be derived from the autonomous creatures who trade in their rights for security – i.e., one must tell a story about the State's utility or service to us, and b) potentially justifies individual and communal resistance to the Behemoth' (Cover 1987: 69). It is not surprising that Western individuals and movements employ the language of rights in their claims against society or the state. Examples range from civil rights groups to women's organizations and gay and lesbian individuals and groups.

9. In 1885 at the Berlin Conference, European powers carved up the map of Africa and created dozens of entirely new countries without regard to existing political entities, ethnic boundaries, economic considerations, historical alliances or geographic and demographic variables (Young 1991).

10. Only Morocco, Tunisia, Ethiopia, Burundi, Rwanda, Madagascar, Swaziland, Lesotho and Botswana have any meaningful pre-colonial territorial identities (Young 1991).

11. This author has argued elsewhere that '[s]ince citizens lack an instinctual and nationalistic bond to the state, those who become rulers pillage it'. Furthermore, '[f]ew Africans owe their allegiance to the emergent state; many identify with an ethnic group – a loyalty that predates colonialism – or the pan-Africanist idea of Africa as home. The colonial state and its successor have been so alienated from the people that the development of national consciousness was not possible' (Mutua 1994: 17).

Other writers have characterized the transformation of the African political and cultural landscape in more modest terms. According to Crawford Young, 'the depth and intensity of alien penetration of subordinated societies continues to cast its shadow'. He notes further that the 'cultural and linguistic impact [of colonialism] was pervasive, especially in sub-Saharan Africa. Embedded in the institutions of the new states was the deep imprint of the mentalities and routines of their colonial predecessors. Overall, colonial legacy cast its shadow over the emergent African state system to a degree unique among the major world regions' (Young 1991: 19–20).

12. For more detailed views of the concept of cultural relativism in human rights, see generally Donnelly 1989; Panikkar 1982; Pollis and Schwab 1979.

13. Rhoda Howard, a well-known Canadian Africanist, refuses to acknowledge that pre-colonial African societies knew human rights as a concept. She emphasizes that 'traditional Africa protected a system of obligations and privileges based on ascribed statuses, not a system of human rights to which one was entitled merely by virtue of being human' (Howard 1990: 159, 167). Howard is so fixated with the Western notion of rights attaching only to the atomized individual that she summarily dismisses arguments by African scholars,

some of whom could be classified as cultural relativists, that individual rights were held in a social, collective context.

14. Francis Deng disagrees with the view 'widely held in the West and accepted or exploited in developing countries, that the concept of human rights is peculiarly Western' (Deng 1990: 261). '[T]o arrogate the concept', writes Deng, 'to only certain groups, cultures, or civilizations is to aggravate divisiveness on the issue, to encourage defensiveness or unwarranted self-justification on the part of the excluded, and to impede progress toward a universal consensus on human rights' (ibid.).

15. Donnelly, for example, dismisses cultural relativists and then declares, rather hastily, that 'human rights are foreign to such communities [African, Native American, traditional Islamic social systems], which employed other mechanisms to protect and realize human dignity' (Donnelly 1989: 118). Unless the contrary is established, this author assumes that all cultures have evolved moral and ethical standards as well as norms and processes that protect the dignity and worth of human beings in both their individual and collective personalities. It is these norms and processes – which manifest themselves in all cultures of the world – that germinate the concept of human rights.

16. Fernyhough notes that this division is ironic because 'both groups take as their starting point a precolonial Africa that they agree was precapitalist and predominantly agrarian, relatively decentralized politically, and characterized by communal social relations' (Fernyhough 1993: 39).

17. Although the majority of pre-colonial authorities in Africa were not rigidly stratified, a number of highly centralized states such Buganda and the Nigerian emirates divided society into the repressive categories of nobles, freemen and slaves (Howard 1984: 175–6). Howard errs, however, when she asserts that the 'picture of precolonial African social relations on which the communal model is based is inaccurate even regarding the past' (ibid.). She deliberately fails to admit that highly centralized societies were the exception, not the norm; most were governed by ideals of communitarianism.

18. An examination of pre-colonial societies yields two basic models. A majority of societies, many of which were agricultural, pastoralist or both, were relatively free of rigid social stratification, although age and gender played significant roles in determining both social and political status. A number of others had developed coercive state structures (Ayisi 1979; Fortes and Evans-Pritchard 1940).

19. A basic contradiction between the European nation-state and pre-colonial African societies lies in the constitution of political society. In distinguishing what he calls 'African cultural-nations' from the modern state, Mojekwu argues that '[w]hile the European impersonal governments were able to accommodate and control peoples from several ethnic, racial, and cultural origins within the nation-state, African cultural-nations controlled kinship groups within their cultural boundaries. A cultural-nation governed through familial chiefs and elders who shared authority with the community at large' (Mojekwu 1980: 87). Few pre-colonial African societies were multi-ethnic.

20. Howard sees no middle ground between individual and group consciousness. She writes, incredibly, that for Africans to 'assert their human rights as individuals would be unthinkable and would undercut their dignity as group members' (Howard 1990: 166).

21. Wiredu defines a right as a 'claim that people are entitled to make on others or on society at large by virtue of their status' (Wiredu 1990: 243).

22. Akans believed that each individual had intrinsic value and was entitled to a measure of basic respect. But individuals were also members of matrilineal kinship lineages which generated duties and obligations. A person could enhance his or her 'individuality' or

'personhood' by executing duties such as participating in public works and sustaining a prosperous household. Conversely, if one failed to make these contributions, one's person-hood diminished. This 'normative layer' in the conception of an individual bears obligations, but it is also 'matched by a whole series of rights that accrue to the individual simply because he lives in a society in which everyone has those obligations' (Wiredu 1990: 247).

23. While all 'people were considered equal in status as human beings', everyone was expected to show strangers 'special generosity' (Muthiani 1973: 18). The age-gradation on which the Akamba were organized was a functional structure based on the level of physical maturity. Equality and democracy were required within each age grade. Women had their own comparable but separate prestige structure which, however, was rarely consulted by the council of elders in matters of public concern (Muthiani 1973: 80–2).

24. On occasion, an election was necessary to determine who in the royal lineage was the rightful heir. The town was the basic unit of government among the Akans. Several Akan towns could group together to form larger governmental units.

25. 'The stool was the symbol of chiefly status, and so the installation of a chief was called enstoolment and his dismissal destoolment' (Wiredu: 1990: 251). The 'destooling' of a chief was governed by certain processes and rules. Charges would be filed and in-vestigations conducted before a decision could be reached (ibid.). On rules governing a chieftainship, see Ayisi (1979: 48). Further evidence of democratic governance in traditional African society is offered by Kobia's description of the political organization among the Meru of Kenya. Members of the *njuri ncheke*, the supreme council of elders, were 'very carefully elected and had to be individuals of unquestionable integrity and in good standing with the society' (Kobia 1993). The chair of the *njuri ncheke*, which held legislative and judicial powers, 'rotated among the *agwe*', leaders of the six sub-groups of the Meru nation.

26. Cattle were highly valued as a measurement of wealth. Among the Maasai, another east African people, the murder of a man was compensated by the fixed fine of forty-nine head of cattle. It is interesting to note that no fine was set for the murder of women because the Maasai almost never murdered women, due to the belief that ill-luck would strike the murderer (Sankan 1971: 14).

27. Wiredu further notes that neither at the 'lineage level nor at any other level of Akan society could a citizen be subjected to any sort of sanctions without proof of wrongdoing' (Wiredu 1990: 252). Even dead bodies were tried posthumously before a symbolic sentence could be imposed.

28. For example, in the Tio kingdom in present-day Brazzaville, the Congo, 'as elsewhere in Africa, a strong tradition of jurisprudence existed, with specific rulings for penalties cited as precedents, such as levels of fines for adultery' (Fernyhough 1993: 62). Among the Akamba, for instance, the offence of assault carried numerous fines, which varied depending on the degree of assault and whether it resulted in the loss of a limb or limbs (Hobley 1971: 79).

29. The concept of 'negritude' was initially coined by Aimé Cesaire and Leopold Sedar Senghor as a reaction to white racism of the French variety. Under the philosophy of negritude, 'collective organizations enfold the individual in Africa. Yet he is not crushed.' What the African knows, Senghor points out, is that 'the realization of the human per-sonality lies less in the search for singularity than in the development of his potential through participation in a community' (Senghor 1977: 257). It emphasizes the importance of the family, nuclear and extended, the role of democratic, consensual decision-making with the community through the council of elders, and respect for nature.

30. The concept of *Ujamaa*, the Kiswahili concept for kinship, was based on three prongs:

(i) respect, where each family member recognized the place and rights of others within the family; (ii) common ownership of property, that all must have the same basic necessities; and (iii) obligation to work, that every family member has the right to eat and to shelter but also the obligation to work (Hyden 1980: 98).

31. In her work on family structures, Sudarkasa groups the cultural factors that account for the cohesion of the African family into four principles: respect, restraint, responsibility and reciprocity. These principles create a complex balance of rights and duties within the family structure (Sudarkasa 1980: 50; Cobbah 1987: 309–31). Special mention must be made of the importance of generosity in traditional society. As noted by Kobia, there was a 'mutual caring for one another, especially strangers and travellers' (Kobia 1993: 13). It was, for example, a 'cardinal custom' in every household to prepare enough food for the unexpected stranger (ibid.). Even in today's economic difficulties, Africans – rural and urban – generally offer food to strangers and visitors.

32. For pre-colonial human rights concepts in Africa, see also Abayomi 1991: 1037–41; Nahum 1982; and Busia 1994.

33. Wai further notes that channels for political participation existed in which '[d]iscussion was open and those who dissented from the majority opinion were not punished ... There was a clear conception of freedom of expression and association' (Wai 1979: 117).

34. In the fire ordeal, the suspect would be asked to lick a red-hot sword to prove his innocence (Hobley 1971: 81).

35. In pre-colonial Africa, women were primarily responsible for housework including childcare. Men generally handled 'public' affairs such as security and governance of the community.

36. Howard attempts to explain away the index of the African notions of rights and duties by making an analogy between the simplicity of feudal Europe and pre-colonial Africa. In 'closed-village societies of premodern Europe, we would also discover that people thought of themselves more as members of their own local groups than as individuals, finding a sense of identity by fulfilling their assigned roles rather than by fulfilling "themselves"' (Howard 1984: 176). To her, what some writers 'view as essentially different African and Western social structures and ways of thinking are actually differences between relatively simple and relatively complex societies' (ibid.). In other words, Howard believes that pre-industrial African societies could not generate the complex concept of human rights.

37. Howard believes that the 'African' world-view, which is 'peasant' and 'traditional', must give way to the 'Western' world-view, which is 'urban' and 'modern' and anchored around the individual. She cites Kenya and Nigeria, the 'more developed economies of contemporary Africa' as examples of societies where the 'traditional concept of solidarity is giving way to individualism' (Howard 1990: 170).

38. Donnelly further writes that '[i]n the Third World today we see most often not the persistence of traditional culture in the face of modern intrusions, or even the development of syncretic cultures and values, but rather a disruptive "Westernization", cultural confusion, or the enthusiastic embrace of "modern" practices and values' (Donnelly 1989: 119).

39. To argue, as Donnelly and Howard do, that the individual in pre-colonial African societies was not entitled, in certain circumstances, to be left alone – for that is what the concept of human rights is partially about – betrays gross and surprising ignorance about African societies.

40. Clawback clauses qualify rights and permit a state to restrict them to the extent permitted by domestic law. Their purpose, apparently, is to place vague constraints on government action against the individual. For an example, Article 6 of the African Charter

provides, in part, that '[e]very individual shall have the right to liberty and to the security of his person. No one may be deprived of his freedom except for reasons and conditions previously laid down by law.' The Charter has also been criticized for the weaknesses inherent in its enforcement mechanisms (Flinterman and Ankumah 1992: 167–9). See generally, Haysom 1994; Ojo and Sessay 1994.

41. For duties imposed on individuals, see African Charter, Arts 27–29.

42. International Commission of Jurists, Human and Peoples' Rights in Africa and the African Charter 27 (1986).

43. The individual's needs, rights, joys and sorrows are woven into a social tapestry that denies singular individuality.

44. The word Bantu consists of *ntu*, a root, which means humanness. Quite often, speakers of Kikamba or Kiswahili will rhetorically ask of an abusive person if he is or has become an animal. An individual is not a *mundu* or a *mtu*, and loses his humanness if he abuses or mistreats fellow community members.

45. In Africa, 'the extended family unit, like family units in nearly all societies, assigns each member a social role that permits the family to operate as a reproductive, economic and socialization unit' (Cobbah 1987: 320). But unlike the West, kinship terminologies in Africa relate to actual duties and obligations borne by members. Furthermore, the terminologies are more encompassing: aunts and mothers, for example, have similar roles within the kinship unit, regardless of biological parentage. The same is true of uncles and older cousins (ibid.).

46. Most pre-colonial African villages were inhabited by people related through blood or marriage.

47. This matrix of group solidarity revolves around respect, based on seniority in age; restraint or the balancing of individual rights with the requirements of the group; responsibility, which requires commitment to work with and help others in return for security; and reciprocity through which generous acts are returned (Cobbah 1987: 322; Sudarkasa 1980: 50).

48. Kenyatta writes that 'early and late, by rules of conduct in individual instances, by the sentiment of the group in which he lives, by rewards and punishments and fears of ceremonial uncleanness, the younger generation learns the respect and obedience due to parents. The older generation do likewise' (Kenyatta 1953: 115).

49. The American Declaration of the Rights and Duties of Man, OAS Res. XXX, International Conference of American States, 9th Conf. (1948), OAS Doc. OEA/Ser. L/V/1.4 Rev. XX (1965), also proclaimed a list of twenty-seven human rights and ten duties (Buergenthal 1988: 128). The American Convention on Human Rights did not follow the same course.

50. Others, such as Haysom, have made blanket condemnations of the concept of duties. Fearing that the concept of duties could be used to suppress rights guaranteed by the African Charter, Haysom has written that the 'interpretation of a duty towards the community as to mean duty towards the state, lends itself to an autocratic style of Government' (Haysom 1994: 6).

51. For a commanding history of the continent, spanning the pre-colonial era to the present, see Davidson 1991; and Mazrui 1986.

52. Hansen defines a nation as 'a group that shares a common history and identity and is aware of that; they are a people, not just a population' (Hansen 1993: 139, 161).

53. According to Busia, the 'new African States are composed of many different tribes. A state can claim to be a common territory for all the tribes within it, but common descent,

real or fictitious, cannot be maintained among tribes, some of which have a history of different origins and migrations, such as the Buale, Senufo, Guro of the Ivory Coast; the Yoruba, Hausa, Ibo of Nigeria; Ewe, Fanti, Dagomba of Ghana ... Instead of the bond of a common culture and language, there are language and cultural differences which tend to divide rather unite' (Busia 1967: 33; Mutua 1994).

54. Although, before the arrival of the Belgians, the Tutsi minority ruled over the Hutu majority and the Twa in a feudal–client relationship, the colonial state 'transformed communal relations and sharpened ethnic tensions by ruling through a narrow Tutsi royalty. The access to resources and power that the Tutsi collaborators enjoyed under the colonial state irreversibly polarized Hutu–Tutsi relations' (Mutua 1994).

55. 'One need not go into the history of colonisation of Africa, but that colonisation had one significant result. A sentiment was created on the African continent – a sentiment of oneness' (Mazrui 1986: 108, quoting Julius Nyerere).

56. Hansen notes that the 'most obvious and powerful expressions of the continued African conceptual reliance on European political forms are the African states themselves. The states are direct and uncritical successors of the colonies' (Hansen 1993: 161).

57. In his discussion of the absence of the requirements of empirical statehood in postcolonial Africa, Jackson has written that, in these 'ramshackle' regimes, '[c]itizenship means little and carries few substantial rights or duties compared with membership in a family, clan, religious sect or ethnic community. Often the "government" cannot govern itself, and its officials may in fact be freelancers, charging what amounts to a private fee for their services' (Jackson 1992: 1).

58. OAU Doc. CAB/LEG/67/3/Rev.1 at 2.

59. Article 29 (1) of the African Charter provides that the individual shall have the duty to 'preserve the harmonious development of the family and to work for the cohesion and respect of the family; to respect his parents at all times, to maintain them in case of need'. The state, however, does not shirk responsibility for the aged and disabled. The Charter gives them 'the right to special measures of protection in keeping with their physical or moral needs' (African Charter, Art. 29, Art. 18, para. 4).

60. In defence of the duty of the individual to parents, the aged, and the needy, Isaac Nguema, the first chair of the African Commission, has rhetorically asked: '[h]ow can society be so ungrateful to people who once helped to build it, on the grounds that they have become a burden, maybe no more than waste?' Isaac Nguema (1989) 'Universality and Specificity in Human Rights in Africa', *The Courier*, Nov./Dec., pp. 16, 17. He pleads for Africa to 'foster the cult and the veneration of the aged'.

61. Article 27(1) of the African Charter provides, *inter alia*, that '[e]very individual shall have duties towards his family'.

62. It would be surprising if the first Africa-wide human rights document did not show sensitivity to the subjugation of African peoples, a condition that has largely defined what the continent is today. Beginning with the invasion, enslavement and colonization by Arabs and later the Europeans, Africans have been keenly aware of the traumatic consequences of the loss of sovereignty over their political and social life. As a general rule, they have not exercised domination over others; that ledger is heavily weighted against them.

63. Although the 'brain drain' is partially a result of the abusive state, the cost of education is so high that a state is entitled to ask its educated elites to contribute to national welfare.

64. Every African is required to 'contribute to the best of his abilities, at all times and at all levels, to the promotion and achievement of African unity' (African Charter, Art. 29,

para. 8). '[A]ll levels' here implies, *inter alia*, unity between different ethnic groups within the same state. This provision reflects a recognition by the Charter of the destructive power of ethnic hatred or tribalism, the term Westerners prefer when referring to ethnic tensions in Africa.

65. The Charter's reference to 'traditional values' cannot in good faith be interpreted as a call for the continued oppression of women. The Charter requires the individual to 'preserve and strengthen positive African cultural values in his relations with other members of the society, in the spirit of tolerance, dialogue and consultation and, in general, to contribute to the promotion of the moral well-being of society' (African Charter, Art. 29, para. 7).

66. 'The state shall ensure the elimination of every discrimination against women and also ensure the protection of the rights of the woman and the child as stipulated in international declarations and conventions' (African Charter, Art. 18, para. 3). Note, however, that the pairing of women and children in this instance is not merely a function of sloppy draftsmanship; it most probably betrays the sexist perception of the drafters.

67. Donnelly, for example, thinks that the Soviet or socialist concept of human rights, reflected in practice and official doctrine, is 'strikingly similar' to African and Chinese conceptions (Donnelly 1989: 55).

68. Articles 39, 50, 51 and 59 of the 1977 constitution of the Union of Soviet Socialist Republics link individual duties to the state with the enjoyment of individual rights (Konst. SSSR, Arts 39, 50, 51, 59, 1977).

69. V. Chkhidvadze (1980) 'Constitution of True Human Rights and Freedoms', *International Affairs*, cited in Donnelly 1989: 55.

70. Individual duties owed to intermediate groups – groups falling between the family and the state such as ethnic, professional and other associational entities – would seem to be implied by Article 27(1) which refers to 'society' and 'other legally recognized communities'. Such a reading could also be attached to Article 10(2) which refers to the 'obligation of solidarity' in associational life. 'Solidarity' is both 'social' and 'national' (African Charter, Art. 29).

71. Article 18(1) compels the state to protect the family, the 'natural unit' of society.

72. According to Benedek: '[t]he human rights approach to be found in traditional African societies is characterized by a permanent dialectical relationship between the individual and the group, which fits neither into the individualistic nor the collectivistic concept of human rights' (Benedek 1985: 63).

73. For other examples of this type of criticism, see Okere 1984: 148–9; Amnesty International 1991: 15; and Shivji 1989.

74. See supra note 40 and accompanying text.

75. Cohen adds that '[m]ore importantly, the dangers of supporting state power as a fundamental "right" are obvious. Indeed, the African record to date on that score provides serious grounds for concern' (Cohen 1993: 15). Donnelly points to the perversion of the ordinary correlation between duties and rights in the former Soviet Union where a totalitarian, undemocratic state manipulated the concept to abrogate individual rights (Donnelly 1989: 55–7). However, this author disagrees with Donnelly when he states that rights are completely independent of duties. The link between rights and duties is a social dialectic; one implies the other.

76. For exhaustive catalogues of human rights abuses by the Kenyan government, see Africa Watch 1991; Robert F. Kennedy Memorial Center for Human Rights 1994; and Kenya Human Rights Commission 1994. For a more conceptual discussion about the

difficulties of creating rights-respecting governments, see generally Aidoo 1993; Shepherd and Anikpo (eds) 1990 (presenting theoretical considerations about emerging rights from the standpoint of political economy); McCarthy-Arnolds et al. (eds) 1994; and Mahmud 1993 (attributing human rights violations in Africa to the African interpretation of human rights and to structural inadequacies).

77. For a comprehensive report on human rights abuses in Zaire, see Lawyers Committee for Human Rights 1990; and Africa Watch 1992.

78. During its first two decades after achieving independence in 1961, Tanzania, under the leadership of Julius Nyerere and the Tanzania African National Union (TANU) and later Chama Cha Mapinduzi (CCM), the ruling party, appeared to be an exception to the kleptocratic oligarchies then prevalent in Africa. The state seemed genuinely committed to the realization of *Ujamaa*, the policy of socialism and self-reliance. See Hyden 1980 (discussing the implementation of *Ujamaa* policies and politics in Tanzania from a political economy perspective with particular focus on the role of the peasants).

79. The misappropriation of tradition by some of Africa's despots and political charlatans to justify coercive measures against individuals should not be a reason for the emotional denunciation of the duty/rights conception. Hastings Kamuzu Banda, the former president of Malawi, used 'traditional courts' to silence his critics, and Mobutu Sese Seko, the long-term Zairian ruler, at one point instituted *salongo*, a thinly disguised colonial practice of forced labour. Both practices, which had nothing to do with pre-colonial values, were cynically designed to increase the state's power over the people (Robert F. Kennedy Memorial Center for Human Rights 1994; Donnelly 1989: 120).

80. Article 45 of the African Charter outlines the mandate of the African Commission, which includes the interpretation of the Charter and the formulation of principles and rules relating to human rights.

81. The African Charter also imposes similar obligations on states: 'States parties to the present Charter shall have the duty to promote and ensure through teaching, education and publication, the respect of the rights and freedoms contained in the present Charter and to see to it that these freedoms and rights as well as corresponding obligations and duties are understood' (African Charter, Art. 25).

82. Benedek observes further that, in traditional African societies, 'the human being could not survive apart from his people, the community, who in turn was dependent on the participation of all its constituent parts' (Benedek 1985: 63). This relationship was one of duality, 'not one of subordination but of complementarity, participation, and dialogue'. The 'support and allegiance' of these relationships 'are still a predominant factor of the life of most Africans'.

83. Rapporteur's Report, OAU Doc. CM/1149 (XXXVII), Ann. 1, Art. 3, para. 10, quoted in Kiwanuka 1988: 82.

84. Article 1 of both the ICESCR and ICCPR provides: 'All peoples have the right of self-determination. By virtue of that right they freely determine their political status and freely pursue their economic, social and cultural development' (ICESCR, Art. 1; ICCPR, Art. 1). During the drafting of the ICESCR and the ICCPR, Western governments stiffly opposed Common Article 1 because it put at risk the continued domination of the colonies.

85. In its usage of 'peoples', the African Charter neither contemplates internal self-determination, the right of a people to overthrow an oppressive, undemocratic and illegitimate regime, nor the claims of a minority or group within an independent state to its own self-determination or secession. Self-determination in the context of the OAU without a doubt refers to situations of foreign, colonial-type domination (previously the case in

Namibia), or to minority-ruled regimes (formerly the case in South Africa). Ethnic groups or communities within an independent state, such as the Luo or Luhyia of Kenya, are not envisaged by the Charter in this regard. The individual rights guaranteed in the Charter, particularly the rights to political participation, speech, association and assembly, imply the right of citizens to a rule of law, democratic state.

86. Kiwanuka has identified at least four interpretations or usages of a 'people' or 'peoples' in the Charter. They are: (i) all persons within the territorial limits of a colonial state or minority-ruled regime; (ii) all groups of people with certain common characteristics who live within a colonial territory or a minority-ruled state, or minorities within an independent state (external self-determination would not be permitted under the OAU in this case); (iii) the people and the state as interchangeable; and (iv) all persons within the state (Kiwanuka 1988). These are the bearers of collective rights against the state which it has the duty to realize.

87. Chege notes the minimum conditions for the institutionalization of free and popular government which include shared democratic principles, an engaged middle class, and democratic leadership in a reasonably viable state (Chege 1995: 45).

88. *Harambee* has been used in contemporary Kenya as a philosophy to drive domestic development groups. For an example, *harambee* self-help projects in rural communities account for the construction of 70 per cent of Kenya's secondary schools (Gillies and Mutua 1993: 2). *Harambee* projects have been undertaken with little or no state assistance. Conceived originally as 'the social glue binding the state to society', it forced the state to be 'accountable in the realm of social services' because under Kenyatta, the country's first president, it worked as 'an extra-parliamentary bargaining system' for elected politicians to negotiate alliances and attract additional private resources to their constituencies. It acted, in effect, as a redistributive mechanism whereby the influential politician would assemble prosperous friends to make personal monetary contributions or material to self-help projects. However, as the state became more repressive and the political elites more cynical, *harambee* was turned into a 'forced tax and an instrument of patronage' through which senior politicians would extort funds from businesses or frighten away contributors for particular causes or institutions (Gillies and Mutua 1993: 3; Widner 1992).

References

Abayomi, T. (1991) 'Continuities and Changes in the Development of Civil Liberties Litigation in Nigeria', *University of Tol. Law Review*, 22: 1037–41.

Africa Watch (1991) *Kenya: Taking Liberties*, New York: Africa Watch.

— (1992) *Zaire: Two Years without Transition*, Washington, DC: Africa Watch.

Aidoo, A. (1993) 'Africa: Democracy without Human Rights', *Human Rights Quarterly*, 15: 703.

Amnesty International (1991) *Protecting Human Rights: International Procedures and How to Use Them*, New York: Amnesty International.

— (1993) *Amnesty International's Observations on Possible Reform of the African Charter on Human and Peoples' Rights*, New York: Amnesty International.

An-Na'im, A. A. (1990) 'Problems of Universal Cultural Legitimacy for Human Rights', in A. A. An-Na'im and F. M. Deng (eds), *Human Rights in Africa: Cross-Cultural Perspectives*, Washington, DC: Brookings Institution.

Ayisi, Eric O. (1979) *An Introduction to the Study of African Culture*, London: Heinemann Educational.

Benedek, W. (1985) 'Peoples' Rights and Individuals' Duties as Special Features of the African Charter on Human and Peoples' Rights', in P. Kunig et al. (eds), *Regional Protection of Human Rights by International Law: The Emerging African System*, Baden-Baden: Nomos Verlaggesellschaft.

Buergenthal, T. (1988) *International Human Rights*, St Paul, MS: West Publishing.

Busia, K. A. (1967) *Africa in Search of Democracy*, London: Routledge and Kegan Paul.

Busia Jr, N. K. A. (1994) 'The Status of Human Rights in Pre-colonial Africa: Implications for Contemporary Practices', in E. McCarthy-Arnolds et al. (eds), *Africa, Human Rights, and the Global System: The Political Economy of Human Rights in a Changing World*, Westport, CT: Greenwood Press, pp. 225–50.

Chege, M. (1995) 'Between Africa's Extremes', *Journal of Democracy*, 6: 44.

Cobbah, J. (1987) 'African Values and the Human Rights Debate: An African Perspective', *Human Rights Quarterly*, 9: 309.

Cohen, R. (1993) 'Endless Teardrops: Prolegomena to the Study of Human Rights in Africa', in R. Cohen et al. (eds), *Human Rights and Governance in Africa*, Gainesville, FL: University Press of Florida, pp. 3–38.

Cover, R. M. (1987) 'Obligation: A Jewish Jurisprudence of the Social Order', *Jewish Law and Religion*, 5: 65.

Davidson, B. (1991) *Africa in History*, New York, NY: Macmillan.

Deng, F. M. (1990) 'A Cultural Approach to Human Rights Among the Dinka', in A. A. An-Na'im and F. M. Deng (eds), *Human Rights in Africa: Cross-Cultural Perspectives*, Washington, DC: Brookings Institution, pp. 261–89.

Donnelly, J. (1989) *Universal Human Rights in Theory and Practice*, Ithaca, NY: Cornell University Press.

— (1990) 'Human Rights and Western Liberalism', in A. A. An-Na'im and F. M. Deng (eds), *Human Rights in Africa: Cross-Cultural Perspectives*, Washington, DC: Brookings Institution.

Fernyhough, T. (1993) 'Human Rights and Precolonial Africa', in R. Cohen, G. Hyden and W. Nagan (eds), *Human Rights and Governance in Africa*, Gainesville, FL: University Press of Florida, fourth volume in the Carter Studies Series, pp. 39–73.

Flinterman, C. and E. Ankumah (1992) 'The African Charter on Human and Peoples' Rights', in H. Hannum (ed.), *Guide to International Human Rights Practice*, Philadelphia, PA: University of Pennsylvania Press.

Fortes, M. and E. Evans-Pritchard (1940) *African Political Systems*, London: Oxford University Press.

Gillies, D. and M. W. Mutua (1993) 'A Long Road to Uhuru: Human Rights and Political Participation in Kenya', *Report of the International Centre for Human Rights and Democratic Development*, Montreal, Canada.

Gittleman, R. (1982) 'The African Charter on Human and Peoples' Rights: A Legal Analysis', *Virginia Journal of International Law*, 22: 667.

Gluckman, M. (ed.) (1969) *Ideas and Procedures in African Customary Law*, London: Oxford University Press.

Hannum, H. (ed.), (1992) *Guide to International Human Rights Practice*, Philadelphia, PA: University of Pennysylvania Press.

Hansen, A. (1993) 'African Refugees: Defining and Defending their Human Rights', in R. Cohen et al. (eds), *Human Rights and Governance in Africa*, Gainesville, FL: University Press of Florida, pp. 139–67.

Haysom, N. R. L. (1994) 'The African Charter: Inspirational Document or False Start', paper presented at the Bill of Rights Conference, Victoria Falls, Zimbabwe, 14 December.

Hobley, C. W. (1971) *Ethnology of the A-Kamba and Other East African Tribes*, London: Cass.

Howard, R. (1990) 'Group Versus Individual Identity in the African Debate on Human Rights', in A. A. An-Na'im and F. M. Deng (eds), *Human Rights in Africa: Cross-Cultural Perspectives*, Washington, DC: Brookings Institution, pp. 159–83.

— (1984) 'Evaluating Human Rights in Africa: Some Problems of Implicit Comparisons', *Human Rights Quarterly*, 6: 160.

Hyden, G. (1980) *Beyond Ujamaa in Tanzania: Underdevelopment and an Uncaptured Peasantry*, London: Heinemann.

Jackson, R. H. (1992) 'Juridical Statehood in Sub-Saharan Africa', *Journal of International Affairs*, 46: 1.

Kartashkin, V. (1982) 'The Socialist Countries and Human Rights', in K. Vasak and P. Alston (eds), *The International Dimensions of Human Rights*, Westport, CT: Greenwood Press, pp. 631–50.

Kenya Human Rights Commission (1994) *Independence without Freedom: The Legitimazation of Repressive Laws and Practices in Kenya*.

Kenyatta, J. (1953) *Facing Mount Kenya*, London: Secker and Warburg.

Kiwanuka, R. (1988) 'The Meaning of "People" in the African Charter on Human and Peoples' Rights', *American Journal of International Law*, 82: 80.

Ki-Zerbo, J. (1964) 'African Personality and the New African Society', in W. J. Hanna (ed.), *Independent Black Africa: The Politics of Freedom*, Chicago, IL: Rand McNally, pp. 46–59.

Kobia, S. (1993) *The Quest for Democracy in Africa*, Nairobi: National Council of Churches of Kenya.

Lambert, H. E. (1965) *Kikuyu Social and Political Institutions*, London: Oxford University Press.

Laslett, P. (ed.) (1988) *John Locke, Two Treatises of Government*, Cambridge: Cambridge University Press.

Lawyers' Committee for Human Rights (1990) *Zaire: Repression as Policy*.

Legesse, A. (1980) 'Human Rights in African Political Culture', in K. W. Thompson (ed.), *The Moral Imperatives of Human Rights: A World Survey*, Leinham, MD: University Press of America, pp. 123–38.

McCarthy-Arnolds et al. (eds) (1994) *Africa, Human Rights, and the Global System: The Political Economy of Human Rights in a Changing World*, Westport, CT: Greenwood Press.

Mahmud, S. S. (1993) 'The State and Human Rights in Africa in the 1990s: Perspectives and Prospects', *Human Rights Quarterly*, 15: 485.

Marassinghe, L. (1984) 'Traditional Conceptions of Human Rights in Africa', in C. Welch and R. Meltzer (eds), *Human Rights and Development in Africa*, Albany, NY: State University of New York Press, pp. 32–45.

Marie, J.-B. (1986) 'Relations between Peoples' Rights and Human Rights: Semantic and Methodological Distinctions', *Human Rights Law Journal*, 7: 195.

Mazrui, A. A. (1986) *The Africans: A Triple Heritage*, Boston, MA: Little, Brown.

Mbiti, J. (1970) *African Religions and Philosophy*, New York, NY: Praeger.

Mojekwu, C. (1980) 'International Human Rights: The African Perspective', in J. L. Nelson and V. M. Green (eds), *International Human Rights: Contemporary Issues*, Stanfordville, NY: Human Rights Publishing Group, pp. 85–95.

Muthiani, J. (1973) *Akamba from Within*, New York, NY: Exposition Press.

Mutua, Makua wa (1994) 'UN Must Make Rwanda a Priority', *Oakland Tribune*, 25 May, p. A13.

Nahum, F. (1982) 'African Contribution to Human Rights', paper presented at the Seminar on Law and Human Rights in Development, Gaborone, Botswana, 24–29 May.

Nyerere, J. (1968) *Essays on Socialism*, Dar es Salaam: Oxford University Press.

Ojo, O. and A. Sessay (1994) 'The OAU and Human Rights: Prospects for the 1980s and Beyond', *Human Rights Quarterly*, 8: 89.

Okere, B. O. (1984) 'The Protection of Human Rights in Africa and the African Charter on Human Rights and Peoples' Rights: A Comparative Analysis with the European and American Systems', *Human Rights Quarterly*, 6: 141.

Okoth-Ogendo, H.W.O. (1993) 'Human and Peoples' Rights: What Point is Africa Trying to Make?', in R. Cohen et al. (eds), *Human Rights and Governance in Africa*, Gainesville, FL: University Press of Florida, pp. 74–86.

Panikkar, R. (1982) 'Is the Notion of Human Rights a Western Concept?', *Diogenes*, 120: 75.

Paust, J. (1992) 'The Other Side of Right: Private Duties under Human Rights Law', *Harvard Human Rights Journal*, 5: 51–63.

Pollis, A. and P. Schwab (1979) 'Human Rights: A Western Construct with Limited Applicability', in A. Pollis and P. Schwab (eds), *Human Rights: Cultural and Ideological Perspectives*, New York, NY: Praeger, pp. 1–18.

Robert F. Kennedy Memorial Center for Human Rights (1994) *Confronting the Past: Accountability for Human Rights Violations in Malawi*, Washington, DC: Robert F. Kennedy Memorial Center for Human Rights.

Sankan, S. S. O. (1971) *The Massai*, Nairobi: Kenyan Literature Bureau.

Senghor, L. S. (1977) 'Problematique de la negritude', in *Liberte 3: Negritude et civilisation de l'universel*, Paris: Seuil.

Shepard Jr, G. W. and M. O. C. Anikpo (eds) (1990) *Emerging Human Rights: The African Political Economy Context*, New York, NY: Greenwood Press.

Shivji, I. J. (1989) *The Concept of Human Rights in Africa*, London: Codesria.

Sohn, L. B. (1982) 'The New International Law: Protection of the Rights of Individuals Rather than States', *American University Law Review*, 32: 1.

Solomon, J. A. (1994) *Failing the Democratic Challenge: Freedom of Expression in Multi-Party Kenya*, Washington, DC: Robert F. Kennedy Memorial Center for Human Rights.

Sudarkasa, N. (1980) 'African and Afro-American Family Structure: a Comparison', *Black Scholar*, 11: 37.

Umozurike, U. O. (1983) 'The African Charter on Human and Peoples' Rights', *American Journal of International Law*, 77: 902.

United Nations (1993) *Human Rights: A Compilation of International Instruments*, UN Doc. ST/HR/1/Rev. 4.

Vaillant, J. G. (1990) *Black, French, and African: A Life of Leopold Sedar Senghor*, Cambridge, MA: Harvard University Press.

van Boven, T. (1986) 'The Relations between Peoples' Rights and Human Rights in the African Charter', *Human Rights Law Journal*, 7: 183.

Wai, D. M. (1979) 'Human Rights in Sub-Saharan Africa', in A. Pollis and P. Schwab (eds), *Human Rights: Cultural and Ideological Perspectives*, New York: Praeger, pp. 115–44.

wa Mutua, M (1988) 'Tanzania's Recent Economic Reform: An Analysis', *1988 Transafrica Forum*, 69.

— (1993) 'The African Human Rights System in a Comparative Perspective: The Need for Urgent Reformulation', *Legal F*, 5: 31.

— (1994) 'Redrawing the Map Along African Lines', *Boston Globe*, 22 September, p. 17.

Welch, C. and R. Meltzer (1984) *Human Rights and Development in Africa*, Albany, NY: State University of New York Press.

Weston, B. H. et al. (1987) 'Regional Human Rights Regimes: A Comparison and Appraisal', *Vanderbilt Journal of Transnational Law*, 20: 585.

Widner, J. A. (1992) *The Rise of a Party State in Kenya: From 'Harambee!' to 'Nyayo!'* Berkeley, CA: University of California Press.

Wieruszewski, R. (1990) 'National Implementation of Human Rights', in Allan Rosas et al. (eds), *Human Rights in a Changing East-West Perspective*, London: Pinter, pp. 286–7.

Wiredu, K. (1990) 'An Akan Perspective on Human Rights' , in A. A. An-Na'im and F. M. Deng (eds), *Human Rights in Africa: Cross-Cultural Perspectives*, Washington, DC: Brookings Institution, pp. 243–60.

Young, C. (1991) 'The Heritage of Colonialism', in J. W. Harbeson and D. Rothchild (eds), *Africa in World Politics*, Boulder, CO: Westview Press, pp. 19–38.

International Instruments

African Charter on Human and Peoples' Rights, 27 June 1981, OAU Doc. CAB/LEG/67/3/Rev.5 (1981), reprinted in 21 ILM 59 (1982).

American Convention on Human Rights, 22 November 1969, 36 OASTS No. 36, at 1, OAS Off. Reg. OEA/Ser.L/V/II. 23 Rev. 2, reprinted in 9 ILM 673 (1970).

Convention for the Protection of Human Rights and Fundamental Freedoms, 4 November 1950, 213 UNTS 221 (1955).

European Social Charter, 18 October 1961, 529 UNTS 89 (1965).

International Covenant on Civil and Political Rights, GA Res. 2200 A(XXI), UN Doc. A/6316 (1966).

International Covenant on Economic, Social, and Cultural Rights, GA Res. 2200 A(XXI), UN Doc. A/6316 (1966).

Universal Declaration of Human Rights, GA Res. 217 A(III), UN Doc. A/810 (1948).

FOUR

Mediating Culture and Human Rights in Favour of Land Rights for Women in Africa: A Framework for Community-level Action

Florence Butegwa

§ THE last two decades have witnessed sustained efforts by women to claim human rights and fundamental freedoms on the basis of equality with men. Widespread discrimination against women, based on culture and religion or both, remains rampant in Africa, particularly in the area of access and control of land. Many cultural regimes value male members, seeing in them the possibility of survival and identity, while the women are seen as temporary members of the family and/or community, destined to marry into other families or communities. Ensuring that women enjoy a right to equality and freedom from discrimination will require not just a pronouncement of fundamental rights by the state but fundamental change within the respective communities. Existing frameworks for mediating conflict between human rights principles and cultural norms, based on the supremacy and coercive measures of the state, are not likely to lead to this kind of change.

I propose a framework which situates the mediation process in the experiences of the people in the hope of contributing to ongoing discourse about the complex area of mediating perceived conflict between culture and human rights, specifically the human rights of women. I do not seek to contribute to a particular culture, but I will draw upon different aspects of culture and religion from different parts of Africa. Inasmuch as this chapter is not focusing on specific cultures it will suffer from generalities. The issue of women and land provides an example in which culture and human rights, as normative systems, are intrinsically interwoven and provide vivid illustrations of the need for alternative frameworks.

Defining a Complex Situation for Women

It might be useful to start with some rather obvious statements that highlight the problem at hand. Women, like men, are cultural and religious beings. They identify themselves and are identified by others within specific cultures and religions. These cultures and religions not only shape women's and their communities' values, norms and practices, but also are an intrinsic part of each woman. They also define the way in which gender roles are constructed in particular societies. Women are *also* human beings with an identifiable sense of personal dignity, though this diginity is rarely understood or acknowledged. As human beings, women have fundamental human rights and freedoms. Not only is the normative system and practice of any culture potentially different from the norms and practices of religion, but it is also potentially different from human rights norms. Additionally, the values and practices of each of these three variables are dynamic rather than static and are subject to differing interpretations depending on the historical moment, the interpreter and, at times, political expedience. The potential for conflict and therefore the need for mediation are thus based not only on the normative content but also on its interpretation. One author, referring to women in Muslim societies, has stated: 'They [women] are confronted with local religious leaders who, in some cases, have little more schooling than the ordinary believer. Thus what the women are facing – and challenging – is not necessarily religion according to the letter of the Koran, but rather religion as it is explained at the local level' (Thijssen 1984: 19).

Another dimension in this complex situation for women is the nexus between the individual and the broader community within a culture or religion. It is not just a matter of choice of law in which an individual woman chooses a normative system to govern her affairs. Often the decision is taken out of her hands through the appropriation of the woman herself by converting her into the symbol and embodiment of a particular culture or religion. If, for instance, she chooses to conduct her affairs in a manner deemed contrary to the tenets of a religion she is associated with, the entire religious community may see it as an affront and impose sanctions on her. These sanctions are imposed regardless of the woman having a fundamental right to choose. Similarly, if government, as a secular and liberal authority, granted to women a right stemming from human rights principles, this might be seen as an act targeting not just women but the entire religion or culture. The association between the position and conduct of women and notions of cultural and religious identity makes attempts to mediate conflicts in favour of the human rights of women a highly emotive issue, but nevertheless an essential one.

Women and Land in Africa

The concept of women and land in Africa provides a good locus for the discourse attempted in this chapter. The search for legal regimes and bases for African women to own land in their own right has never been more opportune and urgent than it is now. A number of factors have contributed to this opportunity and urgency. First, women increasingly realize that lack of access to land is the major determinant of poverty and social status both in rural and urban areas. In rural areas, land is the main source of livelihood. Second, there has been continued breakdown of traditional family structures, eroding guarantees of resource use and access by women to land at household, family and community levels. Girls and women can no longer rely on unquestioned and guaranteed land user rights on their parents' side if they are unmarried, or on their husband's side if they are divorced. This cultural change is taking place at a time when the economy and market forces are the fora for survival. The welfare state is basically non-existent, and women can no longer expect free services to satisfy their basic needs and to enable them to fulfil their gender roles in the family. Women, like men in Africa, need money and other resources to access services and goods on the market.

Third, although the implementation of economic restructuring programmes has had a negative impact on many poor families, it has also provided women with an opportunity to participate more fully in income generation, albeit in the informal sector. Some of these women now have the independent means to purchase land, or to invest in domestic animals or cash crops. In the case of the latter, the success or failure of their investment may depend on whether they retain access to, and control over, the land on which the crops are planted. There are reports of men selling family land without the knowledge or consent of their wives and/or children. Such transactions are permissible in many jurisdictions since the land belongs to the man. Fourth, traditionally women have collected fuel-wood from common land and forests. With increasing scarcity of such land due to the pressure of an increasing population, commercialization and privatization, women are finding it more and more difficult to find fuel-wood. Governmental and non-governmental agencies are urging families to grow trees on their individual landholdings in order to meet their fuel requirements. Women, whose social role is to provide fuel-wood, are often not able to comply with this governmental dictate since they do not control the land. Fifth, more women in Africa now have the enhanced capacity to analyse their situations or have access to information which leads them to question the status quo. One of the issues women are questioning is the obstacles to ownership of land.

In many African countries, ownership of land is overwhelmingly male-dominated. In Uganda, for instance, it is estimated that only 7 per cent of land is owned by women, despite the statutory law which is apparently gender-neutral (Tamale and Okumu-Wengi 1995: 33). A number of factors contribute to this situation. There is widespread discrimination against girls and women both in law and in the practices of families and communities. Because many families still place a high value on male children, educational opportunities, particularly among poor families, are provided only for boys. This means that more boys than girls are likely to have an education, which in turn enables them to earn sufficient income to purchase land. Customary norms still govern inheritance rights. Family land will often go to the male offspring of a deceased person. Most African cultures regard a male child as perpetuating the family lineage and therefore keep the land within the family. Conversely, girls are viewed in terms of their marriageability – they are destined to leave their respective families and get married elsewhere. This cultural norm applies in most countries regardless of whether or not there is legislation to the contrary. In Uganda, for instance, the Law of Succession Act provides that all children of the deceased (male and female) are entitled to 75 per cent of the parents' net estate on intestacy. In spite of this, many families, even if applying this provision, will give priority to boys when dividing the land. In most cases, however, people are not aware of the legislative provision and apply the custom. The situation is the same in Ghana and Zambia and several other countries on the continent. In Tanzania, the eldest son of the deceased man's first marriage has the primary right to the family land (United Republic of Tanzania 1963). Should there be no son in that marriage, the right passes on to sons from subsequent marriages. In Zimbabwe, the eldest son also has the principal right to be heir to his deceased father and in that capacity is entitled to the family land. This customary practice was based on the premise that female children have to be looked after by the father or brother, or even by another male relative as long as they are unmarried. During marriage, the husband should take care of them, and upon his death, a brother of the deceased, or other male relative, takes care of the women, and then inherits land and other economic resources. This premise is no longer valid, however. Many of those who inherit land use it for their personal use (Uganda Women's Network 1997). The evolution of the modern economy and land as an economic asset means that women's rights in land are no longer secure. Professor Mbilinyi explains this position in the following terms: 'Although men controlled the distribution and allocation of land, so long as women's work was absolutely central in the production and reproductive system, and land had not yet become a commodity, women were relatively indispensable and their security in land rights unlikely to be threatened' (Rwebangira and Mnemey 1995: 50). The culture which treats boys and girls and men and women differently is discriminatory because the distinction is based purely on whether one is male or female (United Nations Human Rights Committee 1989). The basis on which the practice is based is also discriminatory in nature and purport, to condemn women to a state of perpetual minority.

Many African governments have introduced legislation to ameliorate the discrimination against women in matters of land allocation, access and inheritance. In 1984, Burkina Faso decreed that every person has the right to own and use land irrespective of sex. The constitution of Mali proclaims the equality of all citizens in law regardless of, *inter alia*, sex (International Labour Organization 1989). Shortly after its independence, the Zimbabwe government removed the legal distinction between the status of men and women. In Cameroon, the 1974 statutes which govern access to land do not distinguish between men and women (Rwebangira and Mnemey 1995: 50). In spite of these legal provisions, customary attitudes and practices together with low economic status prevent women from enjoying the rights in Africa in matters of access, control and ownership of land. Clearly, law alone is not sufficient to increase and secure women's access to land.

Women have a fundamental right to equality. The Universal Declaration of Human Rights provides that all persons are equal before the law and are entitled without discrimination to equal protection under the law (United Nations, ICCPR, Article 7). The consensus of the international community involved in the drafting of the Universal Declaration of Human Rights was that human rights and fundamental freedoms, including the right to equality and freedom from discrimination, would be enjoyed and protected on a universal basis. Subsequent human rights instruments negotiated at an international (United Nations) and regional levels continue to guarantee this right. The International Covenant on Civil and Political Rights reads: 'All persons are equal before the law and are entitled without any discrimination to the equal protection of the law. In this respect, the law shall prohibit any discrimination and guarantee to all persons equal and effective protection against discrimination on any ground such as ... sex' (Article 20).

States that are parties to the International Covenant on Economic, Social and Cultural Rights undertake to ensure the equal rights of men and women to the enjoyment of all economic, social and cultural rights set forth therein. The Convention on the Elimination of All Forms of Discrimination Against Women further defines the right of women to be protected from discrimination on the basis of sex. It prohibits specific forms of discrimination against women. The Convention explicitly provides that:

1. States Parties shall accord to women equality with men before the law.
2. States Parties shall accord to women, in civil matters, a legal capacity identical to that of men and the same opportunities to exercise that capacity. In particular, they shall give women equal rights to conclude contracts and to administer property. (United Nations, CEDAW, Article 20)

Many African states have ratified these conventions. In addition the African Charter on Human and Peoples' Rights provides that: 'The State shall ensure the elimination of every discrimination against women and also ensure the protection of the rights of the woman and the child as stipulated in international instruments' (United Nations, ACHPR, Article 18[3]; see also Article 2). The language used in this provision, negotiated and agreed upon by African states, allows no exception to this obligation. States are to ensure the elimination of *every* form of discrimination against women (Beyani 1994: 240). Almost all African countries have ratified the African Charter.[1] By so ratifying, African states have assumed an obligation to take all necessary measures to eliminate discrimination against women.

Mediating Conflict Between Culture and Human Rights: Current Practice

It is clear that there is conflict between the norms and practices founded on African culture and those based on human rights scholarship. Of interest in this chapter is how this conflict is sought to be mediated by human rights law and advocates and by proponents of culture or religion. If women are to acquire, hold and control land, thereby enhancing their individual and collective autonomy and opportunities, these conflicts have to be managed and overcome. Mediation in favour of women is both a question of social justice and an economic necessity for Africa. The continent needs the optimum input of all its people in the development process. It is also an imperative for the dignity of women as human beings not to be seen and treated as inferior to men.

The human rights regime has sought to deal with the problem by looking at the different normative systems as forming a hierarchy in which human rights norms are on top. International human rights instruments, by requiring states parties to take all necessary steps to ensure the enjoyment of the guaranteed rights, implicitly expect states to use their power to override other norms constraining or likely to constrain the enjoyment of human rights (United Nations, ICCPR, Article 2; United Nations, CEDAW, 1979). Since the adoption of the Universal Declaration of Human Rights, member states of the United Nations have on numerous occasions made pronouncements on the universal nature and superiority of human rights and the consequent need for customary or religious normative systems to give way in the case of conflict. As early as 1954, the UN General Assembly adopted a resolution calling on member states to eliminate customs, ancient laws and practices contrary to the Universal Declaration of Human Rights affecting the rights of women. The resolution recommended that special efforts be made through fundamental education and through the media to inform the public about these principles and other legislation concerning the status of women. In 1967, the General Assembly declared that discrimination against women by denying or limiting their equality with men is fundamentally unjust and is an *offence* against human rights. It called upon all member states of the United Nations to take all appropriate measures to abolish existing laws, customs, regulations and practices which are discriminatory against women (United Nations 1967). The Convention on the Elimination of All Forms of Discrimination Against Women is even more explicit. Article 5 states that states parties shall take all appropriate measures: 'To modify the social and cultural patterns of conduct of men and women, with a view to achieving the elimination of prejudices and customary and all other practices which are based on the idea of the inferiority or the superiority of either of the sexes or on stereotyped roles for men and women' (United Nations, CEDAW, Article 5).

Article 10 also calls for the elimination of any stereotyped concept of the roles of men and women at all levels. Since in most cases stereotyped roles and consequent status and expectations are intrinsic to a culture, essentially the Convention is calling for the modification of those aspects of culture, thus ensuring the supremacy of the guaranteed rights. The World Conference on Human Rights called for the elimination of gender bias and the eradication of any conflict between the human rights of women and the harmful effects of certain traditional or customary practices, cultural prejudices and religious extremism. The Fourth World Conference on Women reaffirmed this principle by stating that certain modern practices which prevent women from enjoying human rights must be abolished. States committed themselves to review national laws, including customs and customary laws, so as to conform them with the principles of human rights (United Nations Department of Public Information 1995).

The idea of the supremacy of human rights principles can also be found in the African Charter on Human and Peoples' Rights. This doctrine obliges states parties to ensure to all persons within their respective territories the enjoyment of the rights enshrined in the Charter. It specifically imposes a duty on states parties to promote and ensure through teaching, education and publication the respect of the rights and freedoms contained in the Charter and to see to it that these freedoms and rights are understood (United Nations, ACHPR). Implicit in this obligation is the duty for states to modify cultural and or religious norms and practices through education and to publicize the human rights principles found in the Charter. The fundamental nature of the obligation was highlighted by the United Nations Human Rights Committee in the following terms:

> The Committee wishes to draw the attention of States Parties to the fact that the Covenant sometimes expressly requires them to take measures to guarantee the equality of rights of the persons concerned. For example, Article 23 paragraph 4, stipulates that States Parties shall take appropriate steps to ensure equality of rights as well as responsibilities of spouses as to marriage, during marriage and at its dissolution. Such steps may take the form of legislative, administrative or other measures, but it is a positive duty of States Parties to make certain that spouses have equal rights as required by the Covenant. (United Nations 1989)

Clearly, what the Covenant and other instruments prescribe is output (equality). The measures that will enable the achievement of the expected output are left for the states parties to determine, taking into account the cultural contexts and political systems within which they work. This position is quite interesting because it goes beyond the normal narrow concept of human rights as just regulating the relationship between the individual and the state. It includes the private sphere within which the individual must continue to enjoy guaranteed rights.

To buttress the idea of a superior law, the human rights system has in place enforcement mechanisms at the regional and international level to which an aggrieved individual may turn for redress should the state and national level tribunals fail her/him. The Human Rights Committee established under the International Covenant on Civil and Political Rights and the African Commission on Human and Peoples' Rights are good examples of such mechanisms. Although the Committee on the Elimination of Discrimination Against Women has no individual reporting procedure, the fact that states agree to account to it through regular reports shows that it serves a similar purpose (Byrnes 1994).

At the national level, a similar hierarchical ideology exists within legal regimes. Human rights principles or bills of rights are enshrined in the constitutions of many African countries. Such constitutions invariably provide for the supremacy of the constitution over all other laws and normative systems, including culture and customs. Chapter 4 (section 41) of the Nigerian constitution sets out a bill of rights that includes a right to equality and freedom from discrimination. Tanzania has even been more explicit in its intent to implement human rights and override custom in case of conflict. The Constitutional (Consequential, Transitional and Temporary Provisions) Act (1984) obliges courts to interpret customary law (and other laws) with such modifications and qualifications as may be necessary to give effect to the bill of rights in the constitution.

A review of case law in Africa indicates a conscious application of this principle. In *Ephrahim v Pastory Kaizingele* (High Court of Tanzania, 87 ILR 106), the Tanzanian High Court held that a local custom prohibiting females from inheriting and administering clan land was discriminatory on the basis of sex and therefore contrary to the bill of rights and the principles of the Universal Declaration of Human Rights. In Botswana, both the High Court and Court of Appeal refused to uphold legislation which discriminated against women by denying them the capacity to transmit their nationality to their children, even if the legislation was (as was proved by government) based on the patrilineal cultural values and norms of Botswana people (Unity Dow 1995).

The position taken by some states and cultural supremacists has been different. When a state has concluded that a specific human right infringes a cultural or religious norm or practice, the state has either refused to ratify the human rights treaty or has entered reservations on ratification. This is clearly evident with respect to the extent of reservations entered by states on ratifying the Convention on the Elimination of All Forms of Discrimination Against Women. Almost twenty countries have voiced objections with respect to Article 16 which obligates states parties to take all appropriate measures to eliminate discrimination against women in all matters relating to the marriage and the family. The existence of the reservations signify the recognition of the state of its inability to take the necessary measures to comply with the obligation. Malawi's reservation to the Convention, for instance, states as follows: 'Owing to the deep-rooted nature of some traditional customs and practices of Malawians, the Government of the Republic of Malawi shall not, for the time being, consider itself bound by such of the provisions of the Convention as require immediate eradication of such traditional customs and practices.'

Other states and writers have lashed out at a normative system which assumes its own superiority calling it imperialist, foreign and a ploy for the West to impose its individualistic values on African (or, for that matter, Islamic) values.

The position taken by these states is not to deny the existence of human rights but rather to restate the existence of other normative systems, thereby highlighting the need for more informed and sensitive systems of mediation. The positions are also rooted in an evaluation of the political situation and power relations within each state. Can the state carry through the reforms sought by the human rights obligation without turmoil? If an outright ban of a cultural practice or norm would serve no positive practical purpose, what other approach would better serve the interests of gender equality (or other human rights)?

Human rights scholars and advocates support the human rights normative system over others, albeit to varying degrees. Some see no exceptions to the human rights system and advocate the abolition of traditional norms and practices which violate human rights. There are those holding the position that, in general, human rights are universal and a superior set of values and norms, but allow the possibility of challenging theses values on the basis of culture or religion. An-Na'im, for instance, considers this possibility when the legitimacy of the particular human rights norm is fundamentally questionable within the specific culture within which it is to be implemented. He acknowledges, however, the difficulties of allowing culturally-based challenges given the absence of established and objective means of verifying cultural norms and of the differential power relations among those holding opposing views. He calls for a very high standard of proof from those who mount a challenge to an internationally recognized human right (An-Na'im 1994).

There are also those whose proposition is that the mediation of potentially conflicting normative systems must first recognize the possible legitimacy of the conflicting norms. For instance, a religious norm in conflict with a human rights norm may be legitimate from the point of view of freedom to practise one's religion, which is itself a fundamental freedom within the human rights regime. A cultural norm may similarly be defended, at least by its adherents (Sullivan 1992). In addition to formalistic legitimacy, a cultural norm will have legitimacy within its own context. It is in fact this legitimacy which is sought to be vitiated or tempered through mediation. Appreciating that there are two competing rights, or at least that both positions have their own spheres of legitimacy, enables those attempting mediation not to presume the superiority of one over the other or to underestimate the political nature of mediation. Donna Sullivan proposes a framework for resolving conflicts between the right to gender equality and religious norms in which there are six factors to be taken into consideration. The first factor is the relationship between the specific equality right at issue and the overarching goal of gender equality. In other words, is the specific right denied fundamental to achieving gender equality? Second, the same question must be asked of the religious right: is the religious norm or practice a fundamental tenet of the religion? Third, one must analyse the extent to which each norm or practice at issue infringes the other. For instance, does the religion completely prohibit the freedom sought by the goals of gender equality or does it only impose restrictions, and how severe are the restrictions? Fourth, one should ascertain the extent to which the denied right leads to a denial of other human rights. Fifth, although only one right may be at issue, it is necessary to examine other restrictions on gender equality by the religion so as to determine their cumulative effect. Lastly, where the state has taken legislative action either to restrict religious freedom in favour of gender equality or vice versa, the proportionality of the restriction when compared to the need for protection must be considered (Sullivan 1992: 822, 823).

A Framework for Community-level Advocacy for Gender Equality

By proposing the above framework, Sullivan accepts the reality of legitimacy of other normative systems and the need to find objective and fair criteria for overriding them in favour of the right of women to freedom from discrimination on the basis of sex (Richters 1994: 107). Sullivan's approach assumes agreement among the proponents of the religious norm or practice as to its general and specific purport. In other words, the framework does not help in the mediation of competing interpretations within the same culture in deciding which version is to be mediated through the use of the framework. This assumption is not justified, particularly in the context of cultural and religious norms, where conservative and liberal interpretations vie for legitimacy. Sullivan also assumes that women claiming the right to equality are necessarily making the demands from *outside* the religion or culture. Muslim women seeking equality and freedom from discrimination are mostly working from and articulating their concerns within the context of Islam (Hassan 1996).

Similarly, African women are working within their various cultures and traditions to move towards equality and the elimination of discrimination. This trend fits in with observations made at the beginning of this chapter that women are human beings who are also cultural and religious beings. Additionally, the approaches suggested by both Sullivan and An-Na'im may be useful at the formal level – for instance, when parties go to a court of law or other human rights tribunal. Unfortunately, within the African context, very few disputes ever go before such a tribunal, and, if they do, women are rarely represented by legal professionals who can raise these arguments. In the few cases where counsel is involved, there is still no guarantee that the significance of the dispute will be given prominence.

A lot of the work of promoting gender equality, at least in the African context, is being carried out within families, communities and at the national level. There is a need for the emergence of a framework within which the individual woman, man and organization can advocate for the equality of rights between women and men and can make real and practical progress towards this goal. Efforts which target the individuals within a community in mediating between different norms and practices have a threefold purpose. The first purpose is to legitimize conduct which would otherwise be considered deviant within the cultural context. Second, this paves the way for promoting changes in attitudes and behaviour among others by giving reasons for the need for the inevitability of change and the cost to the people and the culture of a no-change stance. Third, an appropriate mediation strategy can forestall any precipitous reactions from forces opposed to the direction of the cultural transformation. Contrary to current approaches, which advocate an omnipotent state using its power to decree what ought to change and how, the framework proposed envisages the possibility of a bottom-up dynamism which is interactive and can be rooted in the realities and experiences of the people within the culture concerned.

At this point I want to propose some key elements of such a framework. The proposition does not negate existing frameworks, particularly those of courts and tribunals as the fora for mediating conflict between human rights and culture. What it seeks to do is provide a tool for those for whom the locus of conflict mediation is within the community itself, particularly those engaged in community-oriented human and legal rights education work. The framework may also be useful for those individual progressive women and men who lead their lives at the cutting edge of a transformed culture in which women and girls have equal rights, opportunities and dignity as human beings.

Within the proposed framework, five key factors should be considered in the effort to mediate any conflict between the human rights principles of equality between women and men and freedom from discrimination on the basis of sex. First, there must be agitation for change towards equality and non-discrimination, and that agitation must come from within the culture concerned. This is key, particularly if the resolution is to be in favour of non-discrimination and equality. Experience has shown that agitation for cultural changes that are perceived as located outside what is considered part of the culture more often serves as fodder for reactionary forces. In this context, the arguments are distorted away from the gist of the conflict to one in which the perceived assault on culture takes centre-stage.[2] The question of belonging to the culture is itself not an easy one and would have to be resolved because conservative elements may try to find ways of justifying the maintenance of the status quo by alleging the 'outsider' status of those agitating for change. This is particularly important with respect to women who tend to be seen as giving up their identities and assuming new ones on marriage. Women proponents of change are also often seen as aping foreign cultures and values. A more complex perspective of this factor, though, is the role of foreign advocates of the right to non-discrimination. I think they can have an important role. For instance, when the people who would naturally agitate from the inside are so oppressed that it is not possible for them to agitate, I can see a role for capacity-building, including skills in problem analysis, organizing and advocacy. The content of their advocacy efforts, including definition of issues and possible solutions, should remain entirely for those working from within. This allows them to define priorities and/or determine those issues which can appropriately be taken up given the prevailing circumstances.

The second factor to be taken into account is the degree, intensity and diversity of agitation. Here one would be looking at the numbers of people involved in calling for change. One would also be analysing their composition and the insistence and intensity with which they are making themselves heard. The more people calling for change in the norms or practices of their own culture, the stronger the case for change. If more and more people are finding the status quo untenable and are determined to do something about it, it may be reasonable to examine the cause of dissatisfaction and the nature of their demands. Diversity may also be relevant by showing that the demands are widespread within the community and cut across individual, sectarian or partisan interests within the culture.

Third, it is also important to do an analysis of the centrality to the overall culture of the particular norm or practice in conflict with the equality principle. I see a difference between a norm or practice that defines the culture itself and one that is designed to preserve a cultural value or other norm. In the latter case, it is possible to explore ways of maintaining the value through other means which are not discriminatory or injurious to the status or dignity of women. The United Nations Population Fund (UNFPA) in Uganda has, for instance, taken an interesting and instructive approach while promoting change in favour of eliminating the practice of female genital mutilation in eastern Uganda. Since the community concerned sees the practice of female genital mutilation as designed to promote and preserve cultural notions of chastity, they are involved in identifying other ways, which are not injurious to the rights and health of women, for achieving that purpose.

Fourth, it is important to analyse the validity and continued relevance of the specific cultural practice or norm given the current socio-economic environment in which it occurs. This process would involve identifying the basis and/or assumptions on which the norm or practice was based and would also examine the continued validity of those bases or assumptions. A good example is one mentioned in an earlier section of this paper. The practice of denying women and girls the right to inherit land and other valuable resources was based on the assumption, justifiable at the time because it applied to most women, that they would be looked after by someone throughout their lives. Male relatives – fathers, brothers, uncles – did discharge their obligation in this respect. The analysis would involve an inquiry into the continued legitimacy of this assumption.

Last, it is important to assess how *desirable* the status quo or the proposed change is for the community given its broader development and survival interests. Many times cultures retain archaic practices not because they want to be recalcitrant, but because they know no other way to act or because they do not have enough information to see a need for change or advantages from such change. Additionally, they may have no assurance that their identity can be retained without the offending practice. They may have no peer communities to observe and appreciate how change can work *for* the community rather than against its cohesion, identity and quality of life. Building within the community skills for critical analysis of their own situation, exposure to other cultures in mid- or post-transformation stage, and strengthening opportunities for real dialogue with those undergoing fundamental change may be crucial in this regard. Additional skills in managing change also become necessary.

The process of mediation requires that the competing rights be weighed against each other using the factors suggested above jointly and severally. For instance, the number of people agitating for change *publicly* may be relatively small due to various factors, but the norm is peripheral to the culture, and it aims to achieve an objective which can be achieved through other acceptable means.

Key Assumptions for the Framework

The framework makes a number of key assumptions. It assumes that cultural norms and practices are legitimate within the community until such time as they are discarded or modified as part of normal response to changing socio-economic environments. This is cultural growth because any culture is essentially dynamic. Another major assumption is the essential legitimacy of human rights principles, including those of gender equality and non-discrimination, as universal values and norms applicable to Africa. Four reasons persuade me of this assumption. First of all, these are values comparable to human rights principles and their overriding purpose existed in African culture before colonialism, even if they may never have been expressed or articulated in similar terminology. The dignity of the individual within the group to which he/she belonged as against other groups was and still remains key in African values. Scholars who have investigated this question have concluded that not only did African culture value groups and group rights, it also protected the individual's dignity and rights, including the right of access to land (wa Mutua 1993: 339).

Second, when African governments consciously set out to devise political and legal instruments founded on African cultural values, they confined the applicability of the human rights principles as we know them today to Africa. The outcome, though introducing the concept of individual duties and group rights, guarantees similar human rights and fundamental freedoms as other human rights instruments. The Charter of the Organization of African Unity stipulates that freedom, justice and dignity are essential objectives of the African peoples. In addition, the African Charter on Human and Peoples' Rights reiterates the right of equality of all people and the right of women to be free from discrimination based on their sex. In fact, the Charter guarantees these rights not only against the state but also within the family – the *locus* of endemic forms of discrimination against women (United Nations, ACHPR, Article 18[3]).

Third, Africa continues to reconfirm these universal principles in various fora. For instance, a significant number of African countries have ratified human rights instruments, thus confirming on behalf of their people not just the belief in the principles but also the obligation to promote and protect the principles. Fourth, the affirmation continues, as was indicated above, in national constitutions through bills of rights. This is so even for countries whose constitutions were negotiated as part of the process leading to independence. They have had several years in which no real attempt has been made to purge the constitution of 'foreign material'.

The third assumption is that human rights principles and norms do not operate from *without* the cultural normative system but from within. This means that the emergence of human rights as an organizing concept and as a rallying point for different groups, including women, is part of on-going *cultural transformation*. If human rights norms were to continue to be seen and projected as an external force or a normative system whose origin and values cannot be traced from within the culture, then their observance could only be expected through coercive means and sustained enforcement (An-Na'im 1994). Any relaxation of policing would see the people return to the 'old' system. There would not be an internalization of the human rights principles and/or the values on which they are based. Ultimately this scenario would be dangerous for women because any period of *forced* observance is likely to be followed by unrelenting backlash when the pressure from authorities or 'outsiders' is reduced or stopped. Recent years have witnessed instances of this nature. In Uganda some groups have been heard to promise vengeance 'after Museveni' because of perceived coercion for significant changes in favour of women.[3]

Conclusion

Land remains a major resource in Uganda, and its value to the holder is fast increasing. In many African cultures, such a valuable resource is under the control of men. Current demands by women, though sound and timely in terms of economics and human rights principles, are perceived as threatening the interests of those privileged to hold the land. African women and men need to join others who actively wonder and ask why it is only when women want to bring about change for their own benefit do culture and custom become sacred and unchangeable (Richters 1992: 125). Selective cultural relativism must be exposed and questioned. The elimination of discrimination against women in matters of land rights can be achieved only through a transformative process in which individual African cultures and the people who make up the culture participate in the change. Coercive strategies can only be secondary and temporary in nature. An acceptable framework for mediating any conflict between cultural norms and the right to equality at the individual and community levels is crucial. Such a framework must be rooted within the people and their experience and aspirations.

Notes

1. Fifty-one out of fifty-two African nations have ratified the Charter.

2. Arguments of this nature by African states, whenever called upon or pushed by Western countries to respect the civil, political and human rights of women, are commonplace. Similar positions are taken by religious groups, states and minorities.

3. President Museveni of Uganda has spearheaded legal and political reforms in favour of women's rights.

References

An-Na'im, A. A. (1994) 'State Responsibility under International Human Rights Law to Change Religious and Customary Laws', in R. Cook (ed.), *Human Rights of Women: National and International Perspectives*, Philadelphia, PA: University of Pennsylvania Press, pp. 167–88.

Beyani, C. (1994) 'Towards a More Effective Guarantee of Women's Rights in the African Human Rights System', in R. Cook (ed.), H*uman Rights of Women: National and International Perspectives*, Philadelphia, PA: University of Pennsylvania Press, pp. 285–306.

Byrnes, A. (1994) 'Towards More Effective Enforcement of Women's Human Rights Through the Use of International Human Rights Law and Procedures', in R. Cook (ed.), *Human Rights of Women: National and International Perspectives*, Philadelphia, PA: University of Pennsylvania Press, pp. 189–227.

Coomaraswamy R. (1994) 'To Bellow Like a Cow: Women, Ethnicity, and the Discourse of Rights', in R. Cook (ed.), *Human Rights of Women: National and International Perspectives*, Philadelphia, PA: University of Pennsylvania Press, pp. 39–51.

Hassan, R. (1996) 'Are Women Equal Before Allah? The Issue of Gender Justice in Islam', in E. Friedlander (ed.), *Look at the World Through Women's Eyes*, Beijing: NGO Forum on Women, pp. 148–56.

International Labour Organization (1989) *Women and Land*, Harare: Women's Resource Centre and Network.

Richters, J. M. (1994) *Women, Culture and Violence: A Development, Health and Human Rights Issue*, Women and Autonomy Series, The Hague: Leiden University.

Rwebangira, M. K. and E. Mneney (1995) 'The Legal Status of Women in Tanzania', in J. Kabeberi-Macharia (ed.), *Women, Laws, Customs and Practices in East Africa*, Nairobi: WLEA.

Sullivan, D. (1992) 'Gender Equality and Religious Freedom: Towards a Framework for Conflict Resolution', *International Law and Politics* 24: 795–856.

Tamale, S. and J. Okumu-Wengi. (1995.) 'The Legal Status of Women in Uganda', in J. Kabeberi-Macharia (ed.), *Women, Laws, Customs and Practices in East Africa*, Nairobi: WLEA.

Thijssen, H. (ed.) (1994) *Women and Islam in Muslim Societies*, Poverty and Development Analysis 7, The Hague: Ministry of Foreign Affairs, Development Cooperation Department.

Uganda Women's Network (1997) *Women and Land Rights in Uganda*, Friedrich Ebert Stiftung.

United Nations (1967) *Resolution Adopting the Declaration on the Elimination of Discrimination Against Women*, Resolution A/RES/2263 (XXII), New York: United Nations.

— (1979) *Convention on the Elimination of All Forms of Discrimination Against Women*, New York: United Nations.

— (1993) *The Vienna Declaration and Programme for Action*, New York: United Nations.

— 'International Covenant on Civil and Political Rights', in *Human Rights: A Compilation of International Instruments*, Vol. 1, pt 1, New York: United Nations.

United Nations Department of Public Information (1995) *The Platform for Action and the Beijing Declaration: Fourth World Conference on Women*, New York: United Nations.

United Nations General Assembly (1962) *Convention on Consent to Marriage, Minimum Age for Marriage and Registration of Marriages*, New York: United Nations.

United Nations General Assembly, *Resolution A/RES/843 (IX)*, New York: United Nations.

United Nations Human Rights Committee (1989) *General Comment 18 of Thirty-seventh Session*, New York: United Nations.

United Republic of Tanzania (1963) *Rule 19, Local Customary Law (Declaration Order), 4.*

— (1982) *The Age of Majority Act.*

Unity Dow (1995) *Attorney General v Unity Dow*, Botswana Court of Civil Appeal, no. 4/91, in Unity Dow, *The Citizenship Case, The Attorney General of the Republic of Botswana vs. Unity Dow: Court Documents, Judgments, Cases and Materials*, Gaborone: Lentswe La Lesedi, pp. 123–95.

wa Mutua, M (1993) 'The Banjul Charter and the African Cultural Fingerprint: An Evaluation of the Language of Duties', *Virginia Journal of International Law*, 35: 339–80.

FIVE

Are Local Norms and Practices Fences or Pathways? The Example of Women's Property Rights

Celestine Nyamu-Musembi

§ IN an earlier article, I argued that in responding to the cultural legitimization of gender hierarchy in developing countries women's human rights actors ought to abandon abolitionist approaches that simply call for an end to cultural practices that contravene international human rights principles (Nyamu 2000). Such abolitionist approaches, I argued, do not encourage a holistic understanding of the context in which these cultural practices are embedded. More importantly for the purposes of this chapter, such approaches assume that the possibility of the realization of women's human rights does not exist in local practice or custom, and can be found only in alternatives offered by national legislation or the international human rights regime (Nyamu 2000: 393). I cautioned that this narrow view of local practice or custom presents difficulties. First, it assumes a radical disjuncture between the sphere of formal law and institutions and the sphere of custom, thereby obscuring the active role that the state apparatus plays in shaping cultural norms at the local level. Second, the assumption that local practices offer no basis for women's human rights pre-empts an open-minded assessment of local practice, which assessment could lead to the recognition and utilization of whatever positive openings are presented by general principles of fairness and justice in a community's value system. Consequently, potential opportunities for collaboration with community members committed to social change that would promote human rights principles generally, and gender equality in particular, are forfeited.

Among the proposals I made is that women's human rights actors must engage the politics of culture in two ways. First, by generating empirical evidence of varied and alternative local cultural practices to counteract negative ideological statements of culture that entrench gender hierarchy. Second, by expanding the scope of human rights practice to include fora it has not traditionally targeted, such as local administrative bodies and informal social institutions whose work plays a fundamental role in articulating cultural norms which impact on people directly at the grassroots level.

Paying attention to local norms and practices is part of the process of internal discourse and cross-cultural dialogue proposed by An-Na'im as necessary for the legitimization of human rights principles in all cultures (An-Na'im 1994: 174). It amounts to recognizing that local norms and practices, not just formal guarantees of rights, produce and redefine ideas about human rights, part of the process that Sally Engle Merry has labelled the 'vernacularization' of human rights (Merry 1997: 29).[1]

This chapter draws from the practices of administrative and informal social institutions at the local level and identifies features that are favourable to the realization of gender equality and features that impede such a realization. The favourable features are, first, affordability and accessibility. In rural areas that are not well served by formal institutions such as courts, these informal and semi-formal fora employing a mixture of customary norms and varied localized understandings of official law offer the forum of first resort for vindication of rights claims. Second, the potential for the realization of gender equality through local norms and processes lies in the fact that local custom is in constant motion. Local norms are constantly changing with practice and adapting to new situations. Flexibility in practice, which contrasts with the rigidity of ideology, allows for responsiveness to the justice of a specific situation rather than a mechanical or rigid application of 'the custom' to all situations. Third, as An-Na'im and Hammond point out in their chapter, people are agents of cultural transformation. Though cultural norms may define the broad parameters within which people may act, they do not dictate behaviour in a deterministic way. I will present evidence of some people's changing perceptions of fairness that explicitly contradict what they and others understand to be the expected cultural practice. Fourth, local norms and processes may grant recognition to claims that the formal legal system does not entertain, or moral claims not acknowledged as 'rights' in the formal legal system.

The features that diminish the possibility of realizing gender equality through these local norms and processes are, first, differences in the power and knowledge required for a person to participate effectively in defining the local norms and to make use of both local fora and formal legal institutions to his/her advantage. The most notable are differences based on socio-economic status and on gender (which often overlap). Second, with respect to intra-family disputes (which make up the bulk of disputes handled by these local fora), embedded ideas about authority and gender roles seem to constrain open deliberation on the facts, and to dictate a resort to idealized statements of custom that necessitate outcomes that disadvantage women. This casts doubt on the ability of these fora to play a transformative role in some aspects of human rights, such as gender equality within the family. Third, women as a social group have limited participation as decision-makers in these local fora.

I will illustrate these arguments with examples drawn from research that I conducted in Makueni district in Kenya between June 1998 and February 1999. The institutions whose work I will refer to are clans, the process of informal dispute resolution before local government administrators, and the quasi-traditional Land Adjudication Committees established by the government in areas currently undergoing formal registration of title to land. The discussion in this chapter is also intended to serve an expository function – to bring to light the existence of these institutions and to highlight their defining role with respect to rights at the local level. The examples I use focus largely on gender relations around access to and control of property (particularly land), since this was the subject of my research.

Defining the Local

It is inaccurate to analyse local norms and practices as though they were separate and insulated from the national or international context. In the present global situation, such a locality would have to be imagined. It is more instructive and reflective of actual practice to view the local, national and global as 'inextricably joined, both as resources and constraints' (Merry 1997: 29, 45).

In the context of this chapter, 'local norms and practices' refers to intra-family and community-based processes for regulating interpersonal relationships, as represented in informal processes for resolving family disputes. It is in these micro-level relations that abstract ideas of rights and justice are given meaning and content and translated into different outcomes for different people. They play a primary role in facilitating or constraining people's ability to claim or exercise whatever rights are available to them under local normative orders, national laws or international human rights principles. Some recent studies have signalled the importance of this focus on micro-level processes by employing empirical research to explore the role of such local disputing processes in shaping gender relations in specific African contexts (Hellum 1999; Griffiths 1997; Hirsch 1998).

The sphere of local norms and practices is best described as being in a relationship of semi-autonomy with the larger social matrix of formal laws. Sally Falk Moore has captured this relationship in her analytical framework of the semi-autonomous social field. This is a framework that she develops for the purpose of analysing issues of law and social change. A social field is any entity that has the capacity internally to generate and enforce norms (rules, customs and symbols) governing the conduct of people living and relating within that social sphere, but which at the same time is permeable to norms (rules and decisions) emanating from the surrounding larger social context (Moore 1978a).[2] Moore characterizes the relationship as one of semi-autonomy precisely because of the simultaneous existence of this internal capacity for norm generation and enforcement, as well as connection to a larger social matrix whose norms it also enforces.

The operation of local norms and practices in contemporary African societies may be characterized in these terms. Far from seeing such normative systems as autonomous entities, this framework demonstrates the symbiotic relationship between local and formal legal norms. They influence and complement each other and are also in tension with each other.

Background on Key Local Institutions in a Kenyan Rural Scene

A brief overview of the institutions involved in articulating custom at the local level in the contemporary Kenyan context is itself a glimpse into the interrelationship between legal and customary, formal and informal, official and unofficial (or semi-official), the local and the national. I use examples drawn from three institutions: the clan, local administration and the Land Adjudication Committee. No doubt there are other less visible intra-family processes of interaction, of which the situations that get presented to these fora are only a small part. Nevertheless, the working of these institutions is a window into the goings-on in those intra-family processes of negotiation and conflict in which local norms are defined.

Clans The clan system is old and it is to be found in most African communities. Few accounts discuss the origins of clan organization.[3] A clan may broadly be defined as a sub-group or section of a larger ethnic group/community, whose members profess a common identity by virtue of a shared ancestry. The degree of actual biological relationship among members varies, since the common ancestors usually date back several generations.[4]

Although individual families in the nuclear sense make up the smallest unit of the clan, the primary unit significant to clan organization is the *mbai ya musyi* (clan at the homestead level, or lineage). *Mbai ya musyi* consists of closely related families, sharing a grandfather or great-grandfather. The oldest living male in the cluster of families is usually regarded as the authority figure for the unit. This could be the great-grandfather, grandfather, oldest great-uncle, uncle or eldest brother. Any issue requiring the intervention of the clan origin-ates at this level. For instance, if a family desires clan mediation to resolve a family dispute, they first involve the *mbai ya musyi*, and if the matter cannot be solved at this level, it is taken to the clan committee at the next level which is the *iko*. *Iko* literally means hearth, and it comprises all the lineages in a par-ticular locality.[5]

The clan is viewed as the quintessential traditional institution. Its authority to make conclusive statements on custom and to pronounce detailed rules for its members is widely recognized. In the Akamba community the role of the clan is relatively strong, and people identify strongly with the clans they belong to, both in rural and urban areas. However, the clan as a force in shaping day-to-day social interaction is felt more in the rural areas, where the clan inter-venes in matters such as division of property in inheritance disputes; mediation in family disputes between spouses, co-wives or in-laws; 'disciplining' husbands who neglect their families or squander their wealth; 'disciplining' unfaithful wives; and responding to witchcraft allegations that arise out of jealousies and mistrust between members of the same family or lineage.

Yet the clan is also a very modern institution. Clans are formally registered under the Registration of Societies Act. The requirement of formal registration of clans dates back to a 1949 directive from the colonial government.[6] Clans maintain a register of members. They also keep accounts of the members' dues and other clan revenues. They hold elections to fill key positions for clan committees at the various administrative levels. Some have written rules, whose formality, scope and detail vary from clan to clan.[7]

Local administration The clan and local administration work closely together and rely on each other's support to boost their respective authority at the grassroots level. When a clan resolves a dispute it must record the agreement in writing and give a copy to the local administration. Similarly, local administrators rely on the clan network to communicate government policy measures. In addition, local administrators are often also leaders in their clans.[8]

By local administrators I mean the chief, assistant chiefs and village headmen. These constitute the lowest rungs of the administration machinery, which is coordinated under the auspices of the office of the president. They are the manifestation of formal law enforcement at the grassroots level. In some rural areas they are often the only such manifestation. Their involvement in social life at the grassroots level further collapses the official (formal) versus unofficial (informal) sphere, and the image of the latter as the only sphere in which custom is made. Through the local administrators, the official (formal) sphere participates just as actively in the making of custom, adding to it an authoritative gait.

The titles of 'chief/assistant chief' must be distinguished from 'chief' in the African communities that did have such titles in the indigenous political structure. The offices that I discuss here are created by government appointment. Their mandate is defined by statute – the Chiefs' Authority Act. They trace their origins to colonial administration and the machinery of 'indirect rule'. At the onset of British colonial rule, largely as a matter of practicality, it was decided that local government would be exercised indirectly through local 'native' institutions. There was a shortage of both personnel and of funds, and therefore little effective control of the vast territory. Native systems of administration, where they could be identified, would be left undisturbed, as long as they did not interfere with the interests of the British crown.[9] In communities where centralized administrative structures did not exist they would be invented.[10]

The local administrators have a broad mandate to maintain law and order at the local level. This loosely defined mandate has come to include facilitation of dispute settlement even though this is not explicitly provided for. In one of the localities covered by my research, the chief's Occurrence Book (where all disputes and any other reported incidents are recorded) recorded 101 disputes between September 1996 (when the current chief took office) and September 1998. Of these, one-third were intra-family disputes.[11] The majority of disputes never get beyond this level. Hardly any disputes reach a formal court.

The format is one of adjudication, where the parties to the dispute each bring two or three *atumia* (elders) who listen to each party and ask questions, and then retreat and deliberate as a panel and agree on a solution. The chief or assistant chief acts as the chair during the proceedings, but does not take part in the elders' deliberations afterwards. The administrators insist that they only provide a forum for the elders' deliberations, and that they are not the ones who actually resolve the disputes.[12] They none the less have an overwhelming influence on the process. Since they keep written records of all disputes that come before them, they serve as the institutional memory for the process. They also serve as an enforcement mechanism. If a person fails to honour the elders' award, or to meet his/her obligations under an agreement that has been filed with the chief's office, there is always the threat of official sanction.

Land adjudication committees Land adjudication is a step in the process that results in official registration of title to land in the former 'African reserve areas' now termed 'trust land areas'.[13] People holding land within the trust land areas are presumed to hold such land under African customary law. The process of introducing private individual titles in the trust land areas has continued from the 1950s to the present. In some parts of the country, this process has been completed; in others, it is still in progress.

Any disputes that arise in the course of land adjudication are brought before a land adjudication committee.[14] The land adjudication committee consists of at least ten 'persons' resident in the area under adjudication. In practice, 'persons' has come to mean male elders; the committees have no women and the average age of the members is at least fifty years.[15] The committee is charged with the duty of adjudicating upon disputes 'in accordance with recognized customary law'.[16]

Pathways: Possibilities for the Realization of Gender Equality Through Local Norms and Practices

In this section I discuss the features I identified in the beginning as favourable for the realization of gender equality. A general observation is that local institutions offer an affordable and accessible forum of first resort for the vindication of claims. Formal legal enforcement is an option only in theory for most people in rural areas, on account of financial cost and restricted access.

Potential in constant change and adaptability The potential for realization of gender equality through local norms and practices lies in the fact that local custom is in constant motion. Local custom represents both ideology and day-to-day social practice. What is said about custom is often a partial truth, whose completeness can be observed or experienced only in actual social interaction. Local practices are varied, and people's day-to-day interactions are more revealing of the 'living' cultural norms. The ideology contained in assertions of culture will often fail to capture all of social reality.

Sally Falk Moore notes that incongruity between social reality and 'ideological systems' (which include laws, procedures, customs, rituals, symbols) is a feature of social life generally, and social scientists have employed various models to analyse it. She characterizes customs, laws, rituals, symbols and rigid procedures as a cultural framework that attempts to capture and represent social life, which social life is difficult to fix because cultural and social change is continuous (Moore 1978b: 37, 39). General statements often present cultural norms in a rigid manner, as immutable and inflexible, applicable in all situations (Moore 1978b: 40). However, individual and situational variations abound: 'For every situation that a person thinks or says, "That cannot be done, it is against the rules, or violates the categories", there is another occasion when the same individual says, "Those rules or categories do not (or should not) apply to this situation"' (Moore 1978b: 39).

What people claim to be the custom does say a lot about expected behaviour and the conventions that exist for ensuring compliance with that expectation. However, stated norms may vary *vis-à-vis* what people actually do. Thus, expressions of customary norms could be analysed as part of a process of 'regularization'; reconciling between ideology (the way in which a community presents itself) and social reality. Articulating custom is a process of producing seemingly durable customs, rules, symbols and categories that in reality serve to mask the indeterminacy and changing nature of the social reality. The articulation may take rigid and precise forms, which diverge from the variation and conflict on the ground.

The production of local custom is a dynamic process and is continually undergoing change. Take the example of inheritance practices. My interviews both in the village survey and in interviews with clan officials elicited a wide range of responses on what Akamba inheritance practices are. For some people it is against tradition for a person to designate shares of property for his family members while he is still living. Such division is to be left to his lineage's elders after his death. Yet others believed that it is better and wiser to lay out one's wishes clearly to avoid the possibility of wrangling after one's death. In some people's experience, married daughters do not feature at all in the division of property in their natal families. In others, although married daughters in general do not acquire interests in land, they could be given livestock.

In spite of the prevailing notion that daughters are not entitled to inheritance, I found that there was a measure of support for the interests of the 'dutiful' daughter, diligent in helping her parents and taking an active role in the affairs of the home. For such a daughter, many people pointed out, provision is justifiable, even though it is not to be demanded by her. As one clan chairman expressed it:

If your father gives it to you no one can ask you. Are you not his child? And who knows? Maybe you are the child who does a lot of good things for him. Maybe you are an obedient child. When he asks you to do something he does not sense resistance or stubbornness. Or maybe you buy him clothes … or you are the one who really takes an interest in his welfare. So he might decide that he too will give you something that you can see (appreciate), like a cow or a piece of land. No one can open his/her mouth against that. What would he/she say? It is your father's land and no one else can claim it from you.[17]

One village headman gave us the example of a man in his village who had declared on his deathbed that his daughter should be given Kshs 100,000 (approximately 1,700 dollars) since she alone had taken care of him during his long illness. The village headman added that if the father had said that she should be given a piece of land, the family would have to follow the father's wishes.[18]

These examples show that listening beyond normative statements and ideology to actual social practices gives a more balanced picture of local norms and practices. It is on the basis of these varied practices that interpretations of custom that accommodate human rights principles (such as gender equality in access to property) can be arrived at. At least they offer a starting point for an internal challenge to abstractions about culture that justify the exclusion of women. This internal challenge is important because abstractions or ideological statements about culture find their way into officialized notions of culture that are embodied in formal legislation, policies and judicial decisions. In the area of family relations in particular, ideological statements about what is properly traditional have played a key role in official interpretations of customary law that have tended to be rigid (Stewart 1998). For this reason, people and groups working for social change should assume the task of making the complex and varied contemporary practices of custom visible in official fora. This will ensure that these are meaningfully represented and taken into account in a manner that reflects balance and fairness.

Culture is not deterministic The dynamism reflected in the variation and flexibility that abound in actual social practice points to the fact that custom/culture is not deterministic. It is not something floating above people's heads and conditioning their actions. I encountered examples of people who held certain opinions or took certain actions, knowing full well that they would be regarded as sailing against the cultural current. People are indeed agents of cultural transformation.

I use the example of the norms and practices around inheritance in polygamous families. All the clan officials I spoke with agreed that the 'traditional'
practice is to divide the property according to the number of wives. If there
are two wives, each household gets half of the property, regardless of whether
one household has ten children (sons) and the other only one. Some clan
officials insisted that this was the fairest division due to the principle that all
the wives should be treated equally. But two of the ten clan officials and some
of the people I interviewed in the survey protested that this practice is unjust
and breeds jealousy and persistent conflict among the children (sons) in the
respective households. One clan chairman noted that a number of people
had complained to him about it. In the chairman's view, the rule on division
of property on the basis of the number of wives was a mistake, and it has had
repercussions since that is what the courts and local administration know to
be Akamba custom, so it will be difficult to change it.[19]

Some cases I encountered in the records of the local administrators suggest
that this practice is changing towards what people perceive to be a more
equitable division of property among children in a polygamous family. In one
case, four stepbrothers had agreed to divide the property equally among them,
rather than between their two households. They came to record the agreement
before the chief and to request a referral letter to present to the Land Control
Board to approve sub-division.[20]

This example shows that people have the agency that enables them to act
against established cultural expectations, therefore opening up the possibility
of departure from interpretations of culture that go against human rights
principles. However, it also raises the issue of relative ability to mobilize change
in local practices. The gradual change in the practice of dividing property in
polygamous families can be attributed to the fact that the practice has drawn
the disapproval of people who are in positions of power, such as the clan
chairman referred to above. If enough relatively powerful people within the
clan complain about a practice then change is more likely. What about complaints by relatively less powerful community members? For example, there is
no recognition of an entitlement to spousal support or to a share of marital
property following the dissolution of a marriage, an issue whose adverse effect
is felt almost exclusively by wives. It is assumed that such a woman's natal
family will provide for her and her children. On this issue, can we expect that
women as a social group (and men who support gender equality) will exercise
enough voice to influence a change of customary norms from within?

This is an issue that would require organizing and identifying allies – people
who will perceive such change as beneficial to them, and whose voices are

listened to. In this case, such allies would be members of natal families that have been forced to bear the additional responsibility of providing for a daughter/sister and her children.[21] This is a process in which human rights actors can become involved in collaborative efforts, and it would also provide a forum for communicating and debating remedies available in formal law as well as deliberating on the inadequacies of both the local norms and the formal laws.

Potential to recognize claims not validated in the formal legal system Claims that the formal legal system fails to characterize as rights may sometimes find recognition in informal fora at the local level, or through interpersonal negotiation. I draw an example from the much-discussed government policy of formalizing and individualizing property rights in land.[22] As a matter of practice, land is registered in the names of male heads of households as sole owners, leaving the interests of other family members unregistered. This is not required under the laws governing formal land registration. On account of this practice, women account for less than 5 per cent of the registered landholders nationally.[23] When disputes have arisen between the title-holder and family members claiming rights under customary law, Kenyan courts have often ruled that formal title extinguishes all other interests in the land, except 'overriding interests' enumerated in section 30 of the Registered Land Act.[24] Among the interests deemed extinguished are interests based on customary law, such as the interests of sons in ancestral land,[25] and the interests of wives that allow them to live on and use family land by virtue of marriage.[26] It seems that, for some reason, labelling the claims 'customary' gives them a meaning that makes it easy for them to be disregarded.[27]

Looking at the statute's definition of overriding interests, I find it difficult to distinguish between the interests protected by section 30(f) and (g), and the claims described as customary. Section 30(f) protects rights of prescription (prescriptive easements), which presupposes long usage, often asserted by family members claiming 'customary' rights to land. Section 30(g) protects the rights of 'a person in possession or actual occupation of land to which he is entitled in right only of such possession or occupation'. If the claimants in a particular family dispute do fulfil these factual criteria, should it matter that they base their claims on customary law? In my view, family members invoke customary law in support of their claims because it is the only medium that allows them to communicate the notion of moral obligations owed to them by the title-holder. It provides them with the ability to express the idea that their claims are not made simply on the basis of a narrow idea of legal rights, but that they are supported by a 'moral order' or 'social order' that binds them as well as the title-holder.

Given the low number of women holding land as registered owners, this dismissal of unregistered interests in land is likely to impact women more as a group compared to men as a group.

Practice at the local level attempts to strike a balance between the freedom that formal title gives the title-holder on the one hand, and the socially recognized interests of other family members, on the other. For example, local customary norms place restraints on individual ownership by requiring consultation at the family level before a decision to sell or mortgage land is taken. This requirement is enforced through the clan structure. I studied the written rules of ten clans and all had this rule, expressed in different ways. One clan rule will serve as an example: '*Atwii* clan: It is not permitted for a member of our clan to sell land without the knowledge and consent of the clan committee. Land belonging to a [member of the *Atwii* clan] must first be offered for sale to the family, and then to other clan members, before it can be offered to outsiders.'[28]

Family members have the option of complaining to the clan authorities if the person in whose name the family land is registered exercises or threatens to exercise his freedom of sale in a manner that prejudices their interests in the land. Among the clan leaders I interviewed and the people I surveyed, there was broad recognition of the power of the clan to intervene in such situations and stop a sale and even require the refund of any money already received by the seller.

There are many instances in which family members (mostly wives and children) were able successfully to invoke the clan's assistance to protect their interests in land. In a formal court they probably would not have had a chance, given the dominant judicial tendency to regard official title as the only legally protected interest. However, there are also instances in which the protection promised by clan practice has proved inadequate or simply inaccessible. I discuss this in the next section on constraints to the realization of gender equality through local norms and processes.

Fences: Limits to the Realization of Gender Equality Through Local Norms and Practices

Local norms and practices offer both opportunities and setbacks in the search for concrete realization of gender equality. This is true of any normative order, including formal national laws and international human rights.

Differences in power and knowledge Legal pluralists correctly observe that people draw from a variety of normative orders in a plural society as it suits their situation.[29] Within the pluralist framework, it is therefore possible to conceive of people being able strategically to pick and choose from formal law and from custom or religion positive elements that benefit them. Women, for example, could, in theory, utilize positive elements of both custom and legislative or administrative procedures (such as the land control board) that give them a voice in transactions involving family property.

In practice, however, the ability to do this may vary on the basis of factors such as class and gender. It would be naive to assume that clans and local administrators are accessible to all people equally, assurances from the relevant officials notwithstanding. One's position within the relevant social network also matters.[30] In the preceding discussion on clan-enforced restrictions on the freedom of a 'family head' holding title to land in which other family members have interests, I noted that clan practice protects interests that formal courts would probably disregard. However, there are instances in which people were constrained in their ability to use this local mechanism to their advantage. Some examples include:

- a young wife with young children, aware of her weak standing in her family and therefore afraid to approach the clan
- a widow who is senior in her lineage, but deterred by social etiquette around keeping family matters private from by-passing her brother-in-law's authority to present her grievances before the clan at the *iko* level
- a poor family, new to the locality, sceptical that they could receive fairness from the clan since they perceive the clan chairman as allied with their richer neighbour with whom they have a boundary dispute.

Another major constraint is lack of knowledge about existing options. For instance, among the 111 people I interviewed in the survey, none had heard of the land control board, an administrative body that operates at the district level. Its function is to screen transactions to ensure sound management of agricultural land. Landholders are required to seek the approval of the land control board for transactions such as sales, mortgages and sub-divisions. Following a presidential directive, land control boards have developed the additional practice of inquiring from applicants whether family members consent to the transaction. This is an avenue that family members, such as wives, could use to object to transactions that jeopardize their interests, yet not many people know of it.

Knowledge about the overarching sphere of formal legality plays a role in shaping interactions in the local sphere and in influencing the choices that people make in specific situations, based on their understanding of the totality of options open to them. This knowledge plays a role in shaping the bargaining landscape in interpersonal relationships at the local level. It becomes one more tool for preserving and broadening existing pathways and creating new ones around the fences erected to preserve gender hierarchy.

No challenge to underlying ideology on authority and gender roles within the family With respect to intra-family disputes (which make up the bulk of disputes handled by these local fora), embedded ideas about authority and gender roles seem to constrain open deliberation on the facts, and to dictate a resort to idealized statements of custom that necessitate a particular outcome. Decision-makers in these local fora are aware of tacitly-defined boundaries of authority within the family. Alice Schlegel defines authority as the 'socially recognized and legitimated right to make decisions concerning others' (Schlegel 1977: 8). Who is viewed as having the legitimate authority to make decisions concerning the family's resources, for instance? In day-to-day social interaction, what forms of authority are seen as legitimately belonging to a woman or man, and which ones are not? Unspoken answers to these questions are at the back of the minds of decision-makers and they appear to dictate outcomes in disputes, in spite of the merits of the evidence presented.

In practice, these boundaries of authority and gender roles are not so rigidly defined, but the power of ideal statements persists in maintaining the perception that they are. In the area of land relations, men and not women are regarded as having the authority to deal with major aspects such as negotiating and financing purchases of land. Where women have exercised such authority, the ideal statements are invoked to cast doubt on or to discredit their claims altogether. Two examples drawn from land adjudication disputes help to clarify this argument.

In the first, a wife sought to be registered jointly with her husband on the grounds that the land in question had been purchased largely with funds that she had contributed from her earnings.[31] The purchases had been made at a time when she was the only income earner, but her husband alone handled the formalities of adjudication and registration, and only his name appeared on the agreements of sale and in the official records. The couple was involved in divorce proceedings before the High Court at the same time as this land adjudication dispute was being heard.

The husband did not explicitly deny that the land parcels were purchased using his wife's earnings. His responses were in fact equivocal and callous: 'I did not use any money from my wife; and even if I did, it was *my wife's* money.' His words suggest that he believed that he was entitled to her earnings as a matter of right by virtue of his authority as a husband.

In deciding the case, the land adjudication officer (LAO) found that the husband admitted having spent money from his wife's income in purchasing the land. Nevertheless, the LAO refused to rule in favour of joint registration, saying that since her name did not appear on the sale agreements, he saw no justification for joint registration, in effect endorsing the husband's implied claim to her earnings. He justified this outcome by means of a disingenuous invocation of custom: 'Under the Kamba customary law property owned by the husband [belongs also to] the wife who is not denied any right to it.' The LAO relied on an abstract statement of 'custom' even when it was obvious in this particular case that she would have no such 'customary right' to benefit from the property, given the acrimonious divorce proceedings between them. Ideal statements of custom that reinforce the perception that the husband is the proper authority in management of family land make it possible for such a decision to be made in spite of the uncontested evidence of her enormous contribution.

The second example arose out of a land adjudication case involving a father and daughter.[32] The daughter had returned to a piece of land owned by her family following her divorce. Her parents moved to a different area, but she stayed on by herself and took care of that piece of land for thirty years, cultivating part of it. At adjudication, her father allowed her to register the cultivated portion in her name, but registered the rest of the land in his own name. She filed an objection stating that the land her father gave her was not enough and that she wanted an additional portion on which she could build her own home and have enough land for grazing. She also based her claim on a sense of entitlement: 'He should give me more land since I am the one who took care of this land. If I had left (when the family moved) it would have been taken by other people'. Without addressing her factual arguments at all, her father responded by resorting to a statement of the custom: 'I cannot [give] more land to her since Akamba do not give daughters land to settle but [only] to cultivate. I have no more [words] to add since even the clan told her the same.' The LAO simply echoed the father's views, reinforcing that as a father he had no such customary obligation towards her. Thus, in spite of what I observed to be a commendable trend in the land adjudication cases, namely honouring claims based on long occupation and development of the land, the 'customary' rule that a daughter does not acquire durable interests in her family's land overrides evidence that would otherwise have fortified her claim. Even though her father justified his decision on custom, our preceding discussion shows that the picture that emerges from practice is much more flexible and varied. If he did choose to give land to his daughter, custom would not stand in his way.

The picture one gets from these two cases is that of a convenient fence of customary ideology erected in the face of attempts by women to present factual evidence in support of entitlements they believe they have justly earned. Although these cases do not, by any means, speak for all local practice, the attitudes they expose cast doubt on the ability of local fora to contribute to a transformative agenda in the area of gender relations within the family. But the cases also show that there are women and men bold enough to make pathways around or through these fences by challenge this underlying ideology. The wife in the first example enlisted the help of the International Federation of Women Lawyers (FIDA-Kenya) in preparing her appeal to the minister, the next level of adjudication under the statute.[33]

The participation of women as decision-makers in local institutions is limited It is important for women to have meaningful input into the affairs of the institutions that play a key role in shaping and enforcing customary norms, especially those concerning family and property relations. The question of voice and participation in shaping and changing custom from within matters a great deal in a plural setting. The internal dynamics of shaping custom through local practice do have an impact on the larger social matrix of national laws. It matters whose articulation or view of custom ultimately counts or is validated in official settings such as court proceedings, government policies such as formalization of landholding or national debate on issues such as reform of family law.

The key institutions at the local level are staffed predominantly by men. The local administration machinery is also almost exclusively male. Some parts of the country have female district commissioners and district officers, but I am not aware of any female chiefs. Clan leadership is almost exclusively male. Two of the ten clans whose officials I interviewed had women in their committees – as secretaries. By this observation I do not intend to suggest that women's participation in decision-making will automatically guarantee change in the absence of a substantive agenda for change towards gender equality.

My concern goes beyond mere absence from visible positions of leadership to perceptions of women's membership status in social institutions that matter, such as the clan. Since clan membership is patrilineal, children belong to their father's clan. Daughters born into the clan are regarded as belonging to the clan, but they do not get registered as clan members and they do not pay dues. The reason for this is that when they get married, they will be registered in their husbands' clans and pay dues there. However, daughters will be required to pay clan dues if and when it becomes clear that they are unlikely to get married. If, for example, a girl has a child or children, and/or she gets to an age that makes it unlikely that she will marry, on her own initiative, or that of her family, she will be enrolled as a member of her father's clan.[34]

In seven out of the ten clans whose officials I interviewed, such member-daughters were not allowed to attend clan meetings, their paid membership notwithstanding.[35] A daughter's full payment of dues does not earn her a voice in clan meetings or participation in decision-making. The officials in these clans were quick to assure me that if such a daughter has any need, she is free to present it before the clan for deliberation and she would be listened to.

Land adjudication committees are staffed exclusively by men. According to the LAOs, the process requires people who are familiar with the history of landholding in a locality, and it is usually the old men who possess this knowledge. If historical knowledge is indeed the important factor, then one would think that old women, too, are competent. After all, women are the ones primarily involved in managing family land. But this is not about competence. *The hen may know how to crow but that is not her business!* It is about perceptions of authority and power. Not all knowledge matters.

It is difficult to respond to the retort that it is not the hen's business to crow, even if she knows how to do so. The solution is not as simple as proving that women are in fact effective decision-makers or leaders. The challenge is a more difficult one of making women's competence count; making women's authority acceptable and legitimate.

Changing this perception will require a major transformation in attitudes. A starting point would be to draw parallels to other key institutions, both informal and formal, in which women play leadership roles. Examples include the few clan committees that do have women. It is likely that the two women who were clan committee members were elected clan secretaries on account of their literacy. Still there is a larger pool of literate men to choose from, so it is remarkable that their clans chose them, and this could be held up as a positive example.

There are examples of women who serve as very active members of the development committee at the sub-location and location levels. These committees were set up by election under the auspices of the Makueni Agricultural Project (MAP), a collaborative project between Kenya's Ministry of Agriculture and the Danish International Development Agency (DANIDA).[36] The development committee in Kathulumbi location (one of the localities covered in my research) has fifteen members, seven of whom are women. The project coordinators made it clear that the committees had to be representative (by village and by gender). Would people have elected the women if the project coordinators had not made it clear that they wished to see gender balance in the committee? Perhaps not all seven, but possibly some of them. Does the committee have legitimacy, or is it simply a strategic move to place the community on good terms with the donor agencies? Will it lead to sustainable change or is it merely superficial? It is too early to tell, but as far as meaningful participation by women is concerned, there is hope in the fact that some of the women who were elected were already active as leaders in other capacities. They all hold positions of leadership in their churches and in local self-help groups. One is a well-respected retired teacher and another is the adult education instructor. Two of them hold key positions in the development committee. One serves as the treasurer and another as the vice-secretary.

Conclusion: Is Engagement with Local Norms and Practices Worthwhile?

The constraints I have identified might lead to scepticism and to a conclusion that any potential gains to be made by engaging local norms and practices in the struggle for women's human rights are rendered illusory. Indeed, some human rights actors may object to the suggestion that institutions such as local administrators have the potential to contribute anything positive to any rights struggle. After all, human rights actors in Kenya have made calls for the abolition of the entire local administration system, charging that it wields excessive power over people at the grassroots level.[37] My approach is pragmatic: as long as the reality of poor access to formal judicial institutions due to cost and inadequate decentralization of institutions persists, people will need some kind of fora to resort to when interpersonal negotiations fail. For now, the semi-formal dispute resolution fora facilitated by local administrators, and the clan-based practices offered by these fora and the role they play, are widely acknowledged.[38] Human rights actors could therefore choose to ignore these local practices altogether or become involved in them, thus expanding the arena of human rights practice.

Beyond this pragmatic concern, there are normative as well as practical reasons why local norms and practices should not be ignored. The normative reason is that it is primarily from their immediate cultural or religious milieu that people draw norms to regulate their interpersonal relationships. Will

Kymlicka argues that a person's societal culture enables meaningful individual choice and supports self-identity: 'Cultural membership provides us with an intelligible context of choice, and a secure sense of identity and belonging, that we call upon in confronting questions about personal values and projects' (Kymlicka 1995: 105).

The further removed the arena of formal law and policy is from this nuanced social practice at the local level, the less legitimacy it will have in people's lives. Similarly, the practice of human rights risks losing relevance and legitimacy if it does not concern itself with what goes on at the local level.

As a practical matter, working towards the incorporation and enforcement of formal guarantees of rights in legislation could be self-defeating if it fails to contend with the force of local institutions whose norms and practices have the potential to complement or contradict the intended goals. This is particularly true of attempts to introduce reforms in the sphere of family relations. The sphere of local practice is not impervious to changes at the formal level, but neither does it respond to such changes in predictable ways. Such reform must take local norms and practices into account.

How do we ensure that these local practices are taken into account in a meaningful way, and not simply as rigid official interpretations of 'custom' or notions that come in handy to rationalize policies that have the effect of deepening gender hierarchy? Human rights actors have to be present in this process of taking local norms into account in order to ensure that practices that offer protection to women (e.g. clan rules that scrutinize a man's decision to sell family land) are included and enhanced. Equally important, we must ensure that practices endorsed as 'custom' but which deepen gender inequality are subjected to intense scrutiny. One way to do this, as I have argued, is to present evidence of practice to the contrary.

Another way is to draw from the larger social matrix by pointing to the aspiration towards gender equality in the constitution. However, the constitutional protection of gender equality is inadequate, particularly with respect to gender relations within the family. The constitutional provision that forbids discrimination makes an exception with respect to the application of customary and religious laws to 'adoption, marriage, divorce, burial, devolution of property on death or other matters of personal law'.[39] In effect, this means that with respect to these matters, customary or religious laws trump the constitution in any proceedings in which discrimination is alleged. The exception shields such personal laws (religious and customary law) from constitutional challenge. People within a particular cultural or religious sub-group are denied access to redress when, *from their perspective*, they have suffered injustice as a result of the application of a cultural or religious norm to their specific situation. These exceptions make it possible (and legal) for cultural barriers to be invoked to justify denial or restriction of women's equal access to and control of economic resources within the family.

The exception limits what should be a dynamic and on-going dialogue in defining social norms in day-to-day interpersonal relationships in a fast-changing social context. Rather, it treats customary and religious norms as already settled and beyond question. It amounts to outright denial of voice to those within the group who may hold a different view of what is culturally proper or what is just in a specific situation. Yet our discussion on constant change and adaptability of local norms shows that culture is not a monolith, experienced in the same way by an entire social group. Prevailing notions of culture may simply be the dominant view at the ideological level, with numerous variations on the ground. Attention to actual local practice enables us to go beyond a critique that simply questions the inadequacy of formal guarantees of gender equality, to one that questions also the representation of customary norms in formal law in a manner that presumes their rigidity.

In conclusion, a genuine engagement with practice at the local level is powerful in dislodging both the abolitionist imagination of the local as the repository of unchanging patriarchal values and the defensive relativist portrayal of local norms as bounded, immutable and well settled.

Notes

I am very grateful to Hani Sayed for useful comments on this chapter and for our continuing conversations on the dilemma of international lawyers compelled to believe in 'the possibility of a meaningful dialogue between civilizations' (in his words).

1. Merry notes that even though the discourse of human rights is based on 'Western liberal-legalist ideas', when non-Western societies, such as indigenous rights movements, utilize the discourse in framing their demands, the concept of human rights is reinterpreted and transformed in a two-way process of incorporation of local understandings and the addition of global discourses. It is this two-way process that she terms 'legal vernacularization'.

2. Moore draws on examples from two different contexts to illustrate this framework of analysis: the loose enforcement of labour regulations in the dress industry in New York, and the Chagga, a community living in the area around Mt Kilimanjaro and their experiences with socialist policy in Tanzania.

3. With respect to the Akamba, the few ethnographic accounts that exist do not concern themselves with the historical origins of clans, except to point out that the clan names suggest a link to particular occupations, which were probably the occupations of the

founders. For instance, Atwii means blacksmiths. Discussions of clan structure are few and sketchy (see, for example, Penwill 1951; Hobley 1971; and Lindblom 1969).

4. In the Akamba community there are at least thirty major clans (*mbai*). In Kathulumbi location alone I noted seventeen clans. Akamba clans are not bounded entities of co-resident families related by blood. They are spread out throughout the country, concentrated in the four districts (Machakos, Makueni, Kutui and Mwingi) predominantly occupied by Akamba. Certain clans may have a prominent presence in one area, and be only thinly spread in another.

5. Presently, the *iko* units coincide with the administrative boundaries for sub-locations. It is not clear what was used as the point of reference for marking out the boundaries of this unit in the period prior to formal administration. Its meaning suggests people who could be traced to the same hearth, or people who cooked together. After the *iko*, there are clan committees at the locational, divisional, district and, for the large clans, national level.

6. Kenya National Archives file reference number DC/MKS/8/12 (District Commissioner, Machakos, notes and correspondence).

7. Some clans' rules are made at the national level and govern all their members nationwide and are distributed in a booklet. Other clans have decentralized rules for each location or sub-location. The rules range from procedural guidelines on the conduct of clan meetings to substantive regulation of the behaviour of clan members, for instance prohibiting alcohol to women and unmarried youths.

8. At the time of my research in Kathulumbi location of Makueni district, all the local administrators were serving in various capacities on their clan committees. Two of the three assistant chiefs were secretaries, the third a committee member, and the chief was his clan's divisional chairman.

9. The official framing of this arrangement was as follows: 'In making Ordinances, the Commissioner shall respect existing native laws and customs, except so far as the same may be opposed to justice or morality.' Section 12(3) East African Order-in-Council, 1902, Vol. IV *East Africa Protectorate Ordinances and Regulations*, at 49.

10. Sir F. D. Lugard (who is credited for the retrospective repackaging of indirect rule as a philosophy rather than as the product of practical necessity) counselled: 'The first step [in establishing indirect rule] is to endeavour to find a man of influence as chief, and to group under him as many villages or districts as possible, to teach him to delegate powers … to support his authority, and to inculcate a sense of responsibility' (quoted in Mamdani 1996: 53). In 1902, the Village Headman Ordinance was enacted to allow the Commissioner to create native authorities and native courts, that would exercise 'traditional' authority.

11. These disputes range from inheritance disputes to accusations of sale of land without family consent, neglect of children, wife-beating, refund of bride-wealth, disputes concerning cohabitation (usually women claiming spousal and child support, and men counter-arguing that they have no such obligation because the cohabitation was not a marriage), and squabbles between mothers and daughters-in-law.

12. Interviews with: Chief Daniel Ileve, 20 January 1999; Assistant Chief Justus Mwanzia, 18 January 1999; Assistant Chief Joseph Kitonyo, 18 January 1999; Assistant Chief Shadrack King'waa, 18 January 1999.

13. The term 'trust lands' has its origins in the colonial period, when land in the use of 'natives' was held in trust for them by the crown, since Africans were considered 'tenants at will' of the crown. Following the 1933 Carter commission's report, the Native Lands Trust Ordinance was enacted in 1938 in a move that ostensibly halted any further allocation of lands occupied by Africans to European settlement, by placing African lands in a trust.

At independence, the trusteeship for these native reserve lands was transferred to the respective counties and municipalities in which those lands were situated, and then renamed 'trust lands'.

14. Appeals from decisions of the land adjudication committees are heard by an arbitration board which is appointed by the provincial commissioner. It consists of elders resident within the district. Parties dissatisfied with a decision of the arbitration board can file objections, which are heard by a land adjudication officer. Appeals from the land adjudication officer's decision may be filed with the minister, who often delegates this role to the respective district commissioners.

15. The explanation I received for this practice is that the old men are the ones who know the history of landholding in the area. Interviews with Thomas Muoka (7 August 1998), Josiah Muinde (10 September 1998) and Joseph Muia (5 August 1998), Makueni District Land Adjudication Department.

16. Section 20(a) of Land Adjudication Act.

17. Interview with Kimatu Kasyula, Aatwii clan chairman, Kathulumbi location, 7 January 1999.

18. Ngolomoto village, interview no. 1. A study by Women and Law in East Africa (WLEA) also documented some favourable views in support of daughters' inheritance in spite of the overall negative aura. Some people interviewed in the WLEA study expressed the view that they would give their daughters plots of land in commercial/urban areas rather than in farmland which was more likely to be challenged as breaking with tradition. See WLEA 1995.

19. Interview with Kimatu Kasyula, Aatwii clan chairman, Kathulumbi location, 7 January 1999; interview with Kiema Kitungi, Aamutei clan divisional chairman, 7 January 1999. The interviewees who opposed the traditional households-based mode of division were emphatic in saying that they would put their wishes in writing, stating clearly that the property should be divided equally among all their sons. Knowing that in the event of clan intervention it is quite possible for the clan to disregard such wishes in favour of the 'traditional' mode of division, some went as far as to state that they would pronounce a deathbed curse on anyone who dared to disregard their wishes.

20. Kathulumbi chief's Occurrence Book, Muema Mutua, Kitheka Mutua, Munywoki Mutua and Pius Mutua (8 November 1996).

21. Out of 111 households covered in a village-based survey that I conducted as part of my research, 23 had daughters who were divorced or who had had children while unmarried. Their natal families assumed the obligation to provide for them (some grudgingly) and none was receiving or expected to receive any support from ex-spouses.

22. For discussion of the policy on introduction of individual title, particularly its impact on gender relations, see, for example, Shipton 1988; Okeyo 1980; Davison 1987; and Karanja 1991.

23. This estimate is given in a study conducted by EarthCare Africa. See 'Land Legislation Shuts Out Women', *Daily Nation*, 7 August 1997, p. 20. My own estimate based on a random sampling of areas of Makueni district in which registration has been completed places the figure for the district at 8 per cent, which includes instances in which women are registered as joint owners.

24. Overriding interests are listed in section 30 of Kenya's Registered Land Act as rights of air, water, way, prescriptions, leases for periods less than one year not requiring registration, and rights of a person in actual occupation.

25. *Esiroyo v Esiroyo* (1973), East Africa Law Reports, 388.

26. *Wanjohi & Wanjohi v Official Receiver and Interim Liquidator (Continental Credit Finance Ltd)*, Civil Application NAI no. 140 of 1988. (Reproduced in the *Nairobi Law Monthly*, 14, February 1989 at 42.

27. This position reflects the dominant trend in the Kenyan judiciary. However, a few decisions of the High Court and Court of Appeal have employed the doctrine of 'constructive trust' to strike a balance between the claims of registered title-holders and family members claiming under customary law. But these decisions are clearly in the minority and are waning. The most recent Court of Appeal case to uphold this view was decided in 1982: *Muthuita v Muthuita* Kenyan Appeal Reports (1982–88), p. 42.

28. *Miao ya Mbai ya Atwii-Athunzu* [Rules of the *Atwii Athunzu* Clan] (Passed on 10 July 1948, revised August 1993), Rule no. 29 (my translation from the Kikamba language).

29. See, for example, Moore 1978a, 1978b; Rwezaura 1995 (pointing out that in spite of the distinct multiple systems of family law based on statute, African customary law and Islam, people rarely confined their actions to one system only, but instead drew from the various systems as it suited them); Hellum 1999; and Moore 1986.

30. In a detailed study of the informal resolution of family disputes in rural Botswana, Anne Griffiths notes that whether talking about local customary fora or formal courts, one's position and ability to mobilize social and economic resources is the crucial factor in deciding what option to pursue and in successfully making use of the forum to one's benefit (Griffiths 1998).

31. Kimundi adjudication section; combined objections nos 210, 211, 212, 213.

32. Kwa Kavisi Adjudication Section, objection no. 105.

33. This woman is educated, is in paid employment in Nairobi and has knowledge of legal aid bodies such as FIDA. Such is not the situation of a majority of the women affected by the decisions of local tribunals. The appeal had not been scheduled for hearing as of the date I left Makueni. FIDA anticipated possible court action for judicial review of the land adjudication decision.

34. From the interviews and conversations I had, it seems to me that the age of the children actually matters more than the age of the woman, in forming the impression that she is unlikely to marry. Customary practice demands that a man who marries a woman who has children must, in addition to making marriage payments to her family, compensate her family for the 'sweat' of raising her children, since the children will be regarded as his after he marries her. The 'sweat compensation' amount increases in proportion to the number of years for which her family has been responsible for the children.

35. Some clan officials believed that they had no power to change the rule excluding daughters from clan meetings because the rule was based on an oath taken a long time ago. Interviews with clan officials: Aatwii, Aakiimii, Aakitutu and Aanziu clans.

36. Ministry of Agriculture, Makueni Agricultural Project, *Participatory Rural Appraisal Report: Kathulumbi Sub-location* (August 1998).

37. The main accusation is that the powers of local administrators are ill-defined in the Chiefs' Authority Act, and have therefore been liable to abuse.

38. In March 2000, the office of the president, through Permanent Secretary Zakayo Cheruiyot, made an abrupt (but hardly uncharacteristic) announcement stating that the offices of assistant chiefs would be abolished in the on-going IMF-required 'right-sizing' of the civil service. Three days later the president reversed this statement in response to strongly-worded protests in the media raising concerns about the absence of clearly worked-

out alternatives. See 'President Overrules Move to Phase Out Chiefs', *Daily Nation*, 16 March 2000 (the *Daily Nation* is available on the web at www.nationaudio.co.ke).

39. Personal law is a collective term used to refer to customary and religious laws. Constitution of Kenya, section 82(4), paragraph (b). See also Constitution of Zimbabwe, Article 23(3), paragraph (a).

References

An-Na'im, A. A. (1994), 'State Responsibility Under International Human Rights Law to Change Religious and Customary Laws', in R. Cook (ed.), *Human Rights of Women: National and International Perspectives*, Philadelphia, PA: University of Pennsylvania Press.

Davison, J. (1987) '"Without land we are nothing": The Effect of Land Tenure Policies and Practices upon Rural Women in Kenya', *Rural Africana*, 27: 19.

Griffiths, A. (1998) 'Reconfiguring Law: An Ethnographic Perspective from Botswana', *Law and Social Inquiry*, 23: 587.

— (1997) *In the Shadow of Marriage: Gender and Justice in an African Community*, Chicago, IL: University of Chicago Press.

Hellum, A. (1999) *Women's Human Rights and Legal Pluralism in Africa: Mixed Norms and Identities in Infertility Management in Zimbabwe*, Oslo: TANO Aschehoug.

Hirsch, S. (1998) *Pronouncing and Persevering: Gender and the Discourses of Disputing in an African Islamic Court*, Chicago, IL: University of Chicago Press.

Hobley, C. W. (1971) *Ethnology of A-Kamba and Other East African Tribes*, London: Cass.

Karanja, Perpetua (1991) 'Women's Land Ownership Rights in Kenya', *Third World Legal Studies*, 109.

Kymlicka, W. (1995) *Multicultural Citizenship: A Liberal Theory of Minority Rights*, Oxford: Clarendon Press.

Lindblom, G. (1969) *The Akamba in British East Africa: An Ethnological Monograph*, New York, NY: Negro Universities Press.

Mamdani, M. (1996) *Citizen and Subject: Contemporary Africa and the Legacy of Late Colonialism*, Princeton, NJ: Princeton University Press.

Merry, S. E. (1997) 'Legal Pluralism and Transnational Culture: The Ka Ho'Okolokolonui Kanaka Maoli Tribunal, Hawai'i, 1993', in R. Wilson (ed.), *Human Rights, Culture and Context: Anthropological Perspectives*, London: Pluto Press.

Moore, S. F. (1978a) 'Law and Social Change: The Semi-autonomous Social Field as an Appropriate Subject of Study', in S. F. Moore, *Law as Process: An Anthropological Approach*, London: Routledge and Kegan Paul, pp. 54–81.

— (1978b) 'Uncertainties in Situations, Indeterminacies in Culture', in S. F. Moore, *Law as Process: An Anthropological Approach*, London: Routledge and Kegan Paul, pp. 32–53.

— (1986) *Social Facts and Fabrications: 'Customary' Law on Kilimanjaro, 1880–1980*, New York: Cambridge University Press.

Nyamu, C. (2000) 'How Should Human Rights and Development Respond to Cultural Legitimization of Gender Hierarchy in Developing Countries?', *Harvard International Law Journal*, 41: 381.

Okeyo, A. P. (1980) 'Daughters of the Lakes and Rivers: Colonization and the Land Rights of Luo Women', in M. Etienne and E. Leacock (eds), *Women and Colonization: Anthropological Perspectives*, New York, NY: Praeger.

Penwill, D. J. (1951) *Kamba Customary Law: Notes Taken in the Machakos District of Kenya Colony*, London: Macmillan.

Rwezaura, B. (1995) 'Tanzania: Building a New Family Law out of a Plural Legal System', *University of Louisville Journal of Family Law*, 33: 523.

Schlegel, A. (1977) 'Toward a Theory of Sexual Stratification', in A. Schlegel (ed.), *Sexual Stratification: A Cross-Cultural View*, New York, NY: Columbia University Press.

Shipton, P. (1988) 'The Kenya Land Tenure Reform: Misunderstandings in the Public Creation of Private Property', in R. E. Downs and S. P. Reyna (eds), *Land and Society in Contemporary Africa*, Hanover: University Press of New England.

Stewart, J. (1998) 'Why I Can't Teach Customary Law', in J. Eekelaar and T. Nhlapo (eds), *The Changing Family: International Perspectives on the Family and Family Law*, Oxford: Hart Publishing.

WLEA, Okech-Owiti et al. (eds) (1995) 'Research Report on Inheritance Laws and Practices in Kenya', WLEA.

SIX

Religious Revivalism, Human Rights Activism and the Struggle for Women's Rights in Nigeria

Hussaina J. Abdullah

§ THE period starting from the mid-1980s in Nigeria has witnessed the emergence of three apparently parallel but ultimately related trends/processes that have become important defining elements of the contemporary socio-political and cultural landscape of the country. The first has to do with the emergence of a host of associations specifically dedicated to the promotion and defence of human rights, civil liberties and legal/constitutional reform. Between 1985, when the National Association of Democratic Lawyers was founded, and 1995, at least thirty other such groups were established in different parts of the country. The second trend/process centres on an unmistakable religious revival entailing the revitalization of many existing religious (particularly Christian and Muslim) structures and networks and, perhaps more significantly, the rapid growth of (North American-type) Pentecostalist/spiritualist churches and 'fundamentalist' activist Islamic organizations. The third trend is connected with the explicit expansion of interest from above (at the level of the state) and from below (at the level of civil society) in the promotion of women's rights and interests.

The state's interest in women has been described elsewhere as signalling the emergence of 'state feminism'[1] and a process of 'femocracy' (Abdullah 1994: 27) linked to the First Lady phenomenon[2] that is rapidly gaining ground in Africa, sometimes with the support of 'developmentally'-oriented United Nations (UN) agencies such as the United Nations Children's Emergency Fund (UNICEF) and United Nations Development Programme (UNDP). With respect to the promotion of women's rights at the societal level, a host of non-governmental groups has been formed or revived explicitly devoted to the promotion of political, legal, cultural and intellectual activism in support of Nigerian women.

The three trends, which have emerged to define the contemporary Nigerian landscape, have unfolded within the context of two important factors. The first of these centres on the prolonged national economic crisis which started in 1981 and which has not been mitigated (some would even argue has been complicated) by the neo-liberal economic structural adjustment programme adopted with IMF/World Bank support in 1986 to contain the crisis. The second factor is the deepening crisis of governance and legitimization most vividly captured by the continuing subjection of the country to progressively worsening forms of military despotism, of which the tyrannical rule of General Sani Abacha's junta is the latest.

The deep-seated crisis in the national economy has not only resulted in the collapse of real incomes for most Nigerians, and a sharp decline in social citizenship, as state-supported social services went into decay on account of the fiscal and government problems confronting the country. It has also provided a fertile framework within which political authoritarianism and militarism thrive (Olukoshi 1993: 5, 6). A perceptible loss of faith in secular authorities has gone hand in hand with the rise of religious fundamentalism. The collapse in personal and household incomes has been accompanied by the growth of the gospel of prosperity (Marshall 1991: 23), economic decline and political dictatorship. The violation of rights associated with these harbingers of cultural decline has fuelled popular concern about the protection of human rights and political liberties and the intensification of corruption among state officials. These indicators are the popular disenfranchisement occasioned by economic decline and political authoritarianism and have eroded the legitimacy of the state and alienated many from state politics. Economic crisis, structural adjustment and political authoritarianism have been central to the transformation of popular identities in contemporary Nigeria. Shifts in the balance among social forces, most of which have been to the detriment of the working poor and the old class of professionals, have not only created a crisis of identities but also spurred activism at the level of religious practices and rights advocacy as individuals and groups attempt to make sense of national decline, protect themselves against its worst effects, and reassert their place and relevance as members of the polity.

This chapter assesses the implications of the growth of human rights/civil liberties activism along with a simultaneous process of religious revivalism, a rising and institutionalized 'state feminism', for the autonomous struggle from below for the protection and advancement of the rights of Nigerian women. It entails an evaluation of the extent to which the concerns and struggles of Nigerian women have been built into the programmes and activities of the growing human rights/civil liberties community and the ways in which activist women's organizations have sought to anchor and deepen the campaign for women's rights amidst the pressures posed by the new 'religiosity' in the country and the authoritarian impulse associated with state feminism.

At one level, the struggles of activist women's organizations have involved the articulation of strategies for responding to the de-politicizing thrust and consequences of state feminism/femocracy while simultaneously attempting to tap potentially positive elements of the process for the benefit of Nigerian women. At another level, it has entailed broadening the campaign for women's concerns and rights with regard to issues of legal and constitutional reform. International networking with other women's groups has also been employed as a strategy for advancing the interests of Nigerian women. Furthermore, there has been an attempt by some women's groups to use the idiom of religion and contestations over doctrinal interpretation to press the case for reforms. In this regard, I will use the experience of the Federation of Muslim Women's Associations in Nigeria (FOMWAN) as a case study to show the possibilities and limits of this specific approach. The struggles of Nigerian women for reform and change still have to contend with resilient patriarchal structures, which aspects of religious revivalism have tended to reinforce. Of particular concern are certain discriminatory practices against women and daily expressions of gender inequality, which the dominant religions tend to justify through their doctrines. The explosion of human rights activism has, so far, been insufficient significantly to challenge the structures of patriarchy. Some of the intellectual and policy challenges posed by this situation will inform the concluding part of this study.

The Emergence and Character of Contemporary Social Movements in Nigeria During the 1980s

In many respects, the human rights/civil liberties associations, establishment and women's activist groups, and radical/spiritualist religious organizations that emerged or were revived in Nigeria during the 1980s, were the products of a process that, in its remote origins, can be dated to the 1970s. Following the end of the Nigerian Civil War (1967–70), the country was, in the course of the 1970s, propelled into an era of unprecedented social and economic expansion, which was underpinned by rapidly growing petro-dollar revenues from oil exports (Olukoshi 1993: 1). The OPEC oil price increases of 1973 and 1977/78 made the huge petro-dollar windfall possible. The revenues, averaging some 12 billion US dollars annually for much of the 1970s, were applied by succeeding governments to finance the reconstruction and rehabilitation of the national economy generally and the war-torn areas in particular and partly to expand the country's physical and social infrastructure, including the supply of modern health and educational services. But a substantial part of the revenues also fed into the 'primitive' accumulation strategies of the Nigerian elite, so much so that 'corruption' or the '10 per cent' culture became almost integral to the socio-economic policies, programmes and practices of the state (Olukoshi 1993: 4).

By the mid-1970s, the Nigerian economy began decisively to take on the character of a 'monocultural' economy with oil increasingly accounting for a disproportionate share of the national revenues. By the end of the 1970s, the country had come to depend on oil exports for over 90 per cent of its total revenues and foreign exchange receipts (Bangura and Beckman 1993: 81). This was in spite of the routine proclamations made by succeeding government regimes, military and civilian, that the diversification of the country's economic base was a matter of national priority. The failure to achieve this objective, therefore, meant that the country was extremely vulnerable to any adverse development in the world oil market. Not surprisingly the Nigerian government was neither prepared for, nor able immediately to cope with, the sudden collapse in the early 1980s of the world oil market. The collapse of the world market price of oil from a high of 42 US dollars at the end of the 1970s, to below $10 at one point during the 1980s, translated into a revenue collapse for the Nigerian state. Given the heavily import-dependent nature of the economy, a major balance of payments and external debt crisis became almost inevitable. Nigeria was, therefore, ushered, inexorably, into a deep-seated recession from which it has still not recovered.

To stem the tide of economic decline, and the social decay that accompanied it, succeeding governments adopted different austerity packages aimed at shoring up the economy.[3] The most radical of these was the International Monetary Fund (IMF) and World Bank-inspired structural adjustment programme (SAP) adopted by the Babaginda military government in 1986. Structural adjustment, as has been argued by many Nigerian scholars, fed into the dynamics of economic decline and social-institutional decay that was already underway in the country. The 1980s in Nigeria, therefore, witnessed several rounds of massive public and private sector retrenchments, the drastic erosion of the standard of living of the majority of people, spiralling inflation and the elimination of subsidies, the imposition of levies for health and educational services, and the collapse of individual and household incomes. The adverse effect of SAP on people's lives and the social unrest it generated (riots in major urban centres, strikes by university teachers, students, doctors, labour unions etc.) were handled in repressive and high-handed ways by succeeding governments (Jega 1993: 102–9). The rapid deterioration of the national economy and the social decay that resulted from it therefore reinforced the structures of political repression and authoritarianism. With the state abdicating its social responsibilities and the economy sliding deeper into decline, even as political repression and corruption blossomed, the basis for the legitimacy of the post-colonial government gradually eroded.

Particularly targeted for repression were associations of Nigerian professionals, workers and youth, whose activism had been central to the construction of a secular, territorial national identity and the containment of the boundaries of political authoritarianism. Most notable among these associations were the Academic Staff Union of Universities, the National Association of Nigerian Students, the Nigerian Medical Association, the National Association of Resident Doctors, and the Nigeria Labour Congress and its forty-two affiliate unions (Jega 1993: 102–9). Members of these associations were also activists in various groups like the Movement for a Progressive Nigeria, Youth Solidarity for Southern Africa and the Socialist Congress of Nigeria. The collapse of the national economy in the early 1980s and the crisis management approaches adopted by the state not only took a heavy toll on the membership of these associations through retrenchments but it also resulted in the collapse of incomes and opportunities of the middle class. Furthermore, as they were in the vanguard of the resistance against austerity, the groups were also at the receiving end of the most repressive political strategies of the state. It was commonplace in Nigeria in the second half of the 1980s to refer to the collapse of the middle class, as it was once known. As a consequence of this, Nigeria witnessed a realignment of social forces in a manner that produced the three trends (religious, human rights and women's activism) I referred to earlier in the essay and which reflected a tension between the forces of secularism and parochialism, democracy and authoritarianism, and centralism and decentralization.

Religious Revivalist Movements: An Overview

Both Christian and Islamic religious revivalist movements, including the fundamentalists, began to enter into the national consciousness from the mid-1970s (Ibrahim 1989). Their emergence signified a new development in religious practices in the country, as their stated aim was to revive and 'purify' both religions by returning to the 'original' theological sources on which they were supposedly founded (Ibrahim 1989; Marshall 1991). In defining their agenda, both strands of the nascent religious revivalist movements were as sectarian and doctrinaire as they were intolerant of each other and of the practitioners of traditional African religions (Ibrahim 1989; Marshall 1991). Yet the assumption that is often made is that the groups are monolithic or homogenous. This is an untenable assumption, as even within each sect there have always existed differences based on their competing interpretations and usage of religious doctrines as well as the strategies that they thought were most suitable for the achievement of their objective of religious purification and revival.

In general, two broad extremes dominate the global Islamic movement, namely, the 'moderates' and the 'radicals'. Within each of these two strands are groups whose doctrines straddle both the moderate and radical divide. The moderates can be characterized as those who are generally accommodating of the government in power, while the radicals on the other hand are critical of and confrontational towards the government and, indeed, all secular authority. They oppose the existing system of politics and governance and view the government's authority as illegitimate arguing that it is corrupt and un-Islamic. According to Azzam, using the Egyptian example, what differentiates these two groups is the basic belief of the radicals in '*Hakimiyya l'allah*, meaning that sovereignty lies only with God, and *jihad*, which is described as the missing pillar (*al-farida al-gha'iba*) in Muslim devotional practice. Muslims are called upon to pursue *jihad* against a ruler deemed to be an un-believer (*kafir*) either by virtue of his not implementing the Shari'a or corruption (*fasad*) or making peace with the Jews' (Azzam 1996: 111). In spite of these differences, both groups believe that Islam is right and the implementation of the Shari'a is the answer.

Although the categorizations used to describe the broad trends in the Islamist movement can be used to classify their Christian fundamentalist counterparts, I have opted instead to use those adopted by Marshall in her study of the Nigerian Christian (fundamentalist) movement. According to Marshall (1991: 22), the movement is made up of two broad streams, namely, the Pentecostals (who are the moderates) and the 'holiness' or 'righteousness' churches (whose members are the radicals). The 'holiness' groups, according to Marshall are, 'highly organised and strongly denominational, and [promote] a doctrine which [stresses] strict personal ethics, a retreat from the "world" and worldly possessions and practices, as well as the imminent second coming of Christ'.

In contrast, the ideological belief of the moderates is based on a doctrine of prosperity, 'in which the spiritual and material fortunes of a believer were dependent upon whether they gave spiritually and materially to God (or his representatives) who would reward them by "prospering" them'. In addition, their doctrine emphasizes experiential faith, the centrality of the Holy Spirit, the spiritual gift of 'speaking in tongues', faith healing and miracles associated with the Pentecost. Although they also stress strict ethical codes and the Second Coming of Christ, they are not as doctrinaire as their 'holiness' brothers.

Nigerian Islamists

If the global Islamist movement is characterized by the two broad currents we described earlier, the Nigerian Islamist movement is made up of three main streams of thought. The first is what Imam refers to as the 'Political Islamist' stream (Imam 1993a: 132). This group represents the interests of the Muslim elite in the Jama'atu Nasril Islam (JNI) and the Supreme Council of Islamic Affairs (SCIA). It is made up of members of the political establishment. The objective of this strand is the political control of the state and its apparatuses, but not for the purpose of imposing radical Islamic reforms. In seeking to maintain their political influence, members of this stream often resort to whipping up religious sentiments with a view to portraying themselves as 'good' Muslims and, thus, winning support for themselves among the members of the more radical, fundamentalist stream. For example, its members played a key role in the 1978 and 1988 Constituent Assembly debates over the application of Shari'a in the country. As Imam has noted, 'the need for mass support' led this group into embracing fundamentalist positions on certain issues: 'the agitation for a Federal Shari'a Court of Appeal equally ranked with the Federal Court of Appeal has been increasingly argued, not simply as for those who wish to apply it, but for the "Muslim communities of Nigeria"' (Imam 1993a: 132, 133). Once in power, the representatives of this stream have often acted to repress challenges from the fundamentalist factions to their authority and the secular basis of the Nigerian state. They are often targeted for this reason by the fundamentalists as corrupt and treacherous. It is under the aegis of this group that FOMWAN, our case study organization, was established.

The second strand is the moderate one represented by the Jamaat Izalat Al-Bidi'awa Iqamat Al Sunna, commonly known as Izala, and its members, the Yan Izala. Ismail Idris, a soldier who served in the Nigerian army as an imam (Kukah 1991: 217) founded this group in the late 1970s. However, the group became synonymous with its grand patron, the late Alhaji Abubakar Gumi, Nigeria's Ambassador to Saudi Arabia in the 1950s, Grand Qhadi of the defunct Northern Nigeria (1963–67), chairman Islamic Pilgrims Board

(1975) and Grand Mufti (the Grand Jurisconsult of Islamic law) of Nigeria in 1976, recipient of the King Faizal International Award for service to Islam (1987). The emergence of this group, according to Kukah, 'was the climax of years of Alhaji Gumi's search for a political platform based on his religious beliefs and the search for an independent political and economic base for himself' (Kukah 1991: 218). With an organizational platform from which to articulate his views, Alhaji Gumi was able to win over new converts through regular preaching in his house, the Sultan Bello Mosque in Kaduna, as well as on the airwaves (Ibrahim 1989: 72). The *raison d'être* of this group is

> based upon a puritanical, 'return to the source' approach aimed to save Islam from syncretist and thus un-Islamic practices. This return to source operates at two levels. First, it involves a frontal attack against remnants of traditional African religious practices still prevalent among Muslim communities. Secondly, it involves a struggle against mystical Practices and the beliefs of Sufi brotherhoods (Darika), mainly the Tijaniyya and Quadiriyya. (Ibrahim 1989: 71)

Thus, it sees its role as partially entailing the re-conversion of the members of the Sufi brotherhoods whom it believes to have been led astray. Other characteristics of this group include its disapproval of ostentatious naming ceremonies, exorbitant marriage payments, the act of prostrating before anybody, as all men (sic) are equal. It also protests the celebration of the prophet's birthday, correct rituals for prayer and fasting, abstention from drugs including alcohol and cigarettes, 'proper' behaviour by women and the discouragement of its members from praying in mosques not managed by its own imams or those with similar beliefs (Imam 1993a: 132). As the group is patronized by the Saudi authorities, it echoes its master's voice by being anti-Ahmadiyya, pro-business and anti-Sufi (Ibrahim 1989: 72).

Since the Yan Izala is opposed to the brotherhoods whose members dominate the Muslim establishment, it sought to recruit its followers from among the growing array of the urban and social poor in Nigeria. The majority of its members was drawn from among the destitute urban poor, including the poorest echelons of the working class, the army of déclassé/lumpen elements, and new and ill-adapted migrants in urban centres from rural areas. These were social categories whose ranks swelled during the 1980s and the 1990s as the Nigerian economic crisis took its toll (Imam 1993a: 132). This is not to suggest that the top leadership of the group lacked influence or had no political clout.[4]

Women account for a significant proportion of the Izala movement's membership. Regular religious classes are organized for them. In fact, the organization's women's programme was incorporated into that of the centre for adult education, which is affiliated to the Ahmadu Bello University, Zaria (Ibrahim 1989: 72). Despite this, Alhaji Gumi had an essentially negative perspective on women's roles in the public domain. Although he urged women to play a positive role in the politics of the aborted Third Republic, he viewed leadership roles as an exclusively male affair. He noted that 'women can be very useful' in some aspects of politics, but 'to make them mix [with men] like Europeans is not acceptable to Islam' (Birai 1993: 196). In continuation of his offensive against women, Alhaji Gumi had categorically stated that it was his hope not to see a woman leading Nigeria while he was still alive.

In contrast to the political Islamists and moderates, the radical strand in the Nigerian Islamist movement rejects the idea of a secular state and constitution and considers the Iranian model of governance as being ideal for Nigeria. Organizations within this strand have close links with the Iranian government and depend on it for both material and financial support. Their basic tenet is that all Muslims should wage a *jihad* until the Shari'a becomes national law, and that the battle for an Islamic state in Nigeria should start with the destruction of the secular state (Birai 1993: 197). The most prominent members of this group are drawn from Mallam Ibrahim El Zakzaky's Islamic Movement (which is based in Zaria) and the Council of Ulama. Both groups metamorphosed from the Muslim Student Society (MSS). El Zakzaky, the leader of the Islamic Movement, was expelled from the Ahmadu Bello University during the 1978 student crisis and has had frequent clashes with the security forces since then (Ibrahim 1989: 73). As for the council of Ulama, it signifies, as Kukah puts it, the 'coming of age, the adulthood of the MSS' from university campuses into mainstream religious discourses (Kukah 1991: 221). The organization attributed its founding in part to the 'growing influence of Zionism as the Federal Government continues to lean more heavily on Israeli security cover, [which] means that hard days lie ahead for Islam' (ibid.).

The MSS was founded in 1954 as an organization of Yoruba Muslim students. It developed, however, into a national organization with branches in most schools and institutions of higher learning. Its objectives at inception were the organization of prayers, fellowship and evangelism among students (Ibrahim 1989: 73). However, since the mid-1970s, a hard-core extremist group has ascended to and retained the leadership of the organization, both at the national level and in the centres of Islamic radicalism in the universities of Zaria, Kano and Sokoto (ibid.). Extremism in the organization started during the 1975–76 academic year over alcohol consumption. It was alleged that dining hall cups that were used in beer drinking parties were not washed properly before being reused by non-drinking Muslim students who found themselves 'drinking' traces of alcohol (ibid.). As a result of this incident, the MSS first launched a campaign against the trading and consumption of beer in the student union premises and later burnt down all student union bars. The organization gained national prominence between 1976 and 1977 during the Constitution Drafting Committee (CDC) and Constituent Assembly debates on Shari'a. The MSS stated that: 'We stand for total application of the Shari'a, both as a legal system and a way of life. The Shari'a is not reducible, nor can it be compartmentalised. Therefore, the Muslims would require nothing less than a total application of the Shari'a and its full entrenchment in the constitution' (ibid.).

The transformation of the MSS from a student prayer group to a national political movement questioning the authority of the state played a significant part in the development of religious fanaticism both in the universities and the wider society. The radical Islamists, like their moderate and political counterparts, can boast of a sizeable female membership. The Muslim Sisters Organization (MSO) is the women's wing of this group. While the political Islamists have a different view on the role and place of Muslim women in society, the moderates and the radicals, despite their differences over the tactics and strategies for achieving their objectives, espouse the same gender ideology. According to Imam:

> These groups are broadly in agreement that women, although having equal souls before Allah, are under the jurisdiction of men as fathers and husbands on earth. These groups also see women as having a different physiology and psychology from men, which fits them essentially for the role of mother and wife. In this role, however, the fundamentalists stress the physical seclusion of women, while the political Islamists are more willing to concede that women may venture out of the home, if only they will dress decently and avoid unnecessary interactions with men. Furthermore, the fundamentalists support education of women primarily in order to enable them to be better teachers to their children and to be able to proselytise among women. The political Islamists accept this objective but also see roles for women in the wider economy – mostly in sex-stereotyped jobs. Fundamentalists defend the right of men to marry barely pubertal girls, political Islamists often advise waiting a little. (Imam 1993a: 133)

Although the political Islamists' interpretation of women's place and role in society is a bit more reasonable than that of the radicals and moderates, it has failed to question the existing gender division of labour and women's subordinate position within it.

Nigerian Christian Religious Groups

The origins of the 'holiness' or radical Christian groups can be traced back to the activities of British and US missionaries between the 1920s and 1950s. Among the earliest churches to be established within this ideological strand were the Faith Tabernacle, the Apostolic Church, the Apostolic Faith and the Assemblies of God (Marshall 1991: 22). Indigenous brands of these churches such as the Redeemed Christian Church of God and the Deeper Life Bible Church (The latter is the only second-wave church, i.e. churches established in the 1970s pursuing the 'holiness' doctrine) were later established as part of the 'holiness' order. Membership was drawn mostly from the literate and semi-literate indigent group. To back up its strict moral doctrine, a strict dress code was established for the female membership, members were forbidden from watching television and wearing jewellery. In addition to the spiritual and moral guidance they provide, these churches have established a social support system to provide succour to members in times of need. For example, the many churches have established nurseries and kindergartens, provide medical services (faith healing) and counselling services. In addition, members cook, mind children and pool resources to help each other whenever the need arises (Marshall 1991: 22, 27).

The Pentecostals emerged on the Nigerian religious landscape in the 1970s and 1980s from their bases in the universities. Unlike their 'holiness' brethren, this brand of the Christian religious movement, which grew out of the academy, was made up of young and highly educated individuals who placed a high premium on material success. It is not surprising, therefore, that the Pentecostals treasure the same symbols of status and prestige (fine clothes, nice cars, foreign goods etc.) that most non-fundamentalists in the wider society fancy.

There is very little difference in the world-views of the 'holiness' and Pentecostal versions of the new Christian movement on the gender roles of women and men, apart from the 'holiness' churches' strict moral and dress code for women, their confinement of women to lower levels of church administration, and their endorsement of most of the popular stereotypes on non-born-again women as 'temptresses', 'witches', 'spendthrift' or 'nymphomaniacs'. Both streams of thought support the spiritual doctrines on the 'submission of women to men and their confinement to the domestic sphere' (Marshall 1991:

22, 29). At the same time, husbands are called upon to treat their wives with respect and consideration by involving them in family decisions, participating in domestic chores, and playing a role in child rearing and caring activities. Despite sanctioning women's subordinate status in relation to their husbands, there is still a sense in which the fundamentalist doctrines which the churches preach could on one level be a partially 'liberating' force in the lives of their female members in the areas of marriage, sexuality and family life. Infidelity, divorce and violence against women, which are rampant in the wider society and which men think are their legitimate rights, are frowned upon and condemned by the Christian fundamentalists. In addition, these churches advocate the use of contraceptives to regulate women's fertility.

At another level, however, their doctrinal injunction for women to obey their husbands reproduces patriarchal structures in a social context where obedience is taken to mean total submission by the woman to the man, including to his arbitrary whims and caprices. Even those women whose husbands are faithful and eschew violence are unable to translate this into a wider struggle for advocating their rights as women because the advantages they gain from membership of the church entail their acceptance of a subordinate position to their husbands in the household. In this sense, the 'liberating' effect of the message of the new Christian movement is a highly partial one, contingent on the willingness of the male members of the church to run a 'responsible' household and lead a responsible life. It is a partial 'liberation' which emerges by default and which collapses should the man change his commitment to the church.

Despite these ideological differences, both groups have some points of convergence. The first is their strong opposition to orthodox denominations. The second is their instinctive hostility to any Christian church that incorporates traditional African beliefs in its teachings and practices. Third is their total disdain for the followers of African traditional religion as well as Muslims (Marshall 1991: 22, 24). Finally, all 'born-again' groups have a strict moral code which embodies the following precepts, 'that true believers do not lie, cheat, steal, quarrel, gossip, give or take bribes, drink alcohol, smoke, fornicate, beat their spouses, lose their temper, or deny assistance to other members in need. Strict marital fidelity is a central tenet and divorce is not sanctioned' (Marshall 1991: 23, 24).

One major difference between the fundamentalist factions of both religions is their attitude towards politics. Unlike their Muslim counterparts, who see their struggle as political, the Christian fundamentalists have, until recently at least, mainly been apolitical. The change in attitude, which has started to take place recently, can be attributed to religious clashes during the 1980s between Muslims and Christians in some parts of Northern Nigeria (see Ibrahim 1989 and 1991). Consequently, the Christian fundamentalists through the Pentecostal Fellowship of Nigeria (PFN) adopted an overtly political approach to issues in which they defined Muslims as their political enemies. As Marshall remarks in her observation on this shift: 'Frequent references were made to "bad politicians" and the "Islamization" of Nigeria through the make up of Babangida's ruling council, incorporation into the Organisation of Islamic Conference, denial of land for church building, and northern religious "fanaticism"' (Marshall 1991: 35).

The Nigerian Women's Movement

Before the 1980s, the Nigerian women's movement was dominated by the existence of one umbrella national women's organization, the National Council of Women's Societies (NCWS) and a host of grassroots village and community-level groupings. However, this situation changed radically in the 1980s with the emergence of Women in Nigeria (WIN) in 1983, the Federation of Muslim Women's Associations in Nigeria (FOMWAN) in 1985, the establishment of the state-funded Better Life Programme for Rural Women (BLP) in 1987, and the growth of a host of national grassroots-community development associations as well as several groups working on women's rights issues.

The NCWS, the government-recognized umbrella organization for women, was created out of the struggle between radical, anti-establishment women and conservative, pro-government women for pre-eminence in, and dominance over, the female space (the arena of female activism). With active government support, the conservative faction won the leadership battle. The NCWS was thus established in 1959 as a non-political and non-religious organization devoted to the promotion of the education, welfare and improved status of Nigerian women (Mba 1982). In recent years, however, the organization has broadened its focus to include women's legal and political rights by promoting political awareness campaigns during elections and demanding changes in some of the laws that dehumanize womanhood (Abdullah 1994: 14).

Although the NCWS sees itself as an advocate for women's rights in Nigeria, the organization's gender ideology, rather than liberating women, reinforces patriarchy. In demanding the recognition of women's rights, the NCWS has always been quick to point out that it is seeking only 'complementary roles for women rather than competitive roles such that when demands are made by women, they are punctuated by assurances that they do not constitute a confrontation with the male establishment or challenge to traditional family patterns' (Kisekka 1992: 116). The organization stresses this point because it does not want to lose the privileges it enjoys from the patriarchal state and its allies. Additionally, some of the NCWS' viewpoints have been detrimental to the advancement of Nigerian women's interests. For example, the organization lobbied politicians against the 1981 bill to legalize abortion and has persistently urged poor Nigerians, especially women, to tighten their belts and endure the harsh economic policies of various governments since 1981 when the Nigerian economy went into crisis (Abdullah 1994: 16; Imam 1992).

In contrast to the NCWS, Women in Nigeria (WIN), Nigeria's first feminist organization, takes a radical and critical stance on the issue of gender in-equalities in society. On the issue of gender subordination in Nigeria, WIN states: 'The majority of women, like the majority of men, suffer from the exploitative and oppressive character of the Nigerian society; women suffer additional forms of exploitation and oppression; women therefore suffer double oppression and exploitation as members of subordinate classes and as women' (WIN Editorial Committee 1985a).

In applying a socialist feminist perspective to the woman question, the organization transformed the debate on gender inequality in Nigeria. It is this defining characteristic that set the organization apart from other women's and left-wing groupings. It further states that 'the liberation of women cannot be fully achieved outside the context of the oppressed and poor majority of the people' (WIN Editorial Committee 1985a: ii). In pursuit of its objective of 'transforming gender relations to achieve gender equality in society', WIN has forged alliances with other popular democratic forces in the country (Abdullah 1994: 46; Imam 1993b: 13; Shettima 1995). The organization's act-ivities are mainly in the areas of research and documentation, dissemination of information, advocacy, political conscientization and project work. The rallying slogan of the organization centres on the notion that, 'every issue is a women's issue [and] every women's issue is everyone's concern' (Imam 1993b: 14). It is on the basis of this that the organization has campaigned against child marriages, purdah, sexual harassment and violence against women. Additionally, WIN has included issues of women's reproductive rights and choice, sexual harassment and violence, and consciousness-raising programmes in its broader discourse on and action programme for Nigerian women (Abdullah 1995).

In 1987, a new trend emerged within the Nigerian women's movement. This trend has had far-reaching consequences both within and outside the movement. The new trend centred on the launch of the Better Life Programme for Rural Women (BLP) by the government of General Ibrahim Babangida (1985–93). The establishment of this programme ushered in a new era in the development of women's groups in Nigeria as it heralded the twin process of state feminism as practised in Nigeria and wifeism.[5] The former refers to the process of direct intervention by the state in the formation and funding of a women's 'development' programme, while the latter refers to the appointment of wives of high-ranking government officials as leaders of the organization set up as part of the project of state feminism (Abdullah 1994: 27).

The BLP's objective, according to its former national coordinator, Mrs Maryam Babangida, was to create a 'new rural woman', economically strong, politically active, socially aware, psychologically fulfilled, and thus equipped to play her role in society to the fullest (Babangida 1991). To achieve these objectives, the BLP organized literacy and vocational training courses, social welfare and health programmes, enlightenment campaigns and income-generating projects for women. But the administrative structure of the project and its ideological orientation supported gender subordination in the society, by mirroring and reproducing the state's conservative image of women as wives, mothers and secondary income earners. Furthermore, the automatic appointment of wives based on their husbands' status in the state political and military hierarchy, regardless of their suitability or merit, was not only undemocratic but also reinforced the prevailing societal image of women as appendages to male power (Abdullah 1994: 26).

To further the policy of state feminism and wifeism, a National Commission for Women (NCW) was established in 1989, with the wife of the president as a life member of the board of the Commission. A National Centre for Women's Development was built and named after the wife of the president. However, after General Babangida was forced out of office in August 1993, the BLP and all that went with it became history. The wife of the new head of state, Mrs Mariam Abacha, launched her own programme, the Family Support Programme (FSP), changed the name of the National Centre and got the NCW upgraded to a ministry (Abdullah 1994: 44). Even though critics of the former regime (such as the change of name of the centre and the upgrading of the NCW) welcomed some of these changes, the ideological orientation of the regime on women's issues did not change. If anything, things have become worse as the Abacha junta has unleashed an unprecedented reign of terror against the generality of Nigerians. For instance, women who were critical of the regime's policy were harassed, detained by the state security service or prevented from travelling abroad to participate in international meetings such as the Fourth World Conference on Women. FSP itself has become the focal point for a personality cult around Mrs Abacha, while the ministry is subject to her arbitrary whims and authoritarian style. Both the BLP and the FSP also pose serious constitutional and governance issues.

The Human Rights and Civil Liberties Movement

Perhaps more than the two social movements previously mentioned, the Nigerian human rights/civil liberties movement was entirely an outgrowth of the socio-economic and political conditions prevailing in the country in the 1980s. In order to understand the emergence of this movement, a brief outline of the factors that triggered its emergence in the Nigerian landscape is worth reciting. In this regard, it should be noted that the return of the military, with their disregard for basic civil liberties and human rights at a time of national economic decline and socio-political disquiet, was a factor in the development of the civil rights movement. In their attempt to solve the economic and political problems of the country, the military regime of Generals Buhari and Idiagbon (1983–85) moved against a variety of interest groups throughout the country. Politicians and political activities were banned, several professional and student organizations were proscribed, journalists, activists and politicians were arrested and detained, and decrees were promulgated to limit the press and prevent public discussion of the country's political future, particularly the prospective date for the return to civil rule (Olukoshi 1993). This atmosphere of terror and repression was carried forward by the Babangida administration (1985–93) and is still continuing, with greater intensity than before, under the regime of General Abacha (1993–98).

Given the tense and repressive political atmosphere in the country, as well as the dwindling economic fortunes of most Nigerians, it did not come as a surprise when, in 1987, the Civil Liberties Organization (CLO) was launched as Nigeria's premier national human rights organization. Although the Nigerian human and civil rights movement is made up of over thirty groupings scattered across the country, from the point of view of this chapter, two organizations are particularly important. These are the Legal Research and Resource Development Centre (the LRRDC) and the International Federation of Women Lawyers (FIDA). These organizations were chosen as examples because they are in the forefront of the struggle for women's rights in Nigeria.

The LRRDC is the first human rights NGO in Nigeria to be founded by a woman. Tokunbo Ige, a lawyer, established the organization in 1990. Its objectives are the provision of human rights education and legal services to the poor and the protection and, where possible, the enforcement of their rights. LRRDC's work is mainly among illiterate, poor and marginalized groups in the society. In this regard, women who make up the majority of the poor and illiterate constitute the bulk of the organization's work, as can be seen from its action programmes and its publications. These programmes and publications cover such issues as the custody and maintenance of children, divorce and separation, marriage, rape, and women and the right of residency. Additionally, the organization provides legal aid services to women and trains female paralegals. Despite its pro-women programme bias, the organization sees itself primarily as a human rights organization and not as a women's human rights NGO.

FIDA Nigeria is an affiliate of the International Federation of Women Lawyers. It is an international women's human rights NGO established in Nigeria in 1964. The organization's main project is the provision of free legal services to indigent women and children. Most of the caseloads in FIDA's files relate to custody, abuse and other domestic issues. Although FIDA is a women's human rights NGO, its gender discourse does not threaten the status quo. According to a former executive member of the organization: 'When African women demand equality, we are only asking for our rights not to be tampered with, and the removal of laws that oppress and dehumanise women. We are not asking for equality with our husbands. We accept them as the bosses and heads of the family' (Abdullah 1994: 27).

FIDA's struggle for women's rights is based on the division of society into the private and public spheres. This division of the world into two separate unconnected spheres has relegated discriminatory practices against women into the private domain where it is difficult to regulate.

The Example of the Federation of Muslim Women's Associations in Nigeria (FOMWAN)

In the preceding section, we focused on the emergence and character of three types of associational groups that have dominated the Nigerian political landscape during the 1980s and 1990s. In this section, we now focus our attention on the Federation of Muslim Women's Associations in Nigeria, the first national women's religious organization to be established in the country dedicated to promoting the rights of Muslim women within the framework of Islam. Our critique of FOMWAN's experience will show both the possibilities offered by an approach to advancing women's rights that uses the idiom of religion and the limitations of that approach as set by the doctrinal foundations and practice of religion itself.

FOMWAN: the historical background As pointed out earlier, FOMWAN (or the federation) was founded in 1985. The organization sees itself first and foremost as a Muslim women's religious organization devoted to providing religious education for its members. However, the organization justifies its existence on the grounds of the non-implementation/recognition by the Nigerian Islamic establishment of Muslim women's rights as stated in the Shari'a (for example, their right to education, inheritance, custody of children at divorce, and a woman's right to divorce if the husband is, aong other things, cruel or impotent) and the prevalence of other un-Islamic practices that violate these rights.

Zainab Kabir, one of the members of FOMWAN, stated that it is culture or tradition rather than religion that is responsible for the subordination of Muslim women. Kabir noted that Islam does not sanction the seclusion of women in the home, but it rather encourages women to avoid immoral behaviour and indecent dressing (Kabir 1985). She encourages women to participate in the 'public' domain provided they dress modestly. She noted further that most of the citations used to justify women's subordinate position are based on *hadith* and Shari'a (which are interpretations of learned scholars), and not *suras* (Qur'anic verses). As such, these interpretations must be contextualized within their specific historical framework. She also pointed out that most of the practitioners of *tasfir* (exegesis) were men who interpreted the *suras* and *hadith* without any consideration for women's interests. As a result, she urged women to become scholars and make their own interpretations (Kabir 1985; Imam 1993a: 136).

It is within the context of the contestations over doctrinal interpretation that FOMWAN has attempted to define a role for itself. It can thus be said that the organization was founded with the aim of putting Muslim women's concerns squarely on the national women's agenda. According to a leading FOMWAN activist, the organization was formed: 'to address problems affecting Muslim women such as their education and rights under the Shari'a which can only be satisfactorily dealt with by Muslim women, in co-operation with their male counterparts. Because the problems of a Muslim community can only be cured by Islamic solutions' (Yusuf 1991: 99).

FOMWAN's emergence in the national struggle for women's rights shifted the debate from the secular to the religious arena. The organization's aims and objectives, as outlined in its constitution, are to promote the education and social development of Muslim women; to encourage and propagate Islam; to advance the recognition of Muslim women's right under the Shari'a; to promote unity and cooperation among Muslim women's organizations; and to empower Muslim women to have a positive influence on national matters with a view to safeguarding the interests of Islam (Yusuf 1991: 100).

FOMWAN officials, like the NCWS, have also emphasized that their aim is not to strive for equality between men and women. As Lateefat Okunnu, a former president of FOMWAN observed, the federation does not encourage women to demand equality with men because God has created women and men differently and has thus assigned them different roles in society (Abdullah 1994: 36). The organization has taken this stand because of their narrow perception and definition of equality. Its leaders reason that equality means sameness, not acknowledging that equality in difference. Thus, even as it strives to employ Islam as an instrument in its struggle for the advancement of the rights of Muslim women, FOMWAN's outlook on gender also tends to reinforce existing gender inequalities in a society where the structures of patriarchy are very strong. The contradiction between FOMWAN's attempt to use religion to promote reform in favour of women's rights without embracing the notion of gender equality perhaps explains why the organization's action programmes have been generally downplayed.

The politics of FOMWAN   In discussing the actions the federation has taken to achieve its aims and objectives, we shall also look at the factors that have both hindered and facilitated that process. In furtherance of its objectives, FOMWAN has established schools to educate Muslim women about their rights as provided in the Shari'a. It has also campaigned against practices, such as the *talaq* (the unilateral divorce by husbands) and forced and early marriages, that violate the rights of Muslim women in Nigeria. Furthermore, FOMWAN has actively engaged in *da'wah* (welfare activities), charity works and income-generating projects for Muslim women.

Why is it that, despite twelve years of its existence, FOMWAN has not initiated or demanded any significant changes in the conduct of family and marriage relations for the benefit of those for whom it claims to speak? Apart from the contradiction that expressed itself in FOMWAN's desire to employ Islam to advance women's rights without fighting for gender equality, the federation has not been willing or able to press for far-reaching legal reforms to change existing gender relations. FOMWAN viewed its formation as primarily a political project aimed at countering NCWS and managing change rather than promoting a radical transformatory project (Abdullah 1996). The organization has come out with pronouncements in the press condemning the activities of the NCWS. For instance, it has labelled the NCWS a Zionist grouping because of its alleged domination by Christians (*New Nigerian*, 15 July 1989).

Furthermore, the ideological orientation of its leadership is one that encourages the subordination of women to men. Rather than engaging the state and its allies in its struggle for women's rights, FOMWAN has busied itself more with criticizing and picking holes in every proposal on Nigerian women made by the NCWS, the organization with which it competes for state largesse. For example, NCWS made a proposal to protect the rights of women in marriage (to check the increasing rate of divorce and to protect women's rights at divorce), as most Nigerian women are divorced without alimony or any form of benefit; this measure was criticized by FOMWAN. In the proposal, NCWS wanted the government to require any man who wishes to terminate a marriage that has lasted for ten years or more to relinquish half of his assets to the wife he intends to divorce.

> Most offensive to Muslim women was the assumption that a man had only one wife: the proposal did not allow for the situation of his having up to four wives, most of whom had lived with him for ten or more years. If half a Muslim man's assets were awarded to one divorced wife (assuming she would ever receive the amount), it would result in adverse effects for the children and wives who remained in the family. (Yusuf 1991: 100)

FOMWAN believed the proposal was biased against Muslim women who were in polygamous marriages, and that it was un-Islamic as it failed to recognize the Islamic law of inheritance. Although the proposal failed to recognize the situation of Muslim women and women married under customary law who might be in polygamous relations, and it also displayed ignorance of the Islamic law of inheritance, FOMWAN could have requested a meeting with the NCWS, rather than engaging in a negative war of attrition in the press.

Second, it is impossible for FOMWAN to demand legal reforms for Muslim women with men because it will not only violate its self-appointed mandate and lead to the ultimate loss of support and favour it presently enjoys from the influential Muslim establishment and the state at the local and national levels, but will entail a rethink or revision of its definition of equality in sameness. Since the women in the FOMWAN leadership are not willing to forgo these benefits (and the lifestyle that accompanies them), they have been extremely reluctant to push for changes that will transform the lives of Nigerian Muslim women.

Religious, Human Rights and Women's Movements and the Struggle for Women's Rights in Nigeria: An Assessment

From the discussion so far, it can be deduced that neither the human rights groups nor the women's religious groups and the state feminists/wifeists have concerned themselves sufficiently with issues of the state and family in their struggle for women's rights. Several reasons account for the near neglect of these two institutions as sites for the contestation of women's human rights in Nigeria. First, there is the perception of all these social movement groups (with the exception of WIN) that their roles in society are non-political. Flowing from this perception is the implication that they cannot confront the state with demands to improve and/or transform gender relations in society. Although WIN is an exception in this regard, as it explicitly defines its mission as political, the organization has not been able to infuse its progressive gender ideology into the discourses of its allies in the human rights movement (Abdullah 1994: 46; Imam 1993b: 16). The Christian women, apart from being non-political, are not a unified group dedicated to the promotion of women's rights within the church. Rather, the sermons and doctrines about family and matrimonial life to which they are exposed are designed to prepare them to be good wives for their husbands.

The second reason why the various groups have not sufficiently concerned themselves with reform of the state and family laws centres on the fact that many of the leading organizations such as the BLP/FSP, FOMWAN and NCWS owe their creation and continued existence to the state and its allies. Being dependent on the government and other male-dominated associations for much of their funding, these organizations have tended to be beholden to male interests. Officials of these organizations also tend to depend heavily on state patronage. That being the case, it is inconceivable that they will make demands on the state for radical social transformation.

The family has not been significant in the struggle for women's rights in Nigeria for much the same reason as it is not significant in countries like Lebanon, where, as Joseph observes,

[The] family ... has been pivotal for social, economic, and political existence and well being. This has been so across social classes, regions and religious/ ethnic groups. It is therefore not accidental that human rights movements in the Middle East have fully addressed the family ... While there is increasing recognition that the family is not immune to human rights issues, women's movements in the Middle East have been careful to differentiate their concerns about the family from those of Western feminists whom they often perceive as having been at times, anti-family. (Joseph 1993: 148)

Not surprisingly, most Nigerian human rights groups have focused their attention exclusively on the excesses of the state and the governance of the public arena. Family-related rights concerns such as female circumcision and domestic violence mainly originated from the international arena and took some time before they enjoyed a significant local following. Furthermore, the artificial split of society into the 'private' and 'public' realms has contributed to the near neglect of the family as a site for the struggle for women's human rights in Nigeria. Issues relating to a woman's role in the productive sector and outside the home are discussed in the public sphere, but those regarding her status within the family and her reproductive roles and functions are addressed in the private realm where the state and the many society-based organizations have adopted the notion of respect for privacy and non-interference by the state.

Yet, in ignoring the state and the family as sites for the contestation of women's rights, the various groups that dominate the religious, human rights and women's movements have failed in their quest to promote women's human rights in Nigeria. These two institutions are important in the discussion on women's rights because of their pivotal roles in the construction of rights in society. The state is important as a location for the battle for women's human rights because of its role in promoting or discouraging these rights. The family's role in the protection or disregard of women's human rights is significant because the family in Nigeria, as in most African societies, is the focal social institution for primary social interaction. The family provides its members with social identities with which they come to associate later in life (Joseph 1993: 148).

Within the broad framework of its essentially patriarchal foundation, the attitude exhibited by the Nigerian state towards women has varied from time to time, according to whether the regime in power was more or less conservative than its predecessor. During the Second Republic (1979–83), the overwhelmingly establishment ruling National Party of Nigeria (NPN) was supportive of the conservative views of the NCWS on women's issues. The actions of the austere Buhari–Idiagbon military administration (31 December 1983 to 27 August 1985), which took power in a *coup d'état*, was based on the ruling junta's interpretation of the causes of the Nigerian economic and political crises, an interpretation that had implications for its attitude towards women. According to the junta, the crisis was a result of the corruption and lack of discipline of the civilian population. Hence the regime embarked on a campaign to wipe out these twin 'evils'. Women were targeted in this campaign under the rubric of the 'War Against Indiscipline' (WAI) programme. They were made scapegoats and accused of ruining the economy through profiteering. This led to many women being arrested and having their enterprises destroyed. Women were also implicitly held responsible for the pervading corruption and delinquency of the Second Republic. It was often suggested that men became corrupt in order to satisfy the material demands of women. Consequently, women were admonished to be good wives or citizens or mothers through radio and television jingles. Single women were arrested in several parts of the country and forced to get married. State security forces (Dennis 1987) generally harassed informal sector women, including commercial sex workers.

Although the Babangida regime, which took power in a palace coup and ruled for nine years (27 August 1985 to 27 August 1993), was just as repressive as its predecessor, it took an apparently liberal attitude towards women and women's issues by establishing and funding a state women's programme run by the wives of Babangida and his colleagues in the military junta and political bureaucracy. As has been argued elsewhere (Abdullah 1993; 1994; 1995), the regime's focus on women should be understood within the logic of the SAP it initiated (Abdullah 1993: 32). Although there is very little difference in substance between the political and economic programmes pursued by the Babangida and Abacha (from November 1993 to May 1999) regimes, there is divergence between the two regimes on the 'woman question'. This difference has its roots in the history of petty jealousy and rivalry between the wives of the two men.

During the BLP era, Mrs Abacha, as wife of the then Minister of Defence, was conspicuously absent from the activities of the programme. She concentrated on her role as the chair of the Army Officers Wives Association, a role she inherited from Mrs Babangida after the latter's husband became head of state. It was not surprising, then, that when she assumed the role of Nigeria's first lady she set out systematically to dismantle all structures and programmes that had been established by Mrs Babangida. Thus, the BLP was replaced by the FSP. Unlike the BLP, which had women's 'empowerment' within the existing structures of the state and society as its slogan, the FSP's ideology is based on a conservative, traditional conception of the family, with women's roles being defined primarily as those of mother and wife. As such, the first almanac prepared in 1995 to publicize the programme included a photograph of Mrs Abacha carrying a child on her back.

When the family acts as a provider of economic security and social identity, and as a social institution where members learn the culture and values of their society in their formative years, it defines for its members the initial meaning and parameters of their rights as well as the rewards and sanctions for all kinds of behaviour. Due to the patriarchal character of the family, male members are favoured over women in the construction of rights. This act of privileging males over females feeds directly into the positions of subordination and discrimination that women experience in the wider society.

Conclusion

The three currents in associational life in contemporary Nigeria, which I have reviewed in this chapter, depict the difficulty that continues to prevail in the country with respect to the protection and advancement of women's rights. From their different angles, the various NGOs either showed total disregard for women's rights issues or were incapable of dealing with them. The religious revivalist movement's position represents an essentially right-wing response to the issue of women's role and function in society. Apart from systematically ignoring many women's rights issues in their discourses on women, they also defend the subordination of women to men in all spheres of society. Because the human rights movement works in a purely legalistic and non-political context, it was unable to initiate radical programmes that focus on women's human rights concerns.

Unlike the religious and human rights movements, the women's movement is the most diverse. It has within its ranks a non-religious conservative grouping, a religious conservative organization, conservative state-funded groups and a feminist organization. Apart from the feminist group that addresses women's human rights concerns, the others do not address such concerns for the reasons I discussed earlier. Despite its shortcomings, WIN, the feminist group, is the most successful organization within the women's movement in bringing the women's question to the centre of political discourse in Nigeria, although it has been less successful in persuading its political allies in the pro-democracy movement to embrace its main message.

The inability of the human rights and women's movements to infuse women's human rights concerns into their struggle for women's rights are partly also the result of the continuing dominance of the private/public dichotomy. In order for the international human rights system to be able to incorporate women's rights issues into a radical transformatory project, a reconceptualization of human rights concepts is needed. For example, the questioning by certain groups/communities of their exclusion from the existing human rights framework has challenged the universality of the concept of human rights. What is needed is a more inclusive and holistic concept of human rights that will embrace the needs and aspirations of all minority and historically marginalized groups, including women.

Some attention needs to be paid to the interface between prolonged economic crisis exacerbated by structural adjustment, continuing political authoritarianism and the transformation of popular identities, including religious ones. What are the possibilities open to women, the constraints continuing to face them and the obstacles they have to confront in the context of the underlying changes taking place in African economies, politics and society? This is a critical question that has to be carefully addressed if the struggle for the advancement of the rights and interests of women is to be relevant and meaningful to them. In this regard, the various groups, especially the non-religious ones in the vanguard of the rights struggle in Nigeria, need to make gender central to their analysis. As an analytical concept, it has the same status as class, ethnicity and race, the state and the world system. It deals with the structural relationship between men and women and links this relationship as it is to the state, the economy and to micro and macro processes and institutions (Moghadam 1990: 8).

Few will disagree that, in Nigeria today, women's rights and concerns continue to be trampled upon in spite of the apparent interest in women's affairs expressed at the level of the state. The challenge which this poses to the non-state groups concerned with the promotion of the welfare and rights of women is for them to seek ways of working together on a common, minimum programme for the promotion of the rights of Nigerian women. For all the differences among the non-state groups and the social, organizational and political contexts within which they work, it is still possible to identify a number of action programmes on which the various groups can agree, including areas of legal, political and constitutional reform that will have direct bearing on women's role in the family and polity. As a first step towards the forging of a minimum action programme on which all or most of the non-state groups can agree and which could serve as their campaigning points over the specified period of time, they should convene an all-Nigeria summit on women bringing together the women's human rights and religious groups to develop and adopt such an action programme. Such a summit, if it is to be successful, will necessarily involve a spirit of give and take on the part of all the groups and strands relevant to the struggles of Nigerian women.

Postscript: Democracy, Shari'a and Women's Rights

The transition from military rule to civilian governance, on 29 May 1999, presents both opportunities and challenges in the struggle for women's rights and the enthronement of democracy in Nigeria – ingredients that have been missing in almost sixteen years of military rule.

As mentioned earlier, Nigerians witnessed gross violations of their human rights and personal freedoms. Human rights activists, including women's rights activists, were detained, illegally imprisoned and harassed by the state and its security agencies. In relation to women's activism, the state stifled the development of autonomous initiatives and encouraged the participation of women only as wives, cronies and allies of the military leaders. The present democratic dispensation provides the opportunity to build a system where the rule of law, human rights including women's rights, and fundamental freedoms will be respected. To achieve this, both the government and the people of Nigeria must be ready and willing to address the various challenges that they will confront in their quest for national rebirth and renewal. It is within the framework of the opportunities and challenges that the current political climate presents that the expansion of the Islamic legal system, the Shari'a, is discussed.

The launch of the Islamic legal system, the Shari'a, by the Zamfara State government on 27 October 1999, and its adoption in January 2000,[6] has generated controversy and furore across the country. While proponents of the Shari'a are of the view that it is essentially about Muslims and their fundamental rights, which are inalienable, critics argue that the adoption of the Shari'a is unconstitutional, barbaric and a negation of the political arrangements put in place by the nationalist politicians who negotiated Nigeria's independence as a united entity. This controversy is not new. It surfaced during the constitution drafting process in the political transitions of the 1970s, 1980s and 1990s. These debates focused mainly on the entrenchment of the Shari'a in the constitution as the governing law in aspects of the lives of Muslims. Since the adoption of the Shari'a by the Zamfara State government and other northern states, the discourse has shifted from the total application/adoption of the Shari'a to govern the lives of Muslims, to the legality/constitutionality of the law, to the rights of women, Christians and other religious minorities living in those areas.

It must be noted, however, that the Islamic legal code has been in existence in most of present-day Northern Nigeria since 1804 when Sheik Uthman Dan-Fodio defeated the Habe/Hausa dynasty through his *jihad*. Governance, the system of justice and punishment in the Sokoto caliphate (the empire created by Dan-Fodio), was based on the Shari'a. With the defeat of the Sokoto caliphate by British imperial forces, Islamic law was subsumed within the legal framework of the colonial administration. In its Native Court Proclamation Act of 1900, the British colonial government placed Shari'a courts at par with customary courts and stated that 'these courts are to administer native law and custom prevailing in the area of jurisdiction and might award any type of punishment recognised thereby except mutilation, torture, or any type of punishment which is repugnant to natural justice and humanity' (Kukah 1991: 116). This in effect meant that criminal offences like murder and social vices such as prostitution, adultery/fornication, alcohol abuse and gambling which incurred grave penalties, were no longer to be adjudicated by the Shari'a courts. Thus, Shari'a courts like customary courts made legislation or tried cases only in the area of personal laws (marriage, divorce, inheritance and custody of children). This policy continued until October 1999 when the Zamfara State government extended the scope of Shari'a from Muslim personal laws to incorporate criminal offences and social vices.

At the launch of the Shari'a, the Zamfara State governor, Ahmad Sani, noted that the Shari'a is not 'just a penal code but a way of life'. He stated further that: 'it is the foundation for an entire system of life, covering a whole spectrum of issues which range from specific articles and commandments to general moral teachings, rights and obligations, crime and punishment, personal and public law and a host of other private and social concerns' (*Violence Watch* 2000: 1).

Zamfara and all the states that have emulated its action insist that the application of Shari'a in its entirety will stem social vices (prostitution, alcoholism, gambling, brigandage) and thus reduce society's slide into social and moral decadence. In pursuance of the Shari'a, these states have banned the sale and consumption of alcohol, prostitution, gambling and the mixing of sexes in public spaces. Furthermore, women, whether Christians or Muslims, have been banned from sporting activities, and single women have been given an ultimatum to get married within three months or be relieved of their jobs. Shari'a vigilante groups have been formed to enforce the law, prescribe a dress code for women, the building of Shari'a courts and the segregation of schools. In relation to the latter, the Zamfara State governor stated: 'We will have separate secondary schools for the girls and the boys. And for primary schools, the boys will sit in front and the girls at the back until such a time when we have enough resources to build separate schools for them' (*Tell Magazine*, 15 November 1999). In a recent pronouncement, the governor of Zamfara State stated that women are not permitted to leave their heads uncovered or wear trousers and miniskirts. Women who do not like the law should leave the state. According to reports from the governor's office, a bill prescribing stiff penalties for offenders will be sent to the state legislature.

Since the adoption and implementation of the Shari'a by some states, several people have fallen victim of the law. Mallam Bello Jangebe, the first Shari'a victim, had his right arm amputated on 22 March 2000 for stealing a cow. Other cases include the flogging (five strokes of the cane) of seven prostitutes in Birnin Kebbi in addition to one month's imprisonment with an option of N1,000 (10 dollars) fine, and the male procurer was given ten lashes and sentenced to six months with an option to pay a N2,000 (20 dollars) fine. Two motorbike operators were punished with twenty strokes of the cane each for violating the Shari'a injunction banning men from carrying women on motorbikes. The women were not punished because they were married. A man was given eighty lashes for drinking beer in Minna, the Niger State capital, and Vincent Livinus Obi, a Christian man, was beaten by Shari'a enforcer/vigilantes for assisting his wife in selling alcohol.

However, it was the conviction and public flogging of Bariya Ibrahim Magazu, on 23 January 2001, that drew worldwide condemnation and brought out the gender bias inherent in the Zamfara State (read Nigeria) application of Islamic law. Bariya, a seventeen-year-old girl from Tsafe local government area of Zamfara State, was convicted for fornication in September 2000 when it was obvious that she was pregnant and unmarried. She was thus sentenced to 180 lashes of the cane to be executed forty days after giving birth. The 100 lashes were for engaging in pre-marital sex while the 80 lashes were for *qadhf* (defamation of character) for failing to prove beyond reasonable doubt (in Islamic law the required four eye-witnesses to corroborate her story) that the three men she said were responsible for her pregnancy were indeed the ones. On the other hand, Jamila Sani, a prostitute who gave birth while in police custody in Kano, did not suffer the same fate as Bariya. According to presiding judge Ustaz Ibrahim Isa Rabo:

> When she was brought before me along with others on the January 15, she was not accused of pregnancy outside wedlock and I did not notice any signs of pregnancy in her. For me to judge her for fornication despite the birth she gave, which is concrete proof that she must have slept with a man, a third party has

to institute a case against her, which must be approved by the attorney-general of the state. She is free at the moment until otherwise. (*Guardian*, 17 February 2001)

Jamila might have escaped being whipped because of the national and international outcry from Bariya's case.

Responses to the Shari'a Responses to the expansion of the Shari'a to include criminal offences can be grouped into three main categories, namely, constitutional, religious and human and women's rights perspectives. Both protagonists and antagonists of the Shari'a have used the Nigerian constitution to justify and prove the legality of their actions. In general, those arguing against the criminalization of the Shari'a are of the view that it is unconstitutional as it violates the spirit of the 1999 constitution and Nigeria's federal principle. They also state that it contravenes the Universal Declaration of Human Rights, the Convention Eliminating all forms of Discrimination Against Women (CEDAW) and all other international treaties and conventions to which Nigeria is a signatory. One of the first persons to speak against the adoption of Shari'a in the northern states was the former Chief Judge of Nigeria, Justice Mohammed Bello. He noted that the 1999 constitution is superior to the Shari'a and that Section 1 makes any legal system outside the constitution illegal: 'This constitution is supreme and its provisions shall have binding force on all authorities and persons throughout the federation.' He added: 'If any other law is inconsistent with the provisions of the constitution the constitution shall prevail, and that other law shall to the extent of inconsistency be void' (Justice Bello, quoted in the *Guardian*, 11 February 2000). Pointing out further obstacles to the expansion of the Shari'a, Justice Bello noted that Section 36(12) of the 1999 constitution stipulates that: 'subject as otherwise provided by this constitution, a person shall not be convicted of a criminal offence unless that offence is defined and the penalty therein prescribed in a written law ... a written law refers to an Act of the National Assembly or a law of a state, any subsidiary legislation or instrument under the provisions of a law'. He then added: 'it is clear from the provision of section 36(12) that a person should not be convicted for any Shari'a offence unless that offence and its punishment are enacted by the National Assembly or State Assembly. Accordingly, application of the Shari'a Criminal Law without codification by the National Assembly or State House of Assembly will be unconstitutional.' To buttress the points outlined above, Justice Bello noted: 'It should be stated for the avoidance of doubt that the Shari'a law as stated in the Quran, *Hadith* and other written sources is not a written law within the meaning of Section 36(12) of the 1999 Constitution.'

In his own critique of the Shari'a, another legal luminary, Justice Akinola Aguda, states that the expansion of the jurisdiction of the Islamic legal code to include criminal matters is illegal as it violates Section 10 of the 1999 constitution: 'The government of the Federation or a State shall not adopt any religion as state religion.' He also points out that this negated the principle on which the country's independence was agreed upon: 'In the late 1950s preparatory to independence, the politicians agreed that as a prerequisite for the Northern and Southern regions to be one country, the Northern region could make legislation on Islamic personal laws (Marriage, guardianship of children at divorce, dissolution of marriage and devolution of property) and not on criminal matters' (Justice Akinola Aguda, quoted in *Guardian*, 27 October 1999).

He notes that the Section 262(2)(e) makes an additional proviso that the law would be applied 'Where all the parties to the proceedings being Muslims have requested the court that hears the case in the first instance to determine that case in accordance with Islamic personal law'. Aguda argues that the way Shari'a is practised by the northern states violates Section 38(1), which guarantees the freedom of citizens irrespective of where they live in the country to freedom of worship and other fundamental rights: 'Every person shall be entitled to freedom of thought, conscience and religion including to change his [sic] religion or belief (either alone or in community with others, and in public or in private) to manifest and propagate his religion in worship, teaching, practice and observance.' According to Justice Bello, this provision for conversion or *ridda* is a capital offence (for Muslims who might decide to change their religion) under Shari'a, it is inconsistent with Section 38(1) and, by virtue of Section 1, it is unconstitutional.

For Aguda, the only way a state government can introduce Shari'a (expand the jurisdiction) would be to seek a national consensus on the matter which will invariably lead to the amendment of the constitution. According to him: 'If any state wants to introduce Islamic law, they should call a meeting of politicians to discuss the matter again. They can take it to the National Assembly. If they succeed that would mean creating two judicial systems from the lowest to the highest court – the Supreme Court. We will now have two law schools, two Chief Justices, etc.' Aguda agues further that even if the Zamfara State government goes ahead to apply the law, it will be quashed if the judges of the state abide by their oath of office.

Ahmad Sani and other pro-Shari'a radicals have used the same constitution to justify their actions. Dr Lateef Adegbite, a legal practitioner and secretary-general of the Nigerian Supreme Council of Islamic Affairs, argues that extension of the Shari'a to include criminal laws is constitutional and does not negate the constitution:

> It is not against the constitution. Again, what many people do not realise is that in Nigeria you do not have one criminal code or criminal law for the whole country. There are two important legal instruments that regulate crimes in the country. One is the criminal code, which applies throughout the southern part of Nigeria. The other is the penal code, which applies to the northern part of the country. The two are very similar. The penal code embodies a lot of crimes recognised by the Shari'a. Every legal system of any civilised society forbids stealing and other crimes. That is what we have in the penal code of the North and the criminal code of the South ... it seems to me that what he has done in the area of criminal law is to now add certain crimes that were not embodied in the penal code but which are recognised by the Shari'a and declare them as statutory. For example, it is going to be a criminal offence for you to sell alcohol in the open, because alcohol is forbidden in Islam. It is going to be a crime for you to engage in prostitution, which used to be the case before but has not been embodied in the penal code. The constitution of Nigeria allows such enactment, because the constitution gives power to each state of assembly to make laws for good government. If the people, through democratic means, feel they want to punish certain offences it is within their constitutional rights. But what you cannot do is to say from now on, prostitution is a crime, alcoholism is a crime. They have to define them and write them out because the Nigerian constitution had already stated that unwritten offences will not be punished ... But in doing this, Zamfara State is obliged to keep within the limits of the constitution. (Lateef Adegbite, *Tell Magazine*, 15 November 1999)

States cannot pass laws that infringe fundamental rights, they cannot extend Shari'a to non-Muslims and cannot legislate on matters that are exclusively within the competence of the National Assembly; in concurrent matters, if the National Assembly has dealt with them then the states no longer have any jurisdiction.

Arguing in the same vein, governor Ahmed Sani, in an advertorial in the *New Nigerian* newspaper entitled 'Our Final Stand on Shari'a', states that the action of the government and people of Zamfara State in relation to the Shari'a is constitutional (see Appendix 1 for the full text).

On the religious front, both Christians and Muslims have expressed reservations and warned of the need to tread gently and within the ambit of the constitution. Even though some Muslims do not agree with the expansion of Shari'a, they have refused to voice their opinions publicly because of fear of being branded un-Islamic or anti-Shari'a. Others, such as General Muhammadu Buhari, a former military head of state, and Balarabe Musa, the governor of Kaduna State in the Second Republic, have supported the decisions of some of the northern states in the Islamization of their societies. To them, Shari'a is not just a law. It is a way of life and all Muslims should live under it. However, Ibrahim El-Zakzaky, the notable Shiite leader and an advocate of Shari'a, opposes the action of governor Ahmed Sani and his like because to him Shari'a can be implemented only in an Islamic state. Since Nigeria is not an Islamic state, implementing Shari'a is not feasible because Shari'a should be above the consititution and this is not the case in Nigeria.

> First of all you must have an Islamic environment. Before you have an Islamic environment, you must an Islamic government. Before you have an Islamic government, you have to remove the unIslamic government. The present government running the country, federal or state, is anything but Islamic. Therefore it has to be removed first ... Even when you have an Islamic government in power it doesn't mean that overnight it will implement everything in the Shari'a. It will go about it bit by bit. Because that is how it came, even at the time of the prophet ... if you have some social ills, you don't remove them by law. For example, if people are unemployed, you don't make the law and say therefore anybody who is caught and he [sic] is unemployed he would be punished. You have to provide jobs for people first. When there is no reason for someone to become idle, then being idle becomes a crime. Similarly, if you have prostitutes, you provide a situation whereby there would be no prostitution, and then prostitution will be criminal. Under the present circumstances, people are forced to steal because the society chastises them and forces them to look for what to eat and that might even lead them to committing some crime. If you say now you will punish them for what you have forced them to do, it is nothing but oppression. (Ibrahim El-Zakzaky, *Tell Magazine*, 15 November 1999)

Christians, on the other hand, believe the wholesale adoption of the Shari'a will work against non-Muslims by seeking to change their way of life, affect the outcome when they have legal dealings with Muslims. They do not believe that it is a deterrent to committing offences. Rather they believe that Muslims are gaining undue advantages over other religious groups with the active support of government. They argue that, under Shari'a, if a Muslim brings a case against a non-Muslim, the judge won't accept the evidence of the non-Muslim as his (sic) evidence amounts to nothing. Christians argue that the

Shari'a is repugnant and discriminatory because of the prohibition on mixing of men and women in social gatherings and the stringent punishments such as beheading, amputation and flogging for such offences as adultery/fornication, prostitution and stealing. Summing up the feelings of Christians, the Pentecostal Fellowship of Nigeria states that: 'Christians refuse to be dictated to and dehumanised in these ways. We are not in Afghanistan, Iran or Pakistan. This is not a Moslem country; it is a secular country, by constitution, and all citizens have the right to personal protection, under the law and pursuit of their personal choices without molestation' (*Guardian*, 27 October 1999).

Reacting to the decision of the Zamfara State government, the Cross River State legislature threatened to declare the state a Christian state if Zamfara State is allowed to get away with its plans.

The reaction from women's groups was more varied than those from the religious and constitutional experts. It ranged from outright condemnation and demonstrations against the law to wholesale acceptance of the Shari'a. About 1,000 commercial sex workers staged a peaceful protest march in February 2000 to the Yobe State government house demanding the protection of their fundamental human rights. Their objective was to sensitize government to their plight before the commencement of Shari'a in April. Binta, their spokeswoman, noted that it was the harsh economic conditions and the unwillingness of men to marry them that forced them into the sex trade. She argued that resettling of the women will help them to contribute their quota to the development of the state. She then proposed that the government should launch a resettlement scheme whereby they could be fully engaged in economic activities, provide a marriage grant of between N10, 000 and N20, 000 (1,000–2,000 dollars) and the award of government contracts. Binta assured the governor that they are in support of the Shari'a and, if these conditions are met, they will not be forced to emigrate to non-Shari'a states.

Hundreds of single women (spinsters, widows and divorcees) staged a mass protest in Bunguda LGA of Zamfara State against monogamists. They argue that Shari'a allows Muslim men to have more than one wife. The women pleaded with the Emir (traditional ruler) to use his influence to persuade men to increase the number of their wives as part of their contribution to the implementation of Shari'a in the state. These women took such actions to forestall harassment and scapegoating by Shari'a enforcers and illegal vigilante groups.

In another development, female public office holders in some of the northern states where Shari'a is being enforced are holding clandestine meetings strategizing on how to protect their jobs as they risk losing them if the Islamic legal code is implemented. This is because the Shari'a as implemented forbids women from either holding public office or undertaking jobs that encourage the intermingling of the sexes. According to a report in the *National Concord* newspaper (11 January 2000), the women expect the government to fashion new roles for them so that their hard-earned knowledge through a Western education would not go to waste.

In Kano State, over 10,000 Muslim women took to the street protesting the non-implementation of the Shari'a. They demanded the full implementation of the Shari'a to put an end to prostitution, gambling, alcohol consumption, gambling and other social vices. According to their leader: 'We have abandoned our homes and trekked to your place [i.e. the Emir's Palace] despite the fasting to salvage our religion and the dignity of Islam and the Holy Qur'an' (*Post Express*, 20 December 2000). FOMWAN, our case-study organization whose rallying slogan is the implementation of the Shari'a, placed an advertisement in the newspaper supporting the Islamic legal code (See Appendix 2) without studying its implications for the lives of those Muslim women whose rights it claims to protect. This position contradicts the organization's stance, which is the empowerment and liberation of women within Islam. Shari'a as it is being implementated or advocated, rather than liberating Muslim women, will lead to their disempowerment and continued subordination in society.

Women's groups that have condemned the actions of the pro-Shari'a radicals are those concerned with women's human rights. Galvanized by Ayesha Imam, executive director of BAOBAB for women's human rights, and coordinator for Africa and Middle East for the Women and Law programme of the Women Living under Muslim Law Network, these groups state that the action is not only unconstitutional but also that its provisions violate women's human rights. In her critique of the Shari'a, Imam noted that there is a difference between Islamic law and Muslim law. According to her, the former are laws, which are of decidedly divine origin and which have not been tainted by human, usually male, interventions. Such laws do not usually provoke any contestations in the Muslim world. On the other hand, Muslim laws such as Shari'a are interpretations of religious injunctions by human beings (male) in particular societies at particular times. These variables, she insists, make such laws amenable to fallibility (*Weekly Trust*, 17–23 December 1999).

In her criticism of Bariya Magazu's case, Imam starts by establishing her Islamic credentials and belief in the Shari'a to forestall her critics from labelling her anti-Islam or anti-Shari'a:

> I am a Muslim. I therefore believe that God alone is the Sovereign and that His Law is universal and for all time, because it extends even into the next world.

I believe that the Shari'a is the Command of God, a divinely ordained system to achieve the ideal society. Rules of conduct are thus established concerning religious, economic, domestic, social, family and political life, which place duties on the Islamic State, towards its citizens, towards God, and each other ... I submit unconditionally to the laws and guidance prescribed under Shari'a, as I believe that they are ordained by God as a way of living for those who believe in Islam. These laws are not limited or restricted to criminal penalties and legal instructions, but include acts of worship and moral behaviour. Rights are protected and responsibilities placed upon Muslim rulers to safeguard our faith, lives, families and health. Criminal penalties are therefore not to be viewed as an encroachment on those rights, but as a means of safeguarding them. Consequently, the penalty for theft and robbery is intended to protect rights of others to lawfully enjoy their property. The penalty against adultery and fornication is to protect the family from disintegration, and the society from corruption and decay. These penalties often have extremely exacting conditions for proof, with an intricate system of checks and balances before a sentence is carried out. This situation had even led to the belief by some scholars, that the punishments may have been intended to serve as deterrents, in the ultimate sense. Indeed, Muslims are even discouraged from serving as witnesses to acts of transgression, as authentic *Hadith* exists that conveys clearly that the Holy Prophet (SAW) stated that any person that conceals the faults or weakness of others would have his fault or weaknesses concealed by God on judgement day. I believe, unreservedly, in this law, and cannot be otherwise, for I am a Muslim. (Ayesha Imam, *This Day*, 18 February 2001)

In her criticisms of the actions of the Zamfara State government, Imam notes:

- Bariya's conviction was illegal because the Zamfara penal code states that *zina* (adultery or fornication) is committed when there is no doubt as to the consent and the circumstances of illegality of the act of intercourse between individuals who are not married to each other. Although pregnancy is evidence of sexual intercourse, it is not evidence of willing participation in sex. Pregnancy can result from rape and coerced sex. In Bariya's sex case, considerable doubts were raised about her consent and neither were there witnesses to testify that she had sex.
- The whipping of Magazu was a cruel and deliberate abuse of her rights, which were violated for political expediency. This is because the state government knew that an extension of leave to appeal was being filed on her behalf.

- That Magazu's rights to appeal in Muslim laws, which insist that in *hadd* offences, such as this, there should be no shadow of doubt before convictions are confirmed, were violated. Furthermore, her right to appeal under the Zamfara State penal code and as a citizen of Nigeria in constitutional law were also violated.
- Finally, Imam wanted to know why the Zamfara penal code, which states that when a person under 18 is convicted of any offence, a fine or punishment of 20 lashes can be substituted for the stated punishment, was not applied in Baraga's case. (*The Vanguard*, 7 February 2001, p. 29)

Although the extension of the sphere of Shari'a from personal Muslim laws to incorporate criminal offences is definitely a violation of women's human rights, the fact that it has generated so much controversy even within the Islamic community is a positive sign. Beyond this lies the challenge of making women's human rights issues a priority in the struggle to consolidate democracy in the country.

APPENDIX 1

New Nigerian, 10 November 1999 *'Our Final Stand on Shari'a'*

The Government of Zamfara State of Nigeria wishes to draw the attention of our fellow countrymen and women to very important issues pertaining to the implementation of its Shari'a programme as follows:

A. What is Shari'a? Shari'a is the Islamic Law as ordained by Allah in the Qur'an and as practised through the Hadith and Sunna of the Holy Prophet Muhammed (SAW) and works of the Prophet's companions and other renowned Islamic Scholars. It covers the whole life of a Muslim from the spiritual to the intellectual, political, social and economic spheres. It preaches peace, justice, fairness and equality, it is the only legal system that cannot be amended to suit particular circumstances or time because it is a divine command. We would also like to quote a highly placed Reverend Father and Methodist Minister from the North Eastern part of this country who says 'I understand the word Shari'a itself to mean, literally, path or way. Its religious connotation is that it is the path chosen by Allah for Muslims to follow. Legally, the Shari'a is said to be a comprehensive set of rules, which regulates every aspect of human existence, and prescribes punishments for all crimes committed by Muslims.' This is exactly what Shari'a is all about as defined by the reverend father.

B. What is the position of Islam with regards to Shari'a?   Allah (SWA) has clearly stated in the Holy Qur'an that any Muslim leader or follower who does not accept Shari'a to govern his life is an unbeliever. The Government of Zamfara State therefore must govern Muslims in the state according to the provision of Shari'a.

C. What are the constitutional provisions in support of Shari'a?

1. Section 38(I) of the 1999 Constitution of the Federal Republic of Nigeria states that 'Every person shall be entitled to freedom of thought, conscience and religion (including freedom to change his religion or belief, and freedom either alone or in community with others, and in public or in private) to manifest and propagate his religion or belief in worship, teaching, practice and observance.' Based on this provision, therefore, the Muslims in Zamfara State are guaranteed the freedom to manifest and propagate their religion or belief in worship, teaching, practice and observance (whether alone or in community with others, in public or in private). This is why we must have Shari'a.

2. Section 6 of the 1999 Constitution of the Federal Republic of Nigeria dealing with judicial powers states as follows:

(4) Nothing in the foregoing provisions of this section i.e. section 6 shall be continued as precluding:

a. The National Assembly or any House of Assembly from establishing courts, other than those to which this section relates, with subordinate jurisdiction to that of a High Court.

b. The National Assembly or any House of Assembly, which does not require it, from abolishing any court which it has power to establish or which it has brought into being.

c. Such other courts as may be authorized by law in jurisdiction at first instance or on appeal on matters with respect to which a House of Assembly may make laws.

This is why we established Shari'a courts in Zamfara State with jurisdiction to administer Islamic Law for Muslims.

3. Section 4 (7) of the 1999 Constitution of the Federal Republic of Nigeria dealing with legislative powers states that 'The House of Assembly of a State shall have power to make Laws for peace, order and good government of the State or any part therefore with respect to the following matters', that is to say:

d. any matter not included in the exclusive Legislative List set out in part 1 of the Second Schedule to this Constitution;

e. any matter included in the Concurrent Legislative List set out in the first column of Part II of the Second Schedule to this Constitution to the extent prescribed in the second column opposite thereto; and

f. any other matter with respect to which it is empowered to make laws in accordance with the provision of this Constitution.

This is why Zamfara State House of Assembly passed the Shari'a Bill into Law for peace, order and good governance in the State.

D. Is Zamfara State violating Section 10 of the Nigerian Constitution? No! Because Section 10 states that 'The Government of the Federation or of a State shall not adopt any religion as State Religion'. We are not adopting Islam as our state religion. If we were to do that, there would not be Magistrate Courts or High Courts and even Churches in Zamfara State. But we now have two legal systems. Shari'a Courts to administer Shari'a Laws for Muslims and Conventional Courts (Magistrate and High Courts) to administer Common Law for non-Muslims. There also exist about forty-five Churches for about 9,000 (nine thousand) Christians living in Gusau the State Capital according to the State Chairman of CAN.

E. What is the position of Islam with regard to Non-Muslims? Islam guarantees the rights of non-Muslims to practise their Religion without hindrance and prohibits injustice of any kind against non-Muslims. The Government of Zamfara State will therefore ensure the security of lives and properties of all people residing in the state irrespective of their religion and tribe and will ensure justice and fairness to all.

SIGNED: AHMAD SANI (Yariman Bakura), Executive Governor, Zamfara State

APPENDIX 2

'Shari'a is a Fundamental Right of Muslims'

Press release by the Federation of Muslim Women's Associations in Nigeria (FOMWAN) Iponri Central Mosque, Surulere, Lagos, in *Weekly Trust*, 17–23 March, 2000

The Federation of Muslim Women's Associations in Nigeria, FOMWAN, representing 600 Muslim women's groups in Nigeria, have followed with concern the hostile reaction of non-Muslims to the decision of various state governments to implement Shari'a. It began with a carefully executed anti-Shari'a media offensive. Newspapers had a field day distorting Islam, deriding Muslims and instilling fears in non-Muslims about the dangers of living in an

'Islamic State'. Added to this are the unguarded and provocative pronouncements of Christian clerics who have been threatening war if Shari'a is implemented. Instead of Christians demanding to implement their own divine law, they prefer to adopt the dog in the manger attitude. The worst shade of this was manifested in the unauthorized and rowdy demonstration organized by the Christians in Kaduna marked by harassment of Muslims and shouting of slogans. All God-fearing people must condemn the subsequent carnage, bloodshed and large-scale destruction of property.

We do not understand why Christians should oppose the implementation of Shari'a, which is only applicable to Muslims. In a multi-religious country like Nigeria, this is intolerance and bigotry at its worst. It amounts to sheer injustice to deny Muslims their rights to live in accordance with the tenets of their religion of which Shari'a constitutes the core. Although Shari'a had been in existence before Nigeria came into being, Muslims have for almost a century been subjected to non-Islamic laws such as the common law which is of Christian origin. They are forced to observe Jewish and Christian work free days of Saturday and Sunday. They conceded to use the Gregorian calendar while the school system in many places denies Muslim pupils an opportunity to offer the compulsory Friday prayers. Yet they cannot implement Shari'a because the Christians do not want it and they have the monopoly of intimidation tactics since the media is firmly in their grip. No country can survive on injustice and no amount of intimidation and blackmail can stop Muslims from practicing their faith since the Constitution grants them this right.

As we bury the innocent victims of this senseless carnage and minister to the hoarders of refugees, we must begin a dialogue on the fundamental rights of adherents of all religions, respecting them and defending them. Only then can we chart a genuine path to peace and sustainable development.

Alhaj Airat Oluwatoyin Sadique,
National Amirah, FOMWAN

Notes

1. Before the adoption of Nigeria's brand of state feminism, i.e. the creation and funding of a women's 'development' group and the appointment of wives of top military and political bureaucrats to head these groups, the state provided support to groups that were favourably disposed to it. This came in various forms – annual subvention, political appointments, and inclusion in government overseas trips, office space, and the recognition of the National Council of Women's Societies (NCWS) as the umbrella organizations for women's groups, among others.

2. The policy of appointing the wife of the head of state as leader of state-funded women's groups.

3. These are the economic stabilization policies adopted by various regimes since 1982 to contain the crisis engulfing the economy.

4. Alhaji Gumi had unlimited access to the most influential media organizations in Northern Nigeria, the Federal Radio Corporation, the New Nigerian newspaper, Nigerian Television Authority, Kaduna and the Hausa newspaper, *Gaskiya Ta Fi Kwabo*. He has also, through the marriages of his daughters to powerful and wealthy individuals, created a strong network of family associates. One of his daughters is married to the immediate past Chief Judge of Nigeria, Justice Mohammed Bello. Unfortunately for Alhaji Gumi, a woman was elected as chair of his constituency during the 1989 local government elections

5. This concept was used by Abdullah, in 'Activism and Wifeism', to define the special feature of Nigeria's state feminism (see Abdullah 1995).

6. At least ten of the seventeen northern states have adopted the Shari'a.

References

Abdullah, H. J. (1993) 'Transition Politics and the Challenge of Gender in Nigeria', *Review of African Political Economy*, 56: 27–37.

— (1994) 'Between Emancipation and Subordination: A Study of the Women's Movement in Nigeria', Lagos: Ford Foundation.

— (1995) 'Activism and Wifeism: The Nigerian Women's Movement', in A. Basu (ed.), *The Challenge of Local Feminisms: Women's Movements in a Global Perspective*, Boulder, CO: Westview Press, pp. 209–25.

— (1996) 'Are Nigerian Muslim Women Organizing for Change?', Uppsala: Scandinavian Institute of African Studies.

Azzam, M. (1996) 'The Islamists and the State under Mubarak', in A. S. Sidahmed and A. Ehteshami (eds), *Islamic Fundamentalism*, Boulder, CO: Westview Press, pp. 109–22.

Babangida, M. (1991) Speech at the Africa Prize for Leadership for the Sustainable End of Hunger, *New Nigerian*, 13 October 1991.

Bangura, Y. and B. Beckman, (1993) 'African Workers and Structural Adjustment', in A. Olukoshi (ed.), *The Politics of Structural Adjustment*, London: James Currey, pp. 75–98.

Birai, U. (1993) 'Islamic Tajdid and the Political Process in Nigeria', in M. Marty and S. Appelby (eds), *Fundamentalisms and the State: Remaking Polities, Economies, and Militance*, Chicago, IL: University of Chicago Press, pp. 184–203.

Callaway, B. and L. Creevey (1994) *The Heritage of Islam: Women, Religion and Politics in West Africa*, Boulder, CO: Lynne Rienner.

Dennis, C. (1987) 'Women and the State in Nigeria: The Case of the Federal Military Government, 1984–85', in H. Afshar (ed.), *Women, State and Ideology*, London: Macmillan, pp. 13–27.

Haselgrave, M. (1988) 'Women's Rights: The Road to the Millennium', in P. Davies (ed.), *Human Rights*, London: Routledge and Kegan Paul.

Haynes, J. (1996) *Religion and Politics in Africa*, London: Zed Books.

Ibrahim, J. (1989) 'The Politics of Religion in Nigeria: The Parameters of the 1987 Crisis in Kaduna State', *Review of African Political Economy*, 45/46: 65–82.

— (1991) 'Religion and Political Turbulence in Nigeria', *Journal of Modern African Studies*, 29: 115–36.

Imam, A. (1992) 'The Women's Movement, State and Democracy in Nigeria', Delhi: Akut Workshop on Social Movements and Democracy in the Third World.

— (1993a) 'Politics, Islam, and Women in Kano, Northern Nigeria', in V. Moghadam (ed.), *Identity Politics and Women: Cultural Reassertions and Feminisms in International Perspective*, Boulder, CO: Westview Press, pp. 123–44.

— (1993b) 'The Dynamics of Winning: An Analysis of Women in Nigeria (WIN)', in C. Mohanty and J. Alexander (eds), *Feminist Genealogies, Colonial Legacies, Democratic Futures*, New York and London: Routledge, pp. 280–307.

Itavyar, D. and S. Obiajunwa (1994) *The State and Women in Nigeria*, Jos: University of Jos Press.

Jega, A. (1993) 'Professional Associations and Structural Adjustment', in A. Olukoshi (ed.), *The Politics of Structural Adjustment*, London: James Currey, pp. 102–9.

Joseph, S. (1993) 'Family and Women's Human Rights', *South Asian Bulletin*, 13: 148–51.

Kabir, Z. (1985) 'Women's Liberation: Myth or Reality', paper presented at the Muslim Sisters Conference, Kano, October 1985.

Kisekka, M. (1992) 'Women's Organized Health Struggles: the Challenge to Women's Associations', in M. Kisekka (ed.), *Women's Health Issues in Nigeria*, Zaira: Tamaza Publishing, pp. 105–21.

Kukah, M. (1991) *Religion, Politics and Power in Northern Nigeria*, Ibadan: Spectrum Publishers.

Marshall, R. (1991) 'Power in the Name of Jesus', *Review of African Political Economy*, 52: 21–37.

Mba, N. (1982) *Nigerian Women Mobilized: Women's Political Activity in Southern Nigeria, 1900–1965*, Berkeley, CA: University of California Press.

— (1989)'Kaba and Khaki: Women and Militarized State in Nigeria', in J. Parpart and K. Staudt (eds), *Women and the State in Africa*, Boulder, CO: Lynne Rienner, pp. 69–90.

Moghadam, V. M. (1990) *Gender, Development and Policy: Toward Equity and Empowerment*, Helsinki: World Institute for Development Economics Research, United Nations University.

Olukoshi, A. (ed.) (1993) *The Politics of Structural Adjustment in Nigeria*, London: James Currey.

— (1994) 'The State and the Civilian Liberties Movement in Nigeria, 1985–1993', Kampala: Scandinavian Institute for African Studies.

— (1997) 'Associational Life During the Transition to Civil Rule in Nigeria', in L. Diamond, A. Kirk-Greene and O. Oyediran (eds), *Transition without End: Nigerian Politics, Governance, and Civil Society Under Babangida*, Boulder, CO: Lynne Rienner, pp. 379–400.

Shettima, K. (1995) 'Engendering Nigeria's Third Republic', *African Studies Review*, 38(3): 61–98.

Tomasevki, K. (1993) *Women and Human Rights*, London: Zed Books.

Violence Watch (2000). Quarterly newsletter published by Project Alert (PA) [a women's rights NGO], Lagos, Nigeria.

Williams, P. and T. Falola (1995) *The Religious Impact on the Nation State*, Aldershot: Avebury.

WIN (Women in Nigeria) Editorial Committee (1985a) *The WIN Document: The Conditions of Women in Nigeria and Policy Recommendations to 2000 AD*, Zaira: Ahmadu Bello University Bindery.

— (1985) *Women in Nigeria Today*, London: Zed Books.

Yusuf, B. (1991) 'Hausa-Fulani Women: The State of the Struggle', in C. Coles and B. Mack (eds), *Hausa Women in the Twentieth Century*, Madison, WI: University of Wisconsin Press, pp. 90–106.

SEVEN

Contradictory Perspectives on Rights and Justice in the Context of Land Tenure Reform in Tanzania

Issa Shivji

§ THE purpose of this chapter is to explore the notions of justice, rights, democracy and fairness in the particular context of the current debate on land tenure reform in Tanzania. The process was inaugurated by the Report of the Presidential Commission of Inquiry into Land Matters of which the present author was the chairman. Subsequent to that, the Ministry of Lands published its National Land Policy which formed the basis of the draft Land Act prepared by a consultant, Professor Patrick McAuslan. Although the draft Act has undergone modifications through its various versions, its thrust remains the same. The comments in this chapter are based on the version from August 1996 which was presented at a conference in November of the same year.

It is our position that the issue of land tenure reform cannot be separated from the question of democracy. No major law can work satisfactorily if it does not speak to the major grievances of the large majority of land users – the peasant and pastoral communities. Land tenure reform is not simply a matter of law; it is also an issue of justice. The central question to ask, therefore, is: does the draft bill embody the notions of justice, rights and fairness of the people themselves or is it an imposed version of justice with typical top-down bureaucratic approaches and notions of 'administrative' justice?

In the first section, I briefly review the Western and colonial notions of justice. The next sections then go on to compare the notions of justice/rights which form the basis of the Commission's report and those that inform the Land Act. This is done by selecting a few areas – such as the vesting of radical titles, dispute-settlement machinery and village adjudication – as examples.

The Colonial Heritage

Ali Mazrui has written that, 'post-colonial Africa has a triple heritage of law: indigenous/customary law, Islamic law, and the legal and judicial systems which came with Western acculturation' (Mazrui 1989: 252). The last is what constitutes largely, if not exclusively, state law, while Islamic law is often subsumed under customary law. Academic discussions of 'competing' notions of justice and fairness in Africa are constructed around the triple heritage, that is the notions of justice and fairness embedded in Western law (state law), customary law and Islamic law. To be sure, state law and customary law did not have some kind of separate and independent existence; they were constructed in the course of social struggles and changing material and social relationships. 'Customary law' was used as a resource or ideology of resistance, both against the imposed state law as well as within African communities, as the societies became increasingly differentiated with the penetration of commodity economy (Chanock 1991: 3). Nevertheless, the colonial state law ultimately prevailed. It was the dominant logic and, therefore, what was African custom itself was accommodated within the state law. As Channock observes: 'What was ultimately allowed to develop as "custom" and what was not depended on what the State would accommodate' (Chanock 1991: 80).

While customary law – and the notions of justice and rights underlying it – was a contested terrain, some of the more recent literature has tended to exaggerate the contest by ignoring or de-emphasizing the dominant contest which was with the colonial state (law). Thus, stereotyped notions of customary law portraying communal consensus, while a little exaggerated, may still be closer to the truth. This is certainly so when contrasted with the notions of rights and justice of Western law constructed around the fetish of the abstract individual (Fine 1984).

In Western jurisprudence, the construction of rights is rooted in two sets of theories. One has its origins in the Enlightenment. These Enlightenment rights are based on contractarian constructs, the opposite of the legal contract based strictly on commodity exchange. In this situation rights are the rights of contracting parties (juristic persons) arising from contractual relations (private law) and constructed around, to use Marx's phrase, 'freedom, equality, property and Bentham'. It is this, coupled with the Dicean notion of parliamentary supremacy/rule of law, which is strongly present in the rights discourse within the positivist/empiricist tradition dominant in Britain. In the hands of English courts, the natural law theories of the Enlightenment period were transformed into largely procedural rights under the rubric of principles of natural justice.

Substantive rights continued to be constructed around the building block of private contract.

Natural law theories and the notions of natural rights were more influential in the American and French revolutions, which have had greater influence on the discourse on substantive rights and the entrenching of the doctrines of rule of law/separation of powers. The colonial state law was strictly constructed in the most crude positivist tradition as a collection of rules to transmit force. 'Freedom' and 'equality' were confined to private law contractual relations, while public law did not exist beyond the criminal code, which itself was drained of any rights content, as its operation was predominantly an administrative rather than a judicial affair. The colonial executive was the legislature, the administrator and the judge (fusion of power). During much of the colonial period, constitutional law and administrative law (both in the realm of justifying and restraining state/administrative power) were very undeveloped. Thus, colonial law was predominantly a self-sufficient body of rules giving discretionary powers to officials to exercise power. In other words, colonial law was a thinly veiled exercise of state force without being disguised in ideologies of justice, rights and fairness.[1] Colonial state law is, then, a despotic law. The colonial state, to the extent that it did seek legitimacy, was not on the legal terrain but rather the cultural, the racial and the religious.

The post-colonial state inherited and further sharpened the authoritarian character of the law. There is considerable literature showing the authoritarian character of African law (Ghai 1986). The post-colonial state sought legitimacy in various nation-building and developmentalist ideologies (Wamba dia Wamba 1991). In the case of Tanzania, the ideology of *Ujamaa* could be considered hegemonic (Shivji 1995). The 'law' as such was not the terrain for the construction of legitimacy; rather, its main function was to control and regulate (Shandi 1985). The legal order exhibited much more of the tyranny of rules than the rule of law. The post-independence state law continued to be in the positivist tradition, tempered, at best, only by principles of natural justice. In the absence of an enforceable bill of rights, even the constitutional notions of (human) rights (and justice) were, until recently, irrelevant. Equality, justice and rights were constructed on non-legal terrain in the realm of the statist ideology of *Ujamaa*. Within the limitations of its strong statist and top-down character, the ideology of *Ujamaa* had far greater resonance among the large majority of popular classes than any liberal notions of human rights and democracy have had since.

However, within the official academic and political discourse, customary law has had very little presence except as a nuisance to be modernized at the earliest convenience. Thus, customary law is much more a lived experience, subtly expressing itself in day-to-day perceptions of people and, probably, more sharply, in conflictual situations. Academic research on customary law as a terrain of alternative perspective on rights and justice is scanty. This chapter is, therefore, not able to draw on any body of secondary material so far as Tanzania is concerned.

This chapter explores people's perspectives on justice and rights underlying their complaints and grievances presented to the Presidential Commission on Land Matters chaired by the author (United Republic of Tanzania 1992). Land is the major resource and the site of the construction of culture, custom and conflicts. The actually existing perceptions on land would, it is hoped, be able to give us a fair picture of the alternative, and possibly competing, perspective on rights and justice.

I have further explored how the rights and justice perspectives of the people were translated into policy, and into the institutional and legal recommendations of the Commission for a land tenure reform. Since the publication of the report, the government, through the Ministry of Lands, has published a National Land Policy (NLP) paper. Based on this paper, a consultant from the United Kingdom, Professor McAuslan, was hired to draft a comprehensive law to effect reform and regulate land tenure in the country. Having written the draft, he took the opportunity of delivering the Third Alistair Berkeley Memorial Lecture (hereinafter 'the lecture') at the London School of Economics on 30 May 1996 to make jurisprudential observations on his work and provide academic justifications for his policy choices (McAuslan 1996a). The government policy, the draft Land Act and the lecture together supply excellent material to unravel the dominant state law perspectives on rights and justice. I try to do this in this chapter by taking a few selected areas addressed by the Commission's report and the draft Land Act.

The Terrain of Contradictory Perspectives: The Land Tenure Reform Experience Background to Land Law

The land tenure regime in Tanzania mainland was established by colonialism in a short piece of legislation called the Land Ordinance of 1923. This is the law which still forms the overall legislative framework for land tenure and 'land rights' in the country. The most important provisions are those which declared all lands in the country to be public lands at the disposal of the governor (now president), and that no occupation of land shall be valid without the consent of the governor (Section 4). The effect was to expropriate control over land from the indigenous and colonized and vest it in the executive arm of the state. Much of the later development of land law and the tenure system, whether by way of legislation, judicial law-making or administrative practices, was built around this major premise.

The governor was empowered to grant land by way of a right of occupancy (defined as a right to occupy and use land) for a period of up to ninety-nine years. This came to be called the 'granted right of occupancy' and was the main basis for alienating land to foreign companies, settlers and other immigrants, both in the plantation sector and urban areas. The genius of colonial judiciary (with the assistance of the privy council) regularized the indigenous occupation of land by small peasants and pastoralists by inventing the category of the 'deemed right of occupancy' which referred to the occupation of land by indigenous people governed by their respective customary law. The courts assumed consent on the part of the governor that indigenous landowners could use and occupy land. The legal regime was also aided by a large peasant sector producing for a metropolitan market.

What is more interesting for the purposes of this chapter is the relationship between the dual land tenure regime (statutory and customary) and the state. The relationship between the state as the grantor and the occupier as the grantee of the right of occupancy was contractual. A civil relationsip based on the fundamental notions of Western legal justice determined the rights of the parties. Any breach of the contract (dispute) went to civil courts manned by professional magistrates and judges, and the highest recourse was to the privy council. Where the courts found gaps in statutes they resorted to principles of common law and equity, modifying them according to local circumstances as empowered to do so under the reception clauses. The statutory land regime thus developed. Like much colonial jurisprudence, the notions of human rights and justice were strictly jurisprudentially positivist, philosophically empiricist and legally contractual where, to paraphrase Marx, 'Freedom, Equality, Property and Bentham' reigned while human rights were nothing but 'nonsense on stilts' (Bentham).

The relationship of the customary occupier with the state was statutory (as opposed to contractual). His/her occupation of land, as the courts said, was permissive, and was almost at the mercy of the state. The relation between the state and the customary occupier was administrative (Lyall 1973: 86).[2] The predominant function of the state in this regard was one of control while it operationalized its regulatory function through the customary law. The relationship of customary owners among themselves (*inter se*) was governed by customary law; with the state this relationship was administrative and, in relation to the statutory/contractual occupier, inferior. Customary landowners went to traditional courts (chiefs) for redress.

Both customary law and customary courts were subordinate to the colonial state executive. First, as the reception clause made clear, criminal customary law was not applicable. When state force appeared on the surface and, therefore, made notions of justice and rights more open – as in penal law and more generally public law – the colonial state kept its control intact. Customary law regulated land relations as a matter of personal, rather than private or public law. Even here, the higher colonial/civil court had powers to disallow a rule of customary law if it was repugnant to 'justice, morality and good conscience'. While it is true that the so-called customary law was a reconstructed one and embodied the struggles of the people, this was not some process of 'negotiation' or 'dialogue' as post-modernist language would deem it.

Second, the producer, production on land and its management were under the state. They were sanctioned by penal law through various regulations and by-laws passed by 'native authorities' on 'advice' (in practice 'directives') of the provincial commissioner (Williams 1982).[3] Once again, this stands in stark contrast to the contractual/civil relationship, with the grantee of the statutory right of occupancy where development conditions, for example, were incorporated as a covenant in the certificate of title. Thus, customary law as co-opted by the colonial state was both subordinated to it and deprived of its autonomous notions and perspectives of justice.

The post-independence state inherited the land regime outlined above. The most important tenurial reform was to abolish the freehold tenure which covered less than one per cent of land. The freehold land was converted to leasehold (rights of occupancy) tenure. The other reform was to abolish a semi-feudal system in the West Lake Region known as '*nyarubanja*' and to enfranchise the tenants. Both these reforms arose from the philosophy that Nyerere had expounded in the late 1950s in response to the colonial government's proposals to individualize, title and register (ITR) land. Nyerere argued:

> If people are given land to use as their property, then they have a right to sell it. It will not be difficult to predict who, in fifty years' time, will be the landlords and who the tenants. In a country such as this, where, generally speaking, the Africans are poor and the foreigners are rich, it is quite possible that, within eighty or hundred years, if the poor African were allowed to sell his land, all land in Tanganyika would belong to wealthy immigrants, and the local people would be tenants. But even if there were no rich foreigners in this country, there would emerge rich and clever Tanganyikans. If we allow land to be sold like a robe, within a short period there would be only a few Africans possessing

land in Tanganyika and all others would be tenants ... If two groups emerge – a small group of landlords and a large group of tenants – we would be faced with a problem which has created antagonism among peoples and led to bloodshed in many countries of the world. Our forefathers saved themselves from this danger by refusing to distribute land on a freehold basis. (Nyerere 1966: 55, 56)

This was integrated in Nyerere's *Ujamaa* philosophy and policy after independence. In 1962 , Nyerere laid down: 'The TANU Government must go back to the traditional African custom of land holding. That is to say, a member of society will be entitled to a piece of land on condition that he uses it. Unconditional, or "freehold" ownership of land (which leads to speculation and parasitism) must be abolished' (Nyerere 1966: 14).

The translation of the philosophy into law did not go further than the abolishing of freehold tenure, while the basic principles of 'security of land being dependent on use', which both the colonial state as well as the post-independence governments argued was a traditional principle, remained intact. What is most significant, though, is that the overarching ownership of radical titles vested in the state remained and was further reinforced in that the post-independence state was able to legitimate itself as the representative of the people. Second, as has been shown in many studies, the despotic colonial legal regime (rightless law) continued unabated. The imperial presidency with vast unrestrained powers was the pinnacle of the authoritarian state in Tanzania. As I have argued elsewhere, the state sought political legitimacy not so much on the legal terrain – i.e. in the ideology of legal rights and justice – but in developmentalist and nation-building ideologies prevalent then, in the case of Tanzania taking the form of *Ujamaa* (Shivji 1995; see also Shivji 1992).

Ujamaa, drawing its legitimacy from African familyhood, combined in itself notions of human equality (*binadamu wote ni sawa*) and social equity. As the policy of the state party, these tenets were not embedded in law as such, but were translated into action by state or party or both, often contrary to law. The law, on the other hand, continued to operate on the assumptions of the cold-blooded 'freedom, equality and property' of the contract which in practice, as has been argued by critics, means inequity for the propertyless and freedom of the property-owner (Fine 1984). Nyerere often made a similar critique of the law on political platforms, castigating law as a pastime of lawyers. The result, though, was legally unrestrained actions by the state and its bureaucracy and inevitable abuses of power. It is in the most important policy measure of *Ujamaa*, villagization, that the tension between right-less law and the *Ujamaa* variant of social justice revealed itself in the most dramatic fashion around the question of land.

Villagization involved a massive uprooting of peasant/pastoral communities from their original places of residence and resettlement in villages by coercion without consultation or consent of peasant communities. Over nine million peasants were resettled in villages. This was done without any authority in law and without regard to the tenure system. The legal justification, never articulated as such, was simple. Land belonged to the state (*'ardhi ni mali ya umma'*) and, therefore, the state could do with it what it felt was in the interest of the people. As it is, under colonial jurisprudence, customary landholders hardly had secure land rights in law. The post-colonial state took this to its logical conclusion drawing upon its political legitimacy, the ideology of *Ujamaa*. The move backfired, with the liberalization of the 1980s and the abandonment of *Ujamaa* as the richer sections of the former customary owners began to seek redress in law. The upheaval and the potential for social conflict thus created was one of the reasons which led to the appointment of the Land Commission (Shivji 1994).

Nevertheless, the dilemma and tension between concerns of social justice and the law's enormous capacity to co-opt and transform these into, at best, individual procedural rights (natural justice) is constantly faced by even more radical social reformers and activists (Cottrell 1993).[4]

The tension is rendered even more complex because in authoritarian polities, social concerns become statist commands enforced through coercion unrestrained by 'rule of law' which in turn makes the alternative of liberal 'rule of law' an 'unqualified good' to struggle for.

This is precisely the kind of tension and dilemma which was faced by the land commissioners. On the one hand, there were statist structures and practices abusing their powers against the large majority of rural and peri-urban landholders. On the other hand, the alternative offered by the liberal Western law and human rights, in its construct of (individual) rights and procedural notions of equality, freedom and property, fell woefully short of the demands and interests of the village communities and socially disadvantaged groups and classes.

Rights/Justice Perspectives Underlying the Commission's Report and the Draft Land Act

The Land Commission: background The Land Commission visited all districts of Tanzania Mainland (except two) and held some 277 meetings in

145 villages and 132 urban centres which were attended by over 83,000 people. Over 3,000 people submitted their complaints and opinions (United Republic of Tanzania 1992, vol. 1). On the whole, therefore, the Commission was able to get a fairly wide and representative sample of people's grievances against the existing system, their suggestions on reform and their underlying perspectives on rights and justice. The chairman of the Commission in a preface to the published report claims that: '[t]he Wananchi were not only the foundation of inspiration to the Commissioners but the ultimate source of major ideas presented in the Report. What we did was to systematise, articulate and present in a coherent manner what we had gathered from the people in the language of their daily experience and practical wisdom.' Maybe this was a little exaggerated, so far as the institutional and legal structures recommended by the Commission were concerned. But there is no doubt that the basic underlying principles were crystallized from the perceptions and practices of the people as recorded in evidence.

Ownership and control of land The single most important source of complaints/grievances was identified by the Commission as lack of participation and consultation of the people in the decision-making and administrative processes relating to land. '*Hatukushirikishwa*' ('We were not consulted, we didn't participate') was the constant cry. The demand for participation was not made in any general fashion but with respect to specific issues of administration of land.

Non-participation was both the source of complaints and abuses as well as a democratic demand which informed the major recommendations of the Commission on reforming the land tenure structure, institutions and law. A democratic demand to be consulted and participate, as of right, on matters involving the major resource around which the life-conditions, culture and custom of the majority of producers is constructed is a social democratic demand. The core of the conception/perspective on justice may be, albeit inadequately, summed up in the notion of social justice.

I have argued elsewhere that the right to participate and be consulted by the people might be captured within a reconceptualized/reconstructed notion of the right of peoples to self-determination (Shivji 1997). The perception of the villagers in Tanzania, as described here, comes very close to the theoretical arguments made by Archie Mafeje in his intervention on the debate on democracy (Mafeje 1995). Critiquing African scholars who posited values and state structures of liberal democracy as an alternative to the statist one-party authoritarianism in Africa, Mafeje argued that they were simply wrong both in their historical understanding of the democracy discourse as well as the real life-conditions of the oppressed classes (the large majority) in Africa. Arguing that while genuine democracy may be difficult to achieve, it was not difficult to define in the present conditions in Africa. Ordinary people, Mafeje submits, 'only fight when their livelihood is threatened'. In other words, 'they fight in order to guarantee the necessary conditions for their social reproduction'.

> Regarding the present conditions in Africa, this can refer only to two things: First, the extent to which the people's will enters decisions which affect their life chances; and, second, the extent to which their means of livelihood are guaranteed. In political terms the first demand does not suggest capture of 'state power' by the people (workers and peasants) but it does imply ascendancy to state power by a national democratic alliance in which the popular classes hold the balance of power. The second demand implies equitable (not equal) distribution of resources. Neither liberal democracy, imposed 'multi-partyism' nor 'market forces' can guarantee these two conditions. It transpires, therefore, that the issue is neither liberal nor 'compradorial' democracy but social democracy. (Mafeje 1995: 26)

The Commission translated the message embedded in the battle-cry '*hatuku-shirikishwa*' to mean the demand to democratize the land tenure system in which the villagers, the peri-urban and slum dwellers would participate, either directly or through elected representatives, in making major decisions relating to land. The Commission had to face head-on the existing statist land tenure system where the radical title to land, and ultimate control, is vested in the executive arm of the state, which, in practice, meant the Ministry of Lands and its subordinate bureaucracy. On the other hand, there was the market (ITR – individualization, titling and registration) model advocated by the dominant IFIs (international financial institutions), Western donors and their foreign consultants. Neither of these, as was very clear from the grievances and demands of the large majority, answers the essentially social democratic perspectives of the peasant, pastoralist and the so-called squatter communities. The Commission had to recommend policy and institutional and legal reforms in land administration which simultaneously answered the demand of the people as well as provided a feasible alternative of organizing the land tenure system.

The main features of the Commission's recommendations may be summarized as follows.

First, the monopoly of radical title vested in the president should be broken and the radical title should be diversified together with the administration of land. It was recommended that all lands in Tanzania should be divided into national and village lands, that national lands be vested in a Board of Land Commissioners under the National Lands Commission (NLC) which would hold the same in trust for the people of Tanzania. The village lands would be vested in respective village assemblies to be composed of all adult members of the village. Village assemblies would be the ultimate owners, controllers and administrators of village lands. Village assemblies would have a quorum of women.

Second, the NLC would be responsible and accountable to the Parliament (National Assembly), the most representative body at the national level. While the president would nominate the land commissioners and the chief executive of the NLC, they would have to be confirmed by the National Assembly through its land committee.

Third, at the primary level, all the processes dealing with land delivery – surveying, planning, allocation and registration and dispositions of national lands – would be done in public through the participation, and under the supervision, of elected ward and district committees. At the same time, no land would be considered ready and available for allocation unless certified by the circuit land courts. Thus, judicial intervention would not simply be *ex post facto* to provide redress but would prevent abuse as an anticipatory measure.

Both fundamental recommendations of the Commission – that is, its divesting of radical title and vesting of village lands in village assemblies – were unequivocally rejected by the government and have no place in the draft Land Act. The National Land Policy paper described the existing land tenure system, whose main feature is the monopoly of radical title, as 'fundamentally sound' (United Republic of Tanzania 1995: 9). The earlier draft of the policy paper was even more forthright, if rather unsophisticated, in the defence of the monopoly of radical title.

> The existing legislation on land and a long experience and practice of more than 30 years after independence, vesting all land in Tanzania in its President and granting of Rights of Occupancy to the rest of the population has shown that the present land tenure systems [sic] is a sound land tenure for Tanzania. The President is holding the said land in trust for all the citizens of Tanzania and land being a basic element of the State, the Head of State (the President) can easily acquire a piece of land for use for the benefit of the people ... [T]o detach the Head of State from land would be a radical departure from the present land tenure system. Such a change is just like making him and his government beggars for land for implementation of government development policies and projects. (United Republic of Tanzania 1993: 8)

It is curious how the feudal notion of the identity between sovereignty and property in the absolute monarch reappears in the bureaucratic/authoritarian state. In other words, just as a king without land could not be installed in feudal Europe, so an 'imperial' president without control over land is considered a beggar in a republican Tanzania! Professor McAuslan skirts around this issue in his lecture which otherwise tries to justify various policy decisions he says he had to make in drafting the Land Act. At best he offers a lame defence by asserting in his commentary on the draft that 'no government is willing or should be expected to give up that power' (McAuslan 1996a: 14), having in the first place identified the vesting of radical title in the president with the powers of eminent domain (i.e. acquiring land for 'national and public purposes') (see also Mukoyogo and Rutinwa 1994).[5] The historical fact is that the vesting of proprietary title in land in the state was a colonial creation and was recognized as such by some contemporary commentators (Meek 1946). This principle, which both the policy paper and McAuslan's commentary call 'fundamental' and which means, in the words of the commentary, that 'all powers over public land stem from the president', is what is reflected in the draft bill (McAuslan 1996a: 14) The Commissioner for Lands, as a chief delegate, so to speak, of the president's power, has far more powers (spelled out more explicitly and in great detail in the draft Land Act) generally, and particularly over village lands, than the existing political and administrative practices allow. What is clear, though, is that the notions of social justice, equity and rights of the villagers as evidenced in the narratives before the Commission – and which the Commission translated as a demand for the democratization of land tenure – cannot be squared with the detailed legal structure of the draft Land Act. The structure of the Land Act takes the top-down statist approach (i.e. vesting of land in the president) as its primary building block.

The Commission explicitly recommended the detaching of land ownership and administration from the Executive, but the draft Act actually reinforces land ownership, both at the national and village level. The central actor is the Commissioner for Lands in the Ministry of Lands. At the village level, the role of the village assembly is almost totally de-emphasized while the village council (an elected body of twenty-five persons) is the main manager and administrator of village lands. The powers of the village council are regulated with detailed provisions. The ultimate supervisor of these powers is the commissioner. Under certain circumstances, the commissioner can even take over the administration of village land from the elected village council (McAuslan 1996b: 196). In short, rather than the village council (village government) being accountable and responsible to the village assembly (village parliament), the village council is accountable and responsible to the appointed officer of the central government, the Commissioner for Lands.

For example, the village assembly may complain to the commissioner when it feels that the village council is not exercising its functions properly. It is the commissioner who has the legal power to issue directives to the council and, if need be, take over the management of the village land from the village council. At the village level, democracy is inverted by inverting the position of the organ of direct participation (the village assembly) and the elected body (the village council) on the one hand, and by making the elected body, the village council, accountable to an appointed official (the commissioner).

The detailed management, administration and adjudication structure set out by the draft Act is reminiscent of the disastrous 1972 decentralization which was put in place by an American consultancy and management firm, McKinsey & Co. (Coulson 1982: 254). McKinsey decentralized central state bureaucracy to the regional and district level and abolished elected local governments. It was such a disaster that the whole structure had to be reversed six years later, doing irreparable damage to the government machinery (Mushi 1978). The administrative procedures with umpteen forms and constant seeking of directives/advice from the commissioner under the draft Act is nothing less than setting up of 'mini-ministries of land' at village levels. These mini-ministries even by conservative estimates would require at least three to five paid officers: a clerk, a typist, an accountant, a cashier, a messenger and a professional scribe to help villagers fill prescribed forms. They would require constant communication with the commissioner (within set time limits) in Dar es Salaam. This, in a country where many villages are not easily accessible and mail takes weeks to arrive, if it ever does.

In this regard, the draft Act is centrally based on giving powers to state officials, albeit in very detailed provisions, while leaving administration in the hands of village-level elected officials; these elected officials are governed by equally detailed provisions but they have little power or discretion. The draft Act betrays its penchant for positivist legal justice (or, more correctly, 'administrative justice' in the colonial sense) and distrust in ordinary people and their elected representatives, particularly at the local level. In this, the draft Act shares the values, assumptions and biases of modernization and developmentalist scholars, and law and development scholars, whether liberal or authoritarian (Mamdami 1996).

The machinery for dispute-settlement or administering land rights/ justice One of the major findings of the Commission was that the machinery for resolving land disputes had virtually broken down (United Republic of Tanzania 1992). First, there was overlapping jurisdiction between various bodies – including organs and members of the executive and the party involved in resolving disputes. Second, disputes lasted for long periods without final certain determination. Third, organs of justice were remote and inaccessible both physically and socially. Fourth, people showed great dissatisfaction with the decisions of judicial organs; they did not find them just or fair. The following narrative before the Commission is typical:

> My rights are customary. CDA [Capital Development Authority, a parastatal] found me on the land. They allocated the land to the person I regard as an invader. He took me to a court. He produced a certificate as proof of his ownership of the plot. The court ruled against me and awarded the invader my land. I did not accept the injustice and I stayed on the land. The invader took me to court again, this time on a charge of criminal trespass. I was arrested and locked up till I was released on bail. I went to the appellate district court. I lost the appeal. I became very angry to no avail. The invader has since mortgaged my land and secured a bank loan. So I sit on my land as part of the mortgage. (United Republic of Tanzania 1992: 204)

Fifth, government organs, including courts, were accused of nepotism, corruption and bias. In short, people accused the so-called machinery of justice of inefficiency, illegitimacy and injustice. Clearly, the state organs of dispute-settlement had lost credibility. People demanded organs that would be impartial, close, accessible and accountable to them. In this case, the Commission found that the traditional bodies such as elders (*wazee*) still commanded respect and legitimacy as mediators and arbitrators of disputes. In recommending the machinery of dispute-settlement, the Commission was guided explicitly by the principle that people should have faith in the dispute-settlement machinery (legitimacy). The Commission was also guided by the principle that the organs of justice should be accessible, approachable and understandable. These institutions should be open, transparent and institutionally impartial and independent. In a word, the Commission was both conscious of, and deliberately tried to move away from, the Western positivist bias for professional dispensers of justice ('qualified, competent, efficient, objective').[6]

Combining these principles, the Commission recommended the utilization of the *Baraza la Wazee* (elders council) as the basic village organ with original jurisdiction in all land matters, both civil and criminal. Five *wazee* would be elected by the village assembly for a period of three years, but recallable by the assembly before the end of the term under certain circumstances. The *Baraza* was independent of the assembly and the village council in its operations and determined all disputes (including those against the council) in open meetings in accordance with customary law, principles of natural justice and the community sense of fairness and reasonableness. The *Baraza* would also double as a body to register customary titles (village land registry), again in open meetings. Thus the process of registration is seen as a judicial process.

Appeals from the *Baraza* would go to the circuit land courts which were presided over by a professional magistrate assisted by a panel of *wazee*. The *wazee* would give their own reasoned opinion as to what they considered to be the just and fair outcome of the case before them. While the magistrate would not be bound by the opinion of the *wazee*, he/she was required to give reasons for agreeing or disagreeing. Appeals from the circuit land courts would go to the Land Division of the High Court and there too a judge would sit with a panel of *wazee* who would have a similar role. The Commission explained the role of the *wazee* as follows:

> We see their role as somewhere between the existing system of assessors and the jury system in some common law jurisdictions. It will be noticed that our conception of their role is closer to a jury system than our assessors system. This will allow a fuller participation of the community in the process of adjudication over land. But, even more significant, our expectation is that by exposing the professional personnel (such as magistrates) to the values of justice and fairness of the community, the system will help to develop a more legitimate corpus of law and procedure having roots in the values of the community. (United Republic of Tanzania 1992: 202)

Thus, the Commission tried to bring into the open the competing perspectives on justice between Western-trained legal professionals, representing legal justice, and community elders expressing alternative perspectives. Furthermore, the Commission wanted to move away from the racially structured dualism/dichotomy of colonial times, under which jurisdiction depended on the law applicable or registered land. The assumption was that registered land was governed by statutory/Western law while unregistered land was governed by customary law ('native law and custom') and the 'elders' sat only as some kind of advisers (or appeared as expert witnesses) in matters involving customary law. In the words of the report:

> These dichotomies are in fact a remnant from the colonial past. In the colonial

society the dual judicial structure significantly corresponded to the racial structure. English/statutory law had connotations of superiority over customary law
just as registered land was considered to enjoy greater and legally protected
security of tenure compared to unregistered land. Soon after independence the
court structure was integrated, thus doing away with the overt racial division.
But other dichotomies based on the laws applicable or whether the land was
registered or unregistered, with all its implications, were maintained, and in
some cases resurrected, in post-independence statutes. (United Republic of
Tanzania 1992: 199)

The draft Land Act adopts the terminology of the Commission's report in
setting up the dispute-settlement machinery, while stripping it of all its principles and perspectives on justice, community participation and development
of a more legitimate Tanzanian common law.

In the draft Act, the *Baraza* is composed of persons nominated by the village
council, approved by the village assembly, and confirmed by the judge of the
circuit land court (McAuslan 1996b: cl. 218). Its jurisdiction is only in civil
matters confined to the value of 500,000 shillings, where both parties agree to
submit it to the *Baraza*, and 200,000 shillings when the matter in dispute is
governed by customary law (cl. 219). The circuit land court is headed by a
professional judge who sits with two advisers selected from a panel of regional
customary law advisers. These customary law advisers are appointed by the
Judicial Service Commission 'to assist the circuit land court judges in that
region in determining cases involving an issue of customary land law' (cl.
217[7]).

The circuit land court has jurisdiction in all land cases governed by received
law of value not less than 25 million shillings and cases involving customary law
of value more than 200,000 shillings. It also has appellate and supervisory
jurisdiction over Mabaraza (cl. 215).

The land court (which is at the level of the High Court) is similarly composed of a judge who sits with customary law advisers in matters involving
customary law. It has original and appellate jurisdiction throughout Tanzania
Mainland.

The post-Arusha bill has made further modifications in the machinery for
settlement of land disputes. The *Mabaraza* have disappeared both in name and
substance. At the village level, there are only mediation panels whose jurisdiction is voluntary. Parties to a dispute need not submit to the panel's jurisdiction,
and even if they did, the panel's decisions are not binding. It is the primary
courts that have original jurisdiction in matters of unregistered land within

specified pecuniary value, or in matters governed by customary law. The circuit land courts in the modified draft are called district land courts. The process for settling land disputes is back to what it is at present and the changes are more tangential rather than substantial. The mass of evidence collected by the Commission to the effect that the existing machinery (primary, district courts) is neither efficient nor commands the trust of the people has made no dent.

The draft Land Act in its provisions on dispute-settlement processes reveals in an even more open fashion the biases of Western positivism and its notions of legal justice. To add insult to injury, it resurrects the colonial divisions between received law (not defined, but presumably statutes, common law and principles of equity) and customary law. Professional legal justice is dispensed by professionally trained judges, applying received law in which they are supposed to be well-versed. When matters involve the laws and customs of the community, the judges are not supposed to be well-versed and, therefore, sit with 'advisers'. However, the 'advice', i.e. the notions of justice and fairness to the community, are subject to the sense of justice of the professional judge who has the final decision-making power. Even the decision as to who could be advisers cannot be left to the community concerned but to the professional judgement of the professionally constituted Judicial Service Commission. Where small landholders (who own property not worth more than 200,000 shillings) are concerned, and their matter is governed by customary law, it can be decided by the village-based *Baraza*. Presumably, the quality of justice does not matter where the pecuniary value of the subject matter is small and the disputants are insignificant in the village.[7]

This thinking and the perspective of top-down professional legal justice based on 'received imperial notions' of justice, fairness and reasonableness clash head-on with the perspectives of rights and justice held by the large majority of Tanzanian land users (peasant and pastoral communities) on which was based the structure recommended by the Commission.

Citing precisely the jurisdiction and procedures of the *Mabaraza* as recommended by the Commission, Professor McAuslan observes:

> [T]hese far-reaching proposals involve changes in the law but the clear message of the Presidential Commission was that the new law should be similar to that which it will replace in terms of drafting style; a few broad strokes of the legal pen giving vast powers to totally unqualified people and relying on their innate common-sense and sense of justice to get things done; just like Operation Vijiji in fact. In the light of the evidence uncovered by the Presidential Commission

of the abuse of power and the chaos that accompanied that exercise, the word 'naiveté' comes to mind to describe this approach. This might be unfair; a better analysis is that the approach adopted by the Commission is a classic example of the operation of 'path dependency'. (McAuslan 1996a: 12, 13)

McAuslan then goes on to cite 'path dependency', the relevance of which is difficult to understand, and continues (North 1990: 99):

> Applied to land and the use of law to alter land relations in Tanzania, this tells us that while the policy proposals of the Presidential Commission were indeed far-reaching, the approach to the use of law to implement them was driven, to some extent, by long-standing Tanzanian legal traditions which stretch back to colonial times [sic!]. The real revolutionaries therefore might turn out to be not those who propose radical policies but those who, through the NLP [National Land Policy], propose a radical legal methodology for implementing policies; namely a detailed and inevitably lengthy new land code in which legal rules and checks and balances replace reliance on administrative and political action based on goodwill and common-sense; on the evidence, in short supply where land relations are concerned. (McAuslan 1996a: 13)

It is interesting that the author likens the Commission's approach to law with the colonial tradition. It is true that the drafting style of the Land Ordinance itself was 'a few broad strokes of the legal pen giving vast powers'. The major difference, though, is that these powers were given not to an 'unqualified' mass of 'natives', 'relying on their innate common-sense and sense of justice to get things done', but to the highly qualified servants of the monarch like the Governor and the Commissioner, backed by state force transmitted through law. It is also true that 'Operation Vijiji' was not opera-tionalized through law and there were many abuses. But these abuses were not committed by 'unqualified people' 'relying on their innate common-sense'; rather they were committed by very qualified 'public managers' sent closer to districts and villages in the process of decentralization recommended by another consultant, McKinsey & Co.: 'The "operations" were organized by the Regional Commissioners (or Regional Party Secretaries) assisted by the experienced civil servants who had been sent to the regions and districts in 1972 "decentralization"' (Coulson 1982: 252).

The approach of the Commission to law, legal rules and 'checks and bal-ances' was deliberate and clear. Given the long-standing Tanzanian tradition stretching back to colonial times of giving wide discretionary powers to government organs and officials (including the then governor and now the president), without the consultation of, or reference to, the people's innate sense of justice and fairness, the Commission provided for more rules to control the officials at the top while giving larger discretion to elected organs (for example, *Baraza la Wazee*) and people operating at the bottom. The purpose and aim of this too were clear. The Commission wanted to create an enabling legal framework which would let people's sense of justice, rights, fairness and reasonableness from the bottom jostle for hegemony with the 'imperial/colonial/positivist' notions embedded in received law: 'common law, principles of equity' – innate in the professional dispensers of justice. The Commission recommended that the definition of customary law should be broadened to include custom per se recognized by a Tanzanian community or neighbourhood besides 'native law and custom'. The Commission further recommended that traditional subjecting of customary law to the standards of justice, good sense and morality of 'white' colonial judges (the repugnancy clause in the reception statutes) should be abolished by providing that the received common law and principles of equity should not be 'repugnant to Basic Principles of National Land Policy and principles of justice, fairness and equity held in common by Tanzanian communities' (United Republic of Tanzania 1992). What is more, the *wazee*, selected from the *Mabaraza ya Wazee* and elected by village assemblies, should sit with the magistrate in the circuit land court and the judge in the High Court in all cases, not as advisers on customary law (as if to this day customary law is some law foreign to our judges), but rather they should impart the community's sense of justice and fairness and force the professional judge to take full account of the same.

As for checks and balances, the Commission took a radical step further by applying the venerated liberal constitutional principles of separation of powers and independence of the judiciary at the village level, not confining it to the state level. Thus *Baraza la Wazee* was supposed to be an impartial, independent judicial organ not only when resolving disputes but also in adjudication and registration processes. The draft Land Act, on the other hand, harkens back to the colonial tradition of the hated 'administrative justice' and fusion of power. Thus, the executive organ at the village level, the village council, has powers to impose penalties, including fines, for breaches of conditions although under certain circumstances such remedy has to be approved by another executive organ of the central state, the Commissioner (McAuslan 1996b, cl. 87). Yet, the independent judicial organ, *Baraza la Wazee*, has no criminal jurisdiction whatsoever, thus resurrecting the colonial rationale that the administration of penal/public law could not be entrusted to the 'irresponsible', 'traditional authorities'. The post-Arusha bill has modified slightly the provisions on breaches. The point of principle, however, remains.

Adjudication and issuance of certificates of customary occupancy

Adjudication of land rights and the processes of registration and issuance of certificates of customary occupancy (*hati ya ardhi ya mila*) in the Commission's recommendations is a judicial process involving basic land rights which should be done in an open meeting where any member of the village community has a *locus standi* to object to or support and supplement an application. The Commission reviewed the process of adjudication in Kenya which started in the 1950s to individualize, title and register land held under customary tenure. There have now been a number of studies to show that the virtues attributed to ITR are simply not borne out in practice. What is more, the process works against the interests of the disadvantaged in society.

Furthermore, the whole process is extremely expensive. It means adjudicating and processing millions of titles, hence the Commission recommended against ITR. The Commission opted for a more feasible village-based process of issuing *hati ya ardhi ya mila* which would be done by the village body, the *Baraza la Wazee*, and the records would be kept at the village level.

In the draft Land Act, the adjudication and issuing of certificates of customary occupancy is primarily an elaborate administrative/bureaucratic process under the administration of the executive organ, the village council ('advised' by the village adjudication adviser, a professional person, appointed by the commissioner). The village council is accountable to another executive organ, the Commissioner for Lands. Under certain circumstances, the commissioner may even set aside village adjudication and impose central adjudication.

In many ways, the draft has 'smuggled' in the process of ITR through the back door. For all intents and purposes, the processing of the certificate of customary occupancy is not fundamentally different from processing a granted right of occupancy. In practical terms, such a massive project of titling villagers' lands is virtually impossible. In fact, the whole process is fraught with enormous practical problems and injustices, and these are likely to result in a situation similar to the one that has arisen in Kenya.

The idea of sub-part 4 'land associations' enabling groups to register is reminiscent of Kenya's Land (Group Representatives) Act 1968 and Tanzania's Range Development and Management Act (RDMA) (McAuslan 1996c: 54, 55). The latter, which arose from a UNSAID proposal, was a failure. The Kenyan Act has come under critical review. Some studies have shown that in pastoral areas the Group Representatives Act has meant control by richer members, who have in turn sold off lands to 'outsiders' to the detriment of the majority indigenous people. It is surprising that the draft Act should resurrect Land Associations in spite of this experience and the experience of the RDMA.

Leaving aside the practical and virtually unanswerable argument that the whole section about village adjudication is practically impossible to operate in Tanzanian villages, the concept behind the whole process of adjudication is that it is (1) an administrative/management issue which cannot be trusted to an elected village organ without ultimate control and (2) certainly not to the village judicial organ, *Baraza la Wazee*. That brings me to the final issue of approach to law and, therefore, implicitly to the perspective on rights and justice embedded in it.

Reform through law The Commission's approach was that: (1) the main contours and parameters of the land tenure system should be included in the constitution so as to entrench it in public law and give it visibility; (2) that there should be a basic framework law spelling out the broad principles and rules. Here the approach was to have more rules and procedures requiring transparency and accountability of government officials. The approach also required top organs to be accountable to elected committees and bodies and countervailing bodies to control the exercise of power. At the same time, the Commission's recommendations provided for greater flexibility, discretion and a community sense of fairness to permeate the lower level, as well as exposure of the professional functionaries to the innate wisdom of the people; and (3) the approach continued to apply customary law to village tenure, though the customary law was fundamentally modified by broad democratic principles embodied in the constitution and the Basic Land Law. *Wazee*, for example, are not traditionally elected but the report mandates that they have to be elected. A number of other modifications were also recommended.

In effect, the Commission neither rejected wholly nor accepted uncritically the law or legal methodology to effect radical reform in the tenurial system, but it was minded to reform the statist top-down institutional structures so as to create space for the forces, concepts and perspectives from the bottom. At the same time, the Commission rejected the thoughtless parroting of dominant positivist/liberal market approaches to commoditize land in a blanket fashion. The Commission did this in order to create an enabling environment for the so-called foreign investor. The Commission clearly identified the path of development (national agrarian), the site of accumulation (village), the agency (rich/middle peasantry) and located the tenurial reform in this larger context of political economy.

The approach to law of the Land Act is a far cry from the kind mentioned above. As I have noted, the argument is simply for more law, and that is considered revolutionary. The basic question is, more law for whom? Whether there are issues of social justice and equity involved and how these could be addressed does not seem to be a serious concern, even, in Professor McAuslan's memorial lecture. Normally, it would be unfair to accuse a consultant because he cannot do anything more than translate the policy brief given him. If that had been the sole defence of Professor McAuslan, one would probably be wasting time arguing. But the memorial lecture argues that the consultant was very much involved in policy choices and not simply in the technical task of drafting rules/law. If this is so, it is only proper that he should be academically accountable for the particular choices made by him, which he sets out to defend and justify.

Conclusion

In the final paragraphs of 'Making Law Work', Professor McAuslan turns to the role of academic lawyer and argues that the major challenge for scholarship with respect to land reform in Africa is

> to rise above the merely descriptive and analytical approach to writing about land law and adopt a more policy-orientated and innovative approach which offers new models and creative ideas as solutions to practical problems of land management and if the opportunity presents itself, become involved in the challenging business of turning these ideas and models into legislative drafts; let no one suggest that that is not a scholarly endeavor. Creative not just critical scholarship is needed. (McAuslan 1996a: 38)

Undoubtedly, no one would argue that academics should not be involved in policy debates and in offering creative ideas. That is not new either, for it has been part of the debate by intellectuals in Africa. Although, with the onslaught of a new type of scholarship called 'consultancy', we may be losing the capacity to raise questions of intellectual commitment. This debate on different perspectives on justice and rights embedded in Professor McAuslan's draft and the Commission's report raises a question of a different order than that posed by Professor McAuslan. What kind of perspectives of justice, fairness, and equity are we advancing when we as academic lawyers are involved in law and policy reform? First and foremost, do we accept that (1) there are contradictory perspectives on justice and fairness and that these are neither historically nor socially universal and (2) that by making certain policy choices (even within the narrower confines of paid consultancies) we may be involved in creating methodologies and structures which advance certain perspectives while suppressing or delegitimizing others?

McAuslan concludes with an interesting thought which raises a host of questions for many of us who are involved in the current market-driven reforms at various levels in Africa: 'In sum, while land law reform might, just, still be the preserve of the lawyer, the products of that reform – the new laws – are the property of the nation and the nation must be stimulated whole-heartedly to embrace those laws. Only in this way can law be made to work to restructure land relations in Africa' (McAuslan 1996a: 39)

Why is land law reform still the preserve of the lawyer? Is this because the 'unqualified' people who form the large majority of the nation may find it too technical and, therefore, beyond their reach? Or is it because the legal reforms we are proposing or are involved in have not had their (people's) input? If the challenge of legal scholarship is to be creative and innovative, is it not possible to innovate/reform in a fashion which will translate the interests, perspectives and notions of justice and fairness of the large majority into law? If that is not attempted, then do we have the right to expect such a law to become the property of the nation?

These are precisely the questions that have been raised in this paper. The perspectives of justice, rights and fairness embedded in the law reform recommended in the Commission's report are contradictory to those underlying the draft Land Act. They are not only contradictory but are also locked in struggle. In this contestation, one of the perspectives is undoubtedly proving to become dominant by the logic of force (the state). But whether it can also become the property of the nation, i.e. hegemonic, is a different issue. The draft Land Act and the National Land Policy which forms its basis have not been publicly debated. Rather, they were discussed in closed workshops attended by invited people by virtue of their various qualifications. A call for a public debate (see Shivji 1996) of the policy has been simply ignored while the sponsors of the consultant and other sources have been very keen to see that the draft Land Act is steamrollered through the Parliament as soon as possible.

Have the people really accepted the policy underlying the draft Act? In a few workshops held by HAKIARDHI (an NGO), whose main aim is to popularize and facilitate a debate on the Commission's report, people have largely endorsed the Commission's recommendations. They are wary of what is suggested in the draft Land Act (see *Rai*, February 1997 issues). Clearly, then, such a law, if passed, has little chance of becoming the nation's property.

A national consensual legal ideology cannot be constructed except in contestation between the existing Western/statist/liberal concepts of justice and rights and the social democratic conceptions and perceptions ('*hatukushirikishwa*', right of peoples to life and self-determination) of the large majority, the popular classes.

Finally, it must be emphasized that if the law has to have legitimacy and therefore be workable, it must be debated by the public. What is crucial to its success is how far the people have participated in developing its major basis.

Notes

1. In this regard, I think, Mamdani (1996: 111 et seq.) probably exaggerates the civilizing mission of what he calls civil law in Africa.

2. Discussing the concept of 'public lands' in the Land Ordinance, Van Rees, the Belgian representative of the Permanent Mandates Commission, observed: 'It appears to be more likely that he [the draftsman] did not wish to establish a legal relation between what are known as "public lands" and the State, and that consequently he had in view merely an administrative relation in the sense that these lands have been placed in their entirety under Government control' (quoted in Lyall 1973: 86).

3. There was a plethora of agriculture by-laws providing criminal sanctions against breaches. They mainly dealt with mandatory provisions to cultivate specified acres of food and cash crops, quality controls, 'good' husbandry and so on. This practice continued into the post-colonial era. See, generally, Shivji 1987.

4. This is precisely the kind of dilemma that gives rise to the debate between radical reformers who advocate working through law and revolutionaries who posit an ultimate overthrow of the state. In the 1970s and 1980s these debates were much more prominent than today (see Shivji 1986b, for example). In the human rights context, the whole development of social action litigation in India, now spreading in other Asian jurisdictions, revolves around this tension (see Cottrell 1993).

5. The confusion between the vesting of radical title in the state and the inherent powers of eminent domain is even more pronounced in Mukoyogo and Rutinwa 1994.

6. This study shows that the so-called decentralization stifled and muffled local participation whether direct or indirect through elected representatives. It was the decentralized officials of the central government and party functionaries who reigned supreme in decision-making bodies.

7. In this respect, Mazrui's succinct comparison between the practitioners of Western and customary law is very apposite.

The practitioners of customary law, he says: do not constitute a formal liberal profession (attorneys, solicitors and barristers). Traditional experts of customary law are elders or experienced members of the community, normally without formal qualifications. Nor is there formal licensing for indigenous legal practice. Customary law is much less of a livelihood or money-making occupation than the kind of legal practice which came with Western colonisation. At the other extreme is precisely the legacy which came with Western culture. Under this legacy, one becomes a lawyer by formal training at a university or (where imperially appropriate) an Inn of Court. Laws are codified and precisely formulated in writing. The precise language of the law is often as important as the spirit of the law. Every word matters in the text of the law, or the texts of previous judgments. On the whole, Western law is rooted in the written tradition rather than the oral – although oratorical skills in court are often of considerable relevance. Under the Western umbrella, practitioners of the law are a professional money-making fraternity with some control over qualifications necessary for practice. They also help decide the ethics which are to govern the profession – including a role in awarding or withdrawing licenses to practice. (Mazrui 1989: 252, 253)

References

Chanock, M. (1991) 'A Peculiar Sharpness: An Essay on Property in the History of Customary Law in Colonial Africa', *Journal of African History*, 32: 65–88.

Chossudovsky, M. (1996) 'Apartheid Moves to Sub-Suharan Africa', *Third World Resurgence*, 76: 11–17.

Cottrell, J. (1993) 'Third Generation Rights and Social Action Litigation', in S. Adelman and A. Paliwala (eds), *Law and Crisis in Third World*, London: Hans Zell, pp. 102–26.

Coulson, A. (1982) *Tanzania: A Political Economy*. Oxford: Clarendon Press.

Fine, B. (1984) *Democracy and the Rule of Law: Liberal Ideals and Marxist Critique*, London: Pluto Press.

Ghai, Y. (1986) 'The Rule of Law, Legitimacy and Governance', *International Journal of Sociology of Law*, 14: 179–208.

Lyall, A. B. (1973) 'Land Law and Policy in Tanganyika', LLM thesis, University of Dar es Salaam.

McAuslan, P. (1996a) 'Making Law Work: Restructuring Land Relations in Africa', Third Alistair Berkeley Memorial Lecture (30 May 1996) London School of Economics, London.

— (1996b) 'On a Draft Bill for a Land Act', Second National Land Workshop Organized by the Ministry of Lands, Housing and Urban Development, Arusha, November.

— (1996c) 'Clause by Clause Commentary on a Draft Bill for the Land Act', prepared for the Ministry of Lands, Housing and Urban Development, December.

Mafeje, A. (1995) 'Theory of Democracy and the African Discourse: Breaking Bread with My Fellow-travellers', in E. Cole and J. Ibrahim (eds), *Democratization Processes in Africa*, Dakar: CODESRIA, pp. 5–27.

Mamdami, M. (1996) *Citizen and Subject: Contemporary Africa and the Legacy of Late Colonialism*, Princeton, NJ: Princeton University Press.

Mazrui, A. A. (1989) 'Post-colonial Society and Africa's Triple Heritage of Law: Indigenous, Islamic and Western Tendencies', in N. MacCormick and Z. Bankowski (eds), *Enlightenment, Rights and Revolution: Essays in Legal and Social Philosophy*, Aberdeen: University of Aberdeen Press, pp. 252–70.

Meek, C. K. (1946) 'A Note on Crown Lands in the Colonies', *Journal of Comparative Legislation and International Law*, 28.

Mukoyogo, M. C. and B. Rutinwa (1994) 'Comments on the Report of the Law Tenure Study Group and Professor Shivji's Comments Thereon', Dar es Salaam: University of Dar es Salaam.

Mushi, S. S. (1978) 'Popular Participation and Regional Development Planning: The Politics of Decentralized Administration', *Tanzania Notes and Records*, 83: 63–97.

North, D. C. (1990) *Institutions, Institutional Change and Economic Performance*, Cambridge: Cambridge University Press.

Nyerere, J. K. (1966) *Freedom and Unity: A Selection from Writings and Speeches*, Dar es Salaam: Oxford University Press.

Okoth-Ogendo, H. W. (1991) 'Constitutions without Constitutionalism', in I. G. Shivji (ed.), *State and Constitutionalism: An African Debate on Democracy*, Harare: SAPES, pp. 3–26.

Platteau, J. (1995) 'Reforming Land Rights in Sub-Saharan Africa: Issues of Efficiency and Equity', Geneva: United Nations Research Institute for Social Development Discussion Paper, 60.

Shaidi, L. P. (1985) 'Explaining Crime and Social Control in Tanzania Mainland: An Historical Socio-economic Perspective', PhD dissertation, University of Dar es Salaam.

Shivji, I. G. (1986a) 'Introduction', in I. G. Shivji (ed.), *State and the Working People in Tanzania*, Dakar: CODESRIA, pp. 1–15.

— (1986b) 'Limits of Legal Radicalism: Reflections on Teaching Law at the University of Dar es Salaam', Dar es Salaam: University of Dar es Salaam, Faculty of Law.

— (1987) 'The Roots of the Agrarian Crisis in Tanzania: Theoretical Perspectives', *Eastern Africa Social Science Research Review*, 3(1): 11–34.

— (1992) 'The Politics of Liberalization in Tanzania: Notes on the Crisis of Ideological Hegemony', in H. Campbell and H. Stein (eds), *Tanzania and the IMF: The Dynamics of Liberalization*, Boulder, CO: Westview Press, pp. 67–85.

— (1994) *A Legal Quagmire: Tanzania's Regulation of Land Tenure (Establishment of Villages) Act, 1992*, Pastoral Land Tenure Series 5, London: IIED.

— (1995) 'The Rule of Law and *Ujamaa* in the Ideological Formation of Tanzania', *Social and Legal Studies*, 4: 147–74.

— (1996) 'Grounding the Debate on Land: National Land Policy and its Implications', paper presented at the workshop on land, April 1996.

— (1997) 'Constructing a New Rights Regime: Promises, Problems and Prospects', *Utafiti*, 3: 253–76.

United Republic of Tanzania (1992) *Report of the Presidential Commission of Enquiry into Land Matters*, vols I and II, published in association with the Scandinavian Institute of African Studies: Uppsala, Sweden.

— (1993) Ministry of Lands, Housing and Urban Development, *Draft of the National Land Policy*, Dar es Salaam.

— (1995) Ministry of Lands, Housing and Urban Development, *National Land Policy*, Dar es Salaam.

Wamba-dia-Wamba, E. (1991) 'Discourse on the National Question', in I. G. Shivji (ed.), *State and Constitutionalism: An African Debate on Democracy*, Harare: SAPES, pp. 57–70.

Williams, D. V. (1982) 'State Coercion Against Peasant Farmers: The Tanzanian State', *Journal of Legal Pluralism* 20: 95–127.

EIGHT

The Effects of Land Tenure on Women's Access and Control of Land in Kenya

Akinyi Nzioki

Background and Context

This chapter aims to highlight issues involved in land tenure reform and the effects this has had on women as food producers. It presents an analysis of current gender relations given the land tenure reform, relations that I argue are crucial to formulating policies through which Kenyan women as food producers can advance. Policies concerning women have long been pre-occupied with wage employment, education, health, water and women's role in agriculture, yet the single most important economic factor affecting the situation of the majority of Kenyan women today is the gender gap over land.

Land and land tenure issues have been and continue to be at the heart of events in Kenya. Founded as a settler colony, the colonial government set aside substantial amounts (c. 44,000 square kilometres) of the most productive land for Europeans, while Africans were shunted into reserve areas (Riddell and Dickerman 1986: 85). Demands for land by Africans remained a constant theme in the colonial era, leading to the Mau Mau rebellion. Landlessness, the fragmentation of holdings and crowded conditions increasingly became critical problems in the African reserve, as indeed they are today, despite the extensive programmes of land registration consolidation and resettlement programmes undertaken in the Highlands and other areas since independence.

Land is the basis of Kenya's economy. Despite this fact, an increasing number of Kenyans find themselves without sufficient land to grow food to feed their families or, worse, without land at all. Kenya covers an area of 581,751 square kilometres, of which 571,416 kilometres is dry land and 11,230 square kilometres is open water (Republic of Kenya 1984: 70). As a result of adverse physical conditions, unreliable rainfall and poor soils, over 80 per cent of the land available in Kenya is classified as low potential and therefore unsuitable for crop production (Mathangani 1989: 9). While agriculture is declining, the population growth rate has been advancing. In 1969, Kenya's population stood at 11 million but almost doubled to 21 million in 1989, at a growth rate of 3.8 per cent per year. The current growth rate is 3.34 per cent with an estimated population of 24 million, out of which 21.6 million are in the rural areas (Republic of Kenya 1994: 1, 2). These statistics have more implications for the already severely limited land resource. Given this trend, there is a growing concern over the country's future ability to feed its population.

In order to address these problems and to guide and develop the production of food to meet the country's requirements, the Kenyan government has over the years formulated a series of policies which address various aspects of the agricultural sector. The main goal of this policy on economic management for renewed growth is self-sustenance, growth, employment and diversification (Republic of Kenya 1986: 89; 1989: 22). The Kenyan government's land policy aims at achieving optimum land utilization by intensifying agriculture and adopting the correct management practices to conserve the soil and to sustain the population (Republic of Kenya 1989: 54). Together with this, government policy on nutrition and food security aims to increase and diversify food production at the household level (Republic of Kenya 1989: 22).

In Kenya, as in many other regions of the developing world, women play a crucial role in agriculture as producers and providers of food. More than 80 per cent of the women in Kenya live in rural areas, playing multifaceted roles in this sector as small farmers, income earners and family caretakers (Nadine 1989). They are the prominent economic actors in land-related activities, with a major stake in crop and small stock husbandry, crop preservation, processing and marketing, and food preparation for both domestic consumption and sale. Women contribute 80 per cent of agricultural labour, 70 per cent of hours worked in farming, they carry out 60 per cent of the marketing and produce some 60 per cent of domestically produced food (Jiggins 1988). Land-based opportunity thus remains the basis of incomes and livelihoods in the rural areas. Male migration to urban areas in search of paid employment has left women in charge of small-scale farming activities. Women are, therefore, a critical link in achieving food security, and land is a significant factor in the household food security equation. Supportive agricultural policies recognizing this critical link between women and food production will definitely influence their ability to contribute to household food security.

At this time, when the total production of food in the country is decreasing and cannot adequately feed the growing population, there is an urgent need to look into the constraints of those who produce food in order to identify their needs and address the constraints in order to increase production. Some of the explanations given for Kenya's declining ability to feed itself include drought, desertification, disease, mismanagement and suggestions that there may be a certain endemic incapability on the part of the people involved to feed themselves. The immediacy with which food aid has to be sought obscures the fact that food shortages occur as a result of a multiplicity of factors, each of which perhaps contributes a small percentage to the total deficit in food, and all of which contribute significantly to the suffering that results from empty stomachs (Ndumbu 1985: 32). One of the most neglected factors causing the shortage of food has been the non-availability of production resources to women. Only a few studies have been carried out to determine the debilitating factors in the food deficit for African countries, and even fewer have been carried out to discover how the talents, time and energies of women can be utilized at the national planning levels to stem the food shortage.

Strategies to encourage African agriculture must be multifaceted and must address the various different parts of the farming system. In Kenya, as in most sub-Saharan countries, 'the focus must be on the needs of women farmers for it is on them that the improvement of agriculture and food production will largely depend' (Republic of Kenya and UNICEF 1988: 56). If women are currently the major food producers, then their productivity will depend not only on improving the basic resource (land) which they use in production, but will also be determined by how much access to and control they have over these resources.

At present, the livelihood of over 80 per cent of the Kenyan population is directly dependent on agriculture. Land is, of course, one of the basic factors of production for food and other agricultural products. This poses a dynamic situation in which the rural population and changing technology interact with the existing institutional structures of rural society. This dynamism means that a solution which was appropriate ten years ago may be inappropriate today.

Land has been and continues to be the most significant form of property in rural Kenya and is a critical determinant of economic well-being, social status and political power. The Kenyan government has pursued programmes to transform customary land tenure into statutory freehold tenure through land adjudication, consolidation and registration. It is estimated that by 1984, 1.5 million titles had already been issued, over 6 million parcels of land adjudicated and 5.5 million hectares surveyed for adjudication and registration (Republic of Kenya 1984: 105). The problem is that the titled land is being transferred almost exclusively to individual men, thereby leaving no provision on how women's access rights are to be defined and how women will realize goals of privatization once the land is registered in an individual male's name. Land title deeds not only increase men's control over distribution of land, but also make women dependent on men.

In this scenario, women have access to land only through male kin. The precise nature of those rights is further conditioned by their position in their natal or their husband's lineage, their marital status, and their age. Moreover, derived rights do not include the rights typically associated with ownership rights to use land, to raise loans, to rent, sell, dispose by will or make permanent improvements. Changes in family composition, land law and economic structures increasingly tend to make women's access rights to land less secure. This directly threatens women's ability to produce food and maintain their families. It also means that women cannot treat land solely as an economic asset. Their management, independence and right to the products of land are therefore compromised. As land becomes scarce and begins to assume a capital value, and as pressure builds for increased cash crop production, women and men are affected in different ways. For example, the male rather than the female more often controls intra-family decisions related to agricultural production. Land traditionally allocated for women for food crop production is being reallocated for cash crops. The cash crops are almost always under the control of men. Cash crops are given first priority in terms of soil fertility, number of hectares and distance when allocating family land. Women are left to grow food crops from shrinking and fragmented farmsteads, backyard gardens and poor soils without the resources necessary to increase their productivity.

The pertinent questions in this chapter address four main issues. Has land tenure reform enabled women to own land? What are the negative and positive impacts of land tenure reform with regard to women's ownership of land? What are the effects of land tenure reform on women's decision-making power in agricultural production? How has land tenure reform impacted on the division of family labour? Have women benefited from the objectives of land tenure reform?

Several interconnected arguments support the need for women to have defined rights in arable lands. Studies conducted in Asia indicate that among poor households, women's lack of rights to land is linked to the household's risk of poverty and destitution (Kumar 1978: 207–41; Gulati 1978: A27–A47). Notable differences have been found in how women and men in poor households spend their incomes. Women of poor households typically spend almost all their incomes to purchase goods for the family's general consumption. Men usually spend a significant part on their personal needs like tobacco and liquor (Agarwal 1994: 28–30). A corollary to this gender difference in spending patterns is research which suggests that children's nutritional status tends to be more positively linked to the mother's earnings than the father's.

The risk of poverty and the physical well-being of a woman and her children could depend significantly on whether she has direct access to income and productive assets such as land, and not just access mediated through her husband or other male family members (Agarwal 1994: 6, 7). Within this general argument, the case for rights to land is especially strong. Direct advantages of accessing land are the possibilities of growing crops, trees, vegetable gardens, keeping livestock or practising sericulture. The indirect advantages include the ability to mortgage, sell or rent in times of crisis. Nevertheless, given the noted biases in the intra-family distribution of benefits from household resources, exclusive male rights in land, which would render the household less susceptible to poverty by some average measure, will not automatically provide this protection to all its members, and especially not to its female members. Thus, on the grounds of both women's and children's welfare, there is a strong case for protecting, ensuring and supporting women's rights to land independently of men.

Land tenure reform should favour not just the masses of the rural popula-tion, but women in particular, who represent well over half the agricultural labour force in this country, with an increasing number becoming *de jure* and *de facto* household heads who continue to use land as their primary source of existence, but without titles to the land they are cultivating. In Kenya, although a quarter of the household heads are women, only 5 per cent of women own land in their own names.

Providing women with legal rights to land they cultivate gives them an infrastructural support which could help increase output, by increasing their access to credit and to technology and information on productivity. Thus, the provision of secure land rights could make it easier for women to adopt improved agricultural technology and practices as well as enhance their motiva-tion to do so, and so increase overall production. In addition, the provision of land to women could have other indirect benefits, such as reducing immigration to the cities, both of the women themselves and of the family members dependent on them. Also, improved farm incomes in women's hands could generate a higher demand for non-farm goods that are produced locally, thus in turn create more rural jobs (Jiggins 1988: 10). It is, therefore, critically important to highlight issues regarding women's land rights and to generate suggestions and ideas which may bring about benefits and possible changes, the least of which is increased potential of women in food production. This, in turn, will benefit the whole country irrespective of gender.

It is recognized in the *Kenyan Development Plan 1989–1993* that women have always occupied a central role in African economies, being the main agricultural producers and suppliers of welfare services at the household and community levels. It is further stated in the Plan that the government is working towards the restoration of women's social status which was eroded during the colonial period, to an active role not only in the development of the economy but also in the ownership and control of wealth arising from economic production (Republic of Kenya 1989: 27).

Nevertheless, the above stated plan has not provided guidelines or discussed strategies for intervention. In this chapter, however, I recognize that not all forms of property are equally significant in all contexts, nor are they equally coveted. In an agrarian economy such as Kenya, arable land is the most valuable form of property, for its economic as well as its political and symbolic importance. It is a productive, wealth-creating and livelihood-sustaining asset. For many, land provides a sense of identity and rootedness within the village, and in people's minds land has a durability and permanence which no other asset possesses.

Increasingly, local newspaper reports are beginning to bring out women's voices of lament by highlighting the importance many attach to having rights of access and control to land, such as women divorced or deserted by their husbands and left landless, widows deprived of their rightful shares by prosperous brothers-in-law, left destitute and forced to seek wage work or even beg for survival (*Daily Nation*, 15 December 1988, section II, p. 22; *Kenya Times*, 24 May 1993, p. 10). For a significant majority of rural households, arable land is likely to remain for a long time the single most important source of security against poverty, even if it ceases to be the sole source of livelihood for many. As already stated, land defines social status and political power in the village, and structures relationships both within and outside the household. Yet for most women, effective rights in land remain elusive, even as their marital and familial support erodes and female-led households multiply. Only a small number of women own land, and even fewer can exercise effective control over it. Yet the voice of the disinherited female peasant has, until recently, gone largely unheard, not only by policy-makers, but also by grassroot groups and academics.

Framework of Analysis

I analyse changing gender relations with respect to land rights in the human rights paradigm. The UN Declaration on the Elimination of Discrimination

Against Women includes, among other tenets, the right to equality of men and women in the family and equal rights regarding property and inheritance. At present, there is little evidence to suggest that Kenya is actively pursuing policies of non-discrimination. For example, the Kenyan constitution remains quiet on discrimination on the basis of sex. Nothing so far has been done about cultural values which sometimes are directly antithetical to individual women's rights such as women's equal rights in the family.

Discussion of international human rights includes agreement that economic or subsistence rights are as important as civil and political rights. The rights of rural women to take part in development programmes and to have equal access to agricultural credit and equal participation in cooperatives and agrarian reform schemes are vital. If such economic and social rights in theory were granted in practice, Kenyan women would benefit substantially from the agricultural infrastructural support and services provided for their affectivity in food production.

From a philosophical point of view, if human rights includes the rights of all people by virtue of their humanity, these rights must include women as well as men. From a practical point of view, economic development is unlikely to occur in Africa unless the needs and wants of women are considered. Agricultural projects that ignore the prominent role of women in agricultural production, as well as the differential power of women and men in the home, will not succeed in their goals (Howard 1986: 222). As the culturally-approved view of women's roles is changing as social structures change, women's rights must be protected in law and practice, particularly when real constraints on human rights are hindered by differential access to material resources between women and men.

Land tenure reform, which is part of the agrarian reform adopted by the Kenyan government, includes, among other things, the promotion of equity. Thus, equity remains a central concept in development planning, particularly in terms of creating equal opportunities for everyone, irrespective of gender. Gender equality is a measure of a just society, in which equality of rights over productive resources is an important part. It is within this framework that Kenyan women would like to see themselves as equal partners in the management of both household and national affairs. Although equality of opportunities is granted to all citizens by the Kenyan constitution, women's ability to achieve equality of land rights is disadvantaged by the low status given to women in their families, the community, the nation as a whole and the continued discrimination on the basis of sex (Republic of Kenya Constitution, section 82). These gender gaps need to be bridged if Kenyans are to move towards a more just society. In this chapter, my central argument is that if women are to enjoy equality with men in life-long access to and ownership of land regardless of their marital status, then their land rights must be secure. Providing women with legal rights to land would not only empower them economically, but would also strengthen their ability to challenge social and political gender inequalities. That is, land rights would enhance women's freedom to achieve and give them the opportunity to function in non-economic spheres such as politics.

The Dilemma in Studying Land Tenure Systems in Africa

In Africa, the term 'customary land law' has been used to describe the land tenure system practised by Africans. The common feature of the customary land tenure in Africa is its customary origin and its generally unwritten form (Mitsud 1967: 15). Dealing with customary tenurial systems is not an easy matter since the system is different from property concepts in the West. According to Noronha and Lathem (1983: ii), customary land tenure consists of, 'the rules accepted by a group of the ways in which land is held, used, transferred and transmitted'.

An abundant and available resource prior to colonial occupation, land was rarely 'owned' in the Western sense of exclusive alienable rights invested in one individual in exchange for cash. For this reason there is confusion over terms related to land rights, such as 'tenure' (land holding rights), 'usufruct' (rights to use land), 'freehold' (holding exclusive rights but transferable), and 'ownership' (cash valued land with title for individual or group) (Meek 1946: 90). 'Control' in the African property system was a collective responsibility over land resources which ensured that rights were equitably distributed through time among all members of the society. Okoth-Ogendo, a renowned researcher on land tenure systems, firmly believes that: 'Tenure regimes cannot be adequately explained by directing inquiries into whether or not African social systems knew or recognized the institution of ownership and whether if they did that, ownership was "absolute" or corporate and who in society, the individual, the chief, the family, the clan, the lineage or the "tribe" was the repository of that ownership' (Okoth-Ogendo 1989: 6, 7).

Thus, access related to land use activities carried a varying degree of control exercised at different levels of political organization. This control authority was vested in the grandfather, lineage or clan, but the exercise of this power did not involve exclusive appropriation or distribution 'upon whim and will'.

Western scholars have written about land and customary law with the framework of Anglo-American law, which centres around the concept of 'ownership' during the feudal period when land belonged to the crown and the tillers of land were tenants. In this context, to describe tenure systems as communal, chiefly usufructuary, obviously distorts the very complex relations that rule the customary property law and the manner in which they function (Okoth-Ogendo 1981: 339).

The idea of ownership was important for colonists, who resolved that African rights in land were usufruct only, and that whatever was not under cultivation or occupied was vacant. In the case of Kenya, the sovereign colonial power was free to grant this vacant land to the settlers (Okoth-Ogendo 1979: 23).

Since land systems are dynamic and also vary from community to community, this places obvious limits on the value of broad generalization about African systems of land tenure. The suggested approach to the comparative study of land tenure systems can be conceptualized in the questions: Who holds what interest in the parcel of land? Is the group the holders or owners of land? An apportioned parcel of land owned by a group: is that 'a single and undivided control' over the piece? The village and the community represent a type of customary association that represents itself as a company or a cooperative where the interest holders are the individuals (Bentsi-Enchill 1965).

Antony Allot has suggested that a definition of absolute ownership is a starting point in the light of traditional laws. This is a starting point in order to see if it is possible to isolate the type of interest holders in land (Allot 1958: 34). This view is opposed by Simpson who writes that the word 'ownership' has no God-given meaning. Since ownership is an ordinary English expression, it will be easy to recognize, although Simpson recognizes that one might have difficulties in defining 'rights' which, according to him, have simply not developed into 'ownership' (Simpson 1986: 5).

Shadrack Gutto explains that the term 'ownership' in its present connotation should not be used; instead, 'allodial rights' should be the term used. According to him, this term is more legitimate in that the individual head of the family had the right of occupation and transmission only to members of the family. In this sense, Gutto warns that this type of control should not be confused with the feudal system, since the head of the family had no authority to dispossess the occupier. Neither was the occupier liable to pay rent in terms of labour or otherwise (Gutto 1987: 50).

It is apparent from the literature that the term 'ownership' is fraught with confusion, largely because the popular concept of the term influences perception. Nevertheless, in the African context, the individuals' clans have been allocated defined rights to land and obligations with respect to 'control', 'ownership', exploitation of the resources, and continued attachment of the family.

An Historical Background to Land Tenure Reform in Kenya

Recognizing the broad context of the land reform issue, this section focuses on gender relations with respect to land in Kenya. This land has been modified by a major intrusion of colonialism, accompanied by capitalist notions of production and reproduction. Such conditions of change should be seen within an historical perspective. In this section, therefore, we look at the historical changes that have taken place from the pre-colonial, colonial and present times, and how women have related to land, given the dynamic changes over time.

The pre-colonial system of land tenure

Historical concepts and symbols of land In the period before the advent of colonialism, land was the cornerstone of African civilization. It defined the African way of life, it was the focal point of African solidarity, it determined the spirituality and sense of belonging, and it symbolized the economic status of a people (Wanjala 1995).

In Africa, land assumes many forms that order relationships between people, both living and dead. Land structures relations between groups within society and between people and the supernatural world (Davison 1987a: 15). In this sense, land is sacred and the pre-colonial, pre-capitalist societies recognized this duality. Soil is used in symbolic rituals to express a society's attitude towards sex and gender relations. Previously, human contact with land was structured by religious beliefs that viewed the earth as a sacred female entity. Most of the time, soil symbolizes fertility. For example, among the Bukusu of Western Kenya, boys are smeared with mud during the time of initiation to ensure their future fertility as adult males. The Luo of Western Kenya perform sexual rituals for the earth to ensure the fertility of crops while the Gikuyu of Central Kenya ritualized a marriage ceremony (e.g. *guthinjiro*) whereby an elder linked a woman's family with a man's by mixing soil brought from a man's home with blood from a goat belonging to the man's family (Davison 1987a: 16).

The sacredness of land sometimes extends to the products of land. The '*mugumo*' tree is a sacred shrine to the Gikuyu. The Ibo of Nigeria believe that certain groves of trees and land belong to particular deities. Historically, land was perceived as belonging to the ancestors to be held in perpetuity (Obi 1963: 54).

A generalization has emerged describing African land tenure as 'communal', although there has not been an agreement on how it was politically admin-istered. Nevertheless, at the community level, land was and still is defined in terms of relations between kin and neighbours. In many communities, land was held by a village or family male head of age who had a good knowledge of lineage history and land use patterns and was considered a trustee and not an owner of the group's land (Okoth-Ogendo 1976: 150). It was his respon-sibility, in consultation with lineage elders, to allocate land to heads of families depending upon need and availability.

During a lifetime, a landowner could loan, lease, pledge or pawn a piece of land for temporary use. Land could be promised as a means of paying debts or tribute, it could be pawned in exchange for cash or goods for a wedding, bridewealth or funeral. In some instances livestock were exchanged for temporary use rights (Pala 1978: 27). However, the exchange of goods for land was never viewed as the transfer of permanent rights. Land was not alienated permanently without the consent of the trustee group, whether the group was family, clan or community (Obi 1963: 124; Okere 1983: 97; Moyana 1984: 31). In cases where a portion of land was held throughout a person's lifetime, land rights would revert to the ancestors, lineage group, family and especially to sons in the cases of patrilineal inheritance (Kaberry 1952: 42). Consequently, the degree to which females inherited land depended upon the way gender struc-turing was imposed through male kin (Davison 1987a: 18–19; 1987b: 162–3).

Patterns of land use and tenure   Among African societies there is no single method of classifying land for purposes of use and occupation. Some types of land were classified for residential use, crop land, and pasturage for single families (Sheddick 1953: 57). Schapera makes a distinction between three types of fields: those used by the male compound head, those reserved for the wife or wives, and those designated as common household fields (Schapera 1955: 203). Among the Luo of Western Kenya, land rights have been defined by kinship and length of cultivation. '*Wuon lowo*' refers to rights in lineage land which a person holds throughout his lifetime. Rights in short use is '*kwayo puodho*' (Pala 1978). The Bukusu of Western Kenya also divide rights in long-term occupancy for use by male family members. This is called '*kumukundu*', and short-term cultiva-tion usually by women is called '*silundu*' (Davison 1987a: 12; 1987c: 24). Other classifications are based upon control by occupants; sacred land is controlled by ancestors.

Under adverse conditions of cyclical drought and inherently poor soil conditions, African cultivators developed several survival strategies. They planted drought-resistant crops such as millet, sorghum and tubers. They intercropped legumes and cereal crops to maintain soil fertility and keep down weeds. They practised shifting cultivation and fallowing to allow soil recuperation. They planted in different ecological zones, and when the population outgrew the arable land they migrated to other areas and had first use rights. According to Davison, land was viewed as an economic resource that people had an obligation to use wisely for the good of the community on behalf of the ancestors who were often perceived as spiritual guardians (Davison 1987a: 10).

Thus, customary land occupancy and use practices tended to be inclusive rather than exclusive – that is, no one who needed land went landless. Communal groups and individuals had usufruct rights to land, which were viewed as temporary and redeemable in varying degrees (Davison 1987a: 11). The emphasis was placed on access to land for sustenance of human and social life rather than ownership of land. In this scenario, even strangers gained acceptability in communities by being granted access rights.

Many scholars writing on pre-colonial land tenure systems in Africa have often found it difficult to identify or generalize the system that prevailed during this time. This has been mainly due to lack of authentic literature on the subject, faulty anthropological and historical accounts of Western studies, and mostly because of the diversity and complexities of traditional societies (Kibwana 1990: 231). Okoth-Ogendo writes that:

> Access to land has been specific to a function, for example, cultivation or grazing. Thus, in any given community, a number of persons could each hold a right or a bundle of rights expressing specific range, of functions ... a village could claim grazing rights over a parcel, subject to the hunting rights of another, the transit rights of a third and cultivation rights of the fourth. (Okoth-Ogendo 1976: 154)

One thing is clear, though: each person in a community had rights of access to the land depending on the specific needs of the person at the time. Cultivation rights were generally allocated and controlled at the extended family level, the grazing rights were controlled by a much wider segment of society. To control land was to guarantee rights to allocate it to other members of the community. Those who controlled land did not 'own' land to the exclusion of everybody else (Wanjala and Musymi 1990: 10). Kibwana says that the proper grasp of the principles of land holding reveals that it is conceptually wrong to identify 'chiefs' or 'leaders' in pre-colonial Kenya who 'owned' land or were trustees on behalf of members of an ethnic group (Kibwana 1990: 233)

The family head was responsible for allocating land to families and was accorded great respect and obedience, and those under him had a strong sense of their own rights and obligations. The obligations included a fair distribution of land and settling disputes that arose from land usage. In this way, the family head obtained a position of power in the administration of the land. As distinct societies emerged, gradual changes occurred and loose and non-defined tenures were replaced by definite recognizable land rights attached to individuals, and at times whole communities. Thus, the indigenous tenure arrangements have historically been dynamic and adaptive to economic and technological changes. The tenure arrangements that gradually emerged were governed by principles relevant to pre-industrial economies relying on kinship as the primary organizing factor. The rules governing access and use of land were determined primarily on one's membership and status in the social group controlling a particular territory (Wanjala 1995: 7).

Land rights and gender relations To what extent did women have greater rights to land in the pre-colonial tenure structure? Pala, Okoth-Ogendo and Verhelst claim that the pre-colonial land tenure system benefited women (Pala 1978: 51; Okoth-Ogendo 1982a: 61; Verhelst 1970: 143). On the other hand, Friedl argues that because men have always cleared land in Africa, collectively they have been able to gain land at the expense of women (Friedl 1975: 54). Women were never allowed by themselves to initiate the process of cultivating new or long fallowed land. Thus, first-use rights disadvantaged women. Anthropologist Karen Sacks examines the shifts in the mode of production. She argues that the transition from gathering, hunting and simple horticulture to more complex agriculture resulted in women's loss of power regarding the assignment of labour tasks and allocation of goods because control was increasingly vested in male-dominated kin groups (Sacks 1979: 68).

Boserup asserts that, historically, plentiful arable land coupled with low population density resulted in a gender specialization of agricultural labour that benefited both sexes. While men felled trees and cleared land, women cultivated it. In the pre-colonial period, women had virtual control and monopoly of crop production, given the complementary division of labour between women and men. This led to women having land they controlled for the maintenance of their households. With colonialism, the European agricultural agents, accustomed to male farming systems, engaged African males in export crop production for European markets. Further, Boserup points out that the introduction of cash cropping, with its emphasis upon male-controlled agricultural intensification, is a primary determinant of women's loss of status and power in African agriculture (Boserup 1970: 53–7).

The security of rights to land was guaranteed and protected by the very principle under which the initial rights were acquired – the principles of kinship, residence or allegiance. Land formed the focus of social relations, and as long as these relations which gave rights to land were maintained, the question of insecurity of land seldom became a pertinent issue (Verhelst 1970: 47). For example, Pala, in her study of the Joluo of Kenya, writes that the system provided a daughter 'usufruct' rights (although she was not allocated land) of land belonging to her father's family, while a wife had 'usufruct' rights to her husband's patrilineage. She further describes that such rights conferred (by wives) often lasted for a lifetime. Pala's study states that women as individuals or groups did not have the legal rights to allocate or dispose of land, but neither did the individual men (Pala 1978: 5).

Land was allocated to an individual male and upon his death the land rights were transferred to his sons. Land was, therefore, transmitted only through the permanent members of the family (as women got married outside the family) to guarantee access to the land (Gutto 1987: 49). Although men were considered heads of their families, when they died the land portion that fell directly under their headships remained as family property. Widows held property as trustees for their sons, while the leviratic unions helped the widowed woman to maintain the husband's property. In the case of death/divorce of the mother, the sons still retained the mother's parcel (Pala 1978: 34).

Pala clarifies two concepts of the landowner; one refers to the rights to allocate land to members of the family, and the other refers to the one who invests in a piece of land for productive purposes. In the first category were the heads of families, the men, and in the second category were women (Pala 1978: 39).

Nangendo explains that although land among the Bukusu community was regarded as communally owned, families and clans had specific land rights to certain pieces of land. Each married man demarcated his own portion of land for farming. The man in turn allotted the land to his wife (ves), married sons as well as his grown-up daughters. Daughters did not inherit the land allotted to them for cultivation. In this system, wives had the right to prevent husbands from giving out family land to another person. If the husband was dead, impaired or very old, a woman could sue for trespass, eviction, settle boundaries over disputes of her husband's land and retain all rights to the land until the sons got married (Nangendo 1987: 107).

Okoth-Ogendo draws our attention to the fact that though indigenous property laws excluded women from 'owning' or 'inheriting', this cannot be a mark of an inferior status or chauvinism. Rights over immovable property were trans-generational, and though women were treated as permanent members of the societies in which they were married, the patri-local societies controlled the process of allocations and transmission of land (Okoth-Ogendo 1982a: 16).

Men traditionally gained access to land largely as family members and women gained access as wives. Historically, control over land through inheritance was ascribed to male kinship. Characteristically, men controlled women's access to land and allocated their labour. For example, the more wives a man had, the more land he accumulated and controlled (Guyer 1984). The more land a man controlled, the more wives and children he needed to help cultivate it (Davison 1987a: 18). This joint productive-procreative value of women is symbolized by the exchange of bridewealth to compensate her family for loss of labour, and to assure the future paternity of her children. In turn, her male children inherit the land she cultivates.

It is important to note that, while landholding historically catered for all members of the society, nevertheless, the amount and quality of land acquired or inherited depended upon an individual's status and position in a family and community. For example, there was disparity between land held by a chief and land held by the ordinary member of the community. Likewise, the wives of the chief had access to more land than the wives of ordinary members of the community. Again, the first wife by virtue of her position in the family always had greater access to land than her co-wives. According to Davison, women as a social category cannot be viewed as a single category, even in the pre-colonial period (Davison 1987a: 19). Their social status thus impinged upon their access to and their role in agricultural production.

Male access to land was also based upon social factors like status in the community and size of family, whereas women's access to land still often depended upon their relationship to men and their marital status. What is significant, however, is that the individual members of the family were allocated definite rights and obligations with respect to control, ownership and use of the resource.

The advent of European colonial capitalism drastically altered former patterns of land use and occupancy in many places. The abundant land held by Africans was gradually restricted in many areas by government policies that favoured the consolidation of scattered tracts in the hands of male owners. In this process, women's productive procreative labour has been devalued by capitalist production, given the introduction of cash crop production and less emphasis placed on food production (Davison 1987a: 14, 15).

Nasimiyu argues that the participation of women in the pre-capitalist and post-capitalist mode of production explains why profound changes in the traditional system of the division of labour were brought about by political and economic forces, thereby resulting in a new orientation in rural economies (Nasimiyu 1984: 68). One such development was the introduction of cash crops which brought about changes in the tenure system, resulting in the widening of the economic gap between women and men. According to her, lack of control over land became a major cause of women's economic dependency.

In eastern and southern Africa, colonial capitalist notions of male property ownership brought about a restructuring of gender relations to land in some places, and the intensification of men's control in others. As a result, customary use rights, either communal or individual, were discouraged in favour of legal measures that began to circumscribe land parcels and place them in the hands of individual male owners (Davison 1987a: 14, 15).

The colonial period and land tenure The origins of the tenure reform can be traced back to the Berlin Conference in 1895, when Kenya was declared a British Protectorate; in 1920 it became a crown colony. European settlement was largely a consequence of the construction of the Uganda railway which reached Lake Victoria in 1902. The railway thus opened the way for colonization of the fertile highlands, and European settlement was encouraged by the British Foreign Office because this seemed to be the way in which the railway and the Protectorate could be made to pay. From then on, a series of ordinances followed which eventually alienated large tracts of land from the indigenous people (Wanjala and Musymi 1990: 15).

The colonial era ushered in disruptive changes to the African land tenure systems. Measures were taken to provide land for European settlers, plantation owners and mercantile traders. Acquisition of land was made possible through Crown Land Ordinances. Britain imposed its tenure system through individualization. The indigenous tenure system was transformed. First, the East African Land Order Council in 1901 vested crown lands to the protection of the commissioner and council-general to be held in trust for the queen. This ordinance gave the commissioner the power to make grants or leases of crown land on any terms he thought reasonable, but subject to instructions from the Secretary of State.

The 1902 ordinance opened the way for European settlement in Kenya, making large areas of land alienated for settlers under the principle of ownership of interest. The year 1908 saw the enactment of the Crown Land Ordinance which conferred power upon the commissioner to make grants of ninety-nine-year leases to the settlers.

The Crown Land Ordinance in 1915 further provided for creating and empowering the governor to reserve any crown land which in his opinion was required for the use or support of the colony. The colonial government believed its actions were legal as long as its activities were based on the ordinances. Policies concerning land by the colonial government owe their origin to this period. From this time, there was a systematic and planned imposition of English property law on the colony (United Kingdom 1955: 19).

The settlers, feeling that they were supporting the colonial government's economy as main actors in agriculture, began advocating an English system of property law with regard to transfers, mortgages and leases (Wanjala and Musymi 1990: 14). These demands were implemented by the Transfer of Property Act of India under the Crown Land Ordinance and the Registration of Titles Ordinance. As if this was not enough, the settlers further demanded that all land considered or likely to be 'suitable' for European settlement should be set aside for their exclusive occupation and use, actual or prospective (Okoth-Ogendo 1976: 133). The 1915 ordinance created reserves and empowered the governor to reserve any crown land for use and support of the colony (United Kingdom 1955: 15). The ordinance precipitated further alienation of land. Areas which belonged to Africans were set aside for European settlement, such as Lumbua, Nandi, the southern part of Rift Valley, Seltima, Laikipia, Kenya Province, Kikuyu and Ukamba territories.

All these developments had far-reaching consequences for the indigenous peoples. The alienation of land was followed by the establishment of the African reserves in the same year. Nevertheless, these reserves came into existence without any clear plan of how they were to develop except to provide for cheap and dependable labour for the settlers of plantation agriculture.

Though the effects of land alienation were felt more by communities such as the Maasai, Kalenjin and Kikuyus, who were removed from their ancestral lands, the effects of this alienation later began to spill over to adjacent areas, and this created many repercussions for African land use. For example, problems arose moving both agricultural and pastoral communities who had to struggle to adapt themselves to new ecological conditions. The consequences of this included severe famines, livestock diseases and plagues, particularly among pastoral people. Second, fixed ethnic boundaries established in the creation of reserves restricted shifting agriculture and also led to widespread landlessness. As a result, there was rapid deterioration due to land fragmentation, overstocking, soil exhaustion, erosion, low crop yields, diminishing livestock herds, low income and discontent among the Africans (Okoth-Ogendo 1979: 69). Land disputes also developed and clans and families sought to retain rights of access to ancestral lands. Confronted by these problems, the colonial government seemed set to 'improve' the African reserves at least to divert any major political upheaval (Mwaniki 1975: 10).

It is tempting to assume that it was out of genuine concern that the colonial government improved the deteriorating African reserve. Nevertheless, the settler economy alone was not capable of satisfying the colony's demand. As such, it was imperative that the administration assume wide powers in regulating and directing economic activity in the settler and African areas (Okoth-Ogendo 1976: 160).

Administratively, the colonial government realized during the Mau Mau revolt that individualization could be used to create a solid middle-class population attached to the land. This middle class would have too much to lose by reviving Mau Mau in another form (Sorrenson 1968: 160). The individualization of tenure was therefore aimed at defeating Kenyan nationalization in that a landed class of conservative people was to be created through replacement of customary land tenure with a tenure that permitted a few people to own land. Such a class of people would in turn act as a buffer between the settler and the landless (Kibwana 1990: 237).

Agronomically, the colonial government was advised that the greatest problem in the African reserves was embedded in their land relations which they termed 'communal'. The only answer to these problems was to reform the African tenure system. Arguments made were that the structure of access rights under the African customary land tenure system encouraged sub-division of land, leading to small units of sub-economic size. As a result, they argued, proper husbandry was impossible (Swynnerton 1954: 13).

These arguments led to a land tenure reform programme relentlessly pursued by the colonial government. The solution to the problem lay in the individualization of land tenure.

The Swynnerton Plan and land tenure policy The Swynnerton Plan, completed in 1953 and published in 1954, provided a definitive statement on land tenure policy. Swynnerton argued:

> Sound agricultural development is dependent upon a system of land tenure which will make available to the African farmer a unit of land and a system of farming whose production could support his family at a level, taking into account prerequisites derived from the farm, comparable with other occupations. He must be provided with such security of tenure through an indivisible title as will encourage him to invest his labour and profits into the development of his farm and as will enable him to offer his security against such financial

credits as he may wish to secure from such sources as may be open to him. (Swynnerton 1954: 26)

The goals of the Swynnerton Plan were to create employment, to raise productivity through the use of a title deed as collateral, to access credit, purchase farm implements and increase incomes. Thus, the Plan aimed at intensifying African agriculture on the basis of land tenure reform and production for the urban and export market. According to the colonial government, customary tenure created a barrier to the social and economic advancement of the people. This opinion, later declared by the East African Royal Commission, stated: 'Policy concerning the tenure and disposition of land should aim at individualization of land ownership and a degree of mobility in the transfer and disposition of land which without ignoring existing property rights, will enable access to land for its economic use' (United Kingdom 1955: 23).

The Registered Land Act of 1963 further enhanced the individualization of tenure among indigenous communities. Thus, the introduction of the free enterprise system began with European settlers owning the land, while Africans provided labour. Kibwana rightly observes that the colonial government consciously excluded the participation of indigenous people in the free enterprise system on an equal footing with Europeans (Kibwana 1990: 238). That even when eventually privatization was allowed among Africans, such privatization was on marginal land and a large portion of Kenya had earlier been massively dispossessed.

In this scenario, there is no question that colonial capitalism dramatically transformed the gender relations to land. The solutions imposed by the colonial system aimed at intensifying agriculture and introducing cash crops were primary determinants of women's loss of status and power in agriculture.

The structural changes under colonialism and the later post-colonialism have eroded many rights women enjoyed in their traditional settings, leaving them with the unsupported and unrecognized bulk of agricultural work in the rural areas. Thus, women's role in agriculture and food production was recognized by customary rights of access to land, forests and support from family labour. But with the advent of colonialism, women's position in society began to be exploited. For example, the colonial system set to serve its government barred women from effectively participating in it because of lack of training and education. While the men migrated to urban areas and cash crop farms in search of money to pay for tax, the women were left to do double the amount of work they were already doing in order to feed their families.

The advent of colonial capitalism drastically altered former patterns of land use and occupancy in many areas. Access to agricultural land, which had been in abundance, was now restricted. The consolidated lands were now owned by the men, who most of the time were forced to grow cash crops for export at the expense of food crops for the family. In the same process, while women's labour remained uncompensated, men's labour in agriculture assumed exchange value. The technological innovations that would help women in their productive/reproductive roles remained static while men gained from agricultural technology. The customary rights of women continued to be eroded by the new reforms that promised to generate progress. The end result of colonial capitalism has been the restructuring of gender roles of production. The introduction of cash crops for export has brought about greater gender segregation in labour tasks, with men increasingly becoming agricultural managers or wage labourers (Davison 1987a: 15). In essence, men rather than women have benefited from the reform and restructuring of the customary practices of land tenure.

The Post-colonial Period and Legislation on Land Tenure Reform

The full process of tenure reform involved three distinct stages, namely, adjudication, consolidation and registration of titles. Adjudication is the means by which existing rights in land are ascertained by recognizing and confirming existing rights without creating or altering the right. Consolidation in the context of land reform is usually associated with the fragmentation that arises from different parcels of land in small pieces or fragments. Consolidation was a measure designed to remedy this by forming the fragmented pieces of land into one farm. The registration of titles is done by the Chief Land Registrar who takes responsibility for administering land registries in accordance with the Registered Land Act, Chapter 300. The registrar prepares a register for each person shown in the adjudication register as a landowner. A land certificate is issued in the name which appears on the register.

The whole process from adjudication and consolidation to registration is conducted by men; women's participation in this process has been almost nonexistent. The adjudicators, the consolidators and land committees and boards members are almost always men (Pala 1980: 39). In this context, women's interests and rights in family land are likely to be compromised and ill defined since they are not represented in the land committees. According to Shipton: 'the Adjudication and registration processes themselves require converting multiple, situational and overlapping rights to individual, absolute and exclusive rights. The process can never be free of disagreement, deceit, and difficult compromise, and it can sometimes tear families apart' (Shipton 1987: 48).

The full effect of land registration may not be obvious or known for some time to come, but one thing is clear, that the transition from indigenous land tenure systems to the Western property concept of 'ownership' is not an easy one. People are learning to live with private property, but the land tenure reform has been hard for farmers, and by no means fully successful for the government (Republic of Kenya 1989: 171).

While land tenure reduces disputes about boundaries, it tends to lead to new disputes about the ownership of whole plots; it introduces new possibilities of misunderstandings between local communities and national government, as farmers are suddenly expected to comply with unrealistic rules about recording transactions. The emergent land market is, however, largely unregistered (Shipton 1987: 50).

Nevertheless, the land reform programme is still proceeding with its own momentum, mythology and sub-structure of powerful political incentives. Although some land still remains under customary tenure, the process is underway to convert such land to individual tenure. The courts, on the other hand, have not conclusively decided that adjudication and registration of land initially held under customary tenure eradicates customary land claims altogether. Irrespective of this registration of land in the name of individual male heads of households, evidence has shown that the family continues to enjoy rights of access to the land which existed under customary law (Kibwana 1990: 240).

Land and land tenure constitute a central place in human life and, despite the Kenyan government's emphasis on industrialization, agriculture remains the backbone of the Kenyan economy. Agriculture continues to play a leading role in feeding the Kenyan population, generating employment and incomes, contributing to foreign exchange earnings and inducing growth in other sectors of the economy.

Alongside the tenure reforms, other dynamic social changes have taken place. With a rising population, access to land for subsistence purposes for the majority of the population is no longer guaranteed. Since land does not expand, 'exclusionary' land tenure systems cannot cater for any expansion in the community population; there is no provision for readjustment, rearrangement or reallocation. In effect, the individualization of tenure has led to the 'genesis of landlessness' scenario: employment opportunities in the public and private sectors are not expanding, nor have the multiple interests of those who use the land been taken into account (Kibwana 1990: 230). On the dilemmas brought about by land tenure reform, Kibwana observes: 'It is impossible to translate group rights under customary land tenure to an exact equivalent under individual tenure so that during the conversion process property rights under customary land law will necessarily be extinguished' (Kibwana 1990: 239).

Thus, the dilemma facing the Kenyan courts is that they have two interpretations of the effects of land registration. One interpretation states that all customary land claims are extinguished, the second interpretation states that such claims are merely transformed into another species of rights, and that the registered holder under individual tenure holds the land in trust for those who need access to it under customary law; the latter can still enjoy their rights notwithstanding their non-registration. Whether or not Kenya turns back on its policy, it will have to find alternative arrangements for dealing with those who have been left out of the land tenure reform – women, the majority of the country's citizens. Private property in land has far-reaching consequences for women's relationship to land and their work in agriculture. It is critically important to examine women's rights with regard to land tenure reform and the implications this has for women as food producers.

The individualization of tenure has created potential landlessness (Wanjala and Musymi 1990: 6). It is estimated that two billion people are absolutely landless (about 400,000 families) and this landlessness increases at the rate of not less than 1.5 per cent annually. There is ready cash, and the newly entitled individuals can sell land which was once, or ostensibly still is, family land; there is a trend for poor people to raise money from the sale of land either to pay school fees or for plain subsistence (Shipton 1987). Evidence from the current land reforms suggests that access to land for women is being systematically eroded to a degree where they will be added to the growing hordes of the landless poor, with obvious detrimental consequences to the agricultural industry (ILO 1972: 156). Pala speculates that the women most threatened will be those with families with little or no off-farm income, and this will force them to sell land. Daughters and widows will also be harmed, as they have 'often been defined by land officers as those who do not need much land' (Pala 1983: 16).

A Case Study: Women's Land Rights in Mumbuni Location, Machakos District, Eastern Province of Kenya

In this section, I present a case study to highlight some of the issues already raised regarding women's land rights within the framework of land tenure

reform. The data presented here are mainly drawn from a field survey conducted among women smallholder farmers who live and farm in Mumbuni
Location, Machakos district, 1996/97. The total study sample was 220 women
farmers.

Mumbuni is potentially arable land. Traditionally given to subsistence
farming, the higher areas are increasingly being used for cash crops. This has
led to agricultural intensification and changes in access and use of land for a
majority of women in the area, who need to continue growing food to feed
their families. In Mumbuni, land adjudication and registration have come
into effect while, at the same time, customary land tenure is still in practice.

The impact of land tenure reform on women's land ownership and land rights

Who is consulted during land adjudication and registration? Questions designed to
find out which member of the family was involved or consulted during land
adjudication, consolidation and registration show that women are generally
not involved in the process leading to land tenure reform. Table 8.1 indicates
that out of the total sample of 220, only 6 per cent, 0.9 per cent and 7.3 per
cent of the women were involved in land adjudication, consolidation and
registration, respectively. Fathers-in-law and husbands have the highest score
in terms of involvement during land adjudication and registration. In the
words of Okoth-Ogendo: 'Adjudication and registration processes are conducted on the basis that the power of control in indigenous property laws is
equivalent to ownership in the male members of society without at the same
time imposing obligations towards women on account of their membership in
the society in which they marry' (Okoth-Ogendo 1981: 339).

TABLE 8.1 Family members consulted/involved in the land tenure process

Family Members	Adjudication		Consolidated		Registration	
Self (woman respondent)	15	(6.8%)	2	(0.9%)	16	(7.3%)
Self/husband	1	(0.5%)	1	(0.5%)		
Mother-in-law/husband	4	(1.8%)			3	(1.4%)
Mother-in-law	14	(6.8%)	1	(0.5%)	15	(6.8%)
Husband	51	(23.2%)			45	(20.5%)
Son	2	(0.9%)			10	(4.5%)
Father-in-law	87	(39.5%)	2	(0.9%)	64	(29.1%)
Others	26	(11.8%)			3	(1.4%)
Not applicable	17	(7.7%)	215	(97.7%)	40	(18.2%)

Land tenure reform enactments thus contain serious gender inequalities which clearly need to be addressed. There is a case here for establishing equal rights for both spouses in the ownership of land.

Women, in their status as daughters, are completely left out of this process, while mothers-in-law are involved or consulted only together with their sons. These results clearly indicate that those consulted and involved in the process leading to the land tenure reform are the male members of the family: fathers-in-law, husbands and sons. Wives, daughters and mothers-in-law do not generally participate in the process. Pala rightly points out that, in contrast to past practices, the on-going land adjudication process overemphasizes the structural points of allocation and inheritance of land at the expense of use rights, which is the area in which women cultivators stand to be most adversely affected by the new scheme (Pala 1978: 11).

During the land tenure process, the respondents reported that conflicts often arise between members of the family and between clans regarding land boundaries and rights of ownership. Together with kinship arbitration in case of conflict, the scarcity of land and periodic demands for cash are likely increasingly to limit women's access to land through outright disposal of such land and the produce by the legal owners of the land. This new temptation, which removes the very security the tenure programme was originally set up to strengthen, has created landlessness for members of the family whose interests are not registered. Such conflicts are solved by clan elders and chiefs. Women do not become clan elders. This means that women are not represented in the structures which solve conflicts during the process leading to land registration. Under this new system, women are theoretically protected by the land control boards against unreasonable sales and other disposals by male relatives, but no one has yet demonstrated how effective this protection will be (Shipton 1987: 14)

On the other hand, women's lack of knowledge of the law prevents them from demanding their rights, particularly because the males have the overall decision-making power in the household and in the community. This has reinforced male managerial and financial control over female property.

Who owns land? One of the major concerns of this study was to find out whether land tenure reform had enhanced women's acquisition of land. One justification for the individualization of land tenure is that it allows any person to acquire land, thereby creating equality between the sexes. It is important to determine if women own the land they farm.

Table 8.2 indicates that out of the group sampled of 220, only twenty-six women owned land. Husbands and parents-in-law own most family land. Only one woman respondent out of the whole sample had land registered jointly with the husband. It is important to note that there was no land registered in the name of a daughter. Registration has indeed effected a hardening of men's land rights into absolute ownership, to the exclusion of women and their daughters.

A community-level questionnaire was designed to find out whether women are acquiring land more than in the past. Most of those interviewed said that women rarely acquire land in their own names. There was a general consensus that women who claimed that they own land were mostly widows. Few women had bought land in their own names. Those who claimed to own land (mostly widows) did so in trust for their sons. Once the sons become adults they take over the land. The study also shows that widows continue to cultivate their husbands' land without legally transferring the land title to their own names.

The result of land ownership indicates that, despite registration of family land in individual male heads' names, women by and large do not own the land they farm, but they still have access rights to land which existed under customary law. Despite land tenure laws in the post-independence period that allow women, regardless of marital status, to own land, very few women do. Indeed, there appears to be no rationale for the fact that the new land reform does not provide women with legal protection of their user rights, if not partial ownership, of land that they have been working. On registering of land titles in individual names Pala writes:

The individual, invariably males who have attained the age of 18 years at the time of registration, would be given a land title which gives him a theoretical and practical legal right to dispose of the land by sale or any other means without

TABLE 8.2 Who owns land?

Registered name	Frequency	Percentage
Not applicable	19	8.6
Self (woman respondent)	26	11.8
Husband	82	37.3
Son	1	0.5
Mother/father-in-law	76	34.5
Self/husband	1	0.5
Husband/mother-in-law	1	0.5
Others	14	6.4

necessary recourse to the elders of the patrilineal who would ordinarily have the power to veto in matters of alienation of land by individuals. (Pala 1980: 32).

Land tenure reform has thus transformed the community power which controlled the use of land for the benefit of all its members including women, and placed the power on an individual male owner.

What this means is that land reform has been dominated by male individualized ownership. Two main factors were identified as hindering women from owning land. The women interviewed in Mumbuni still enjoy access rights to family land for agricultural production and see no reason to own land. This is perhaps an indication that the implications of individualized tenure have not been fully understood by the majority of women since they still perform their agricultural activities within the customary tenure system which safeguarded them. Secondly, several women said that they would not buy land in their own names even if they had the money to do so because their husbands would not allow it.

Four women reported that they had purchased their own land. This is an indication that individualization of land may be creating new rights for particular women who are able to purchase land, particularly daughters who did not have such rights under the customary system. Nevertheless, these new rights will tend to give privileges to those women with access to education, good jobs and good salaries, at the expense of those who are poorer, have no access to education and skills for employment. The latter form the majority of women who continue to depend on land for their livelihood.

Women's rights in land

Rights of inheritance Basically, even under the land tenure reform, land is still being inherited by sons and not daughters. It is indicated in Table 8.3 that 63.6 per cent of the women respondents said that their sons will inherit the family land; daughters were expected to marry outside the family and use their

TABLE 8.3 Who inherits land title deed?

Heir to land title deed	Frequency	Percentage
Daughters	7	3.2
Sons	140	63.6
Daughters/sons	63	28.6
Others	8	3.6
Not applicable	2	0.9

husbands' family land. A significant number (28.6 per cent) said both sons and daughters will inherit the land, while a negligible number (3.2 per cent) said it will be daughters. Unmarried daughters, particularly single mothers, are given small pieces of land to use for their survival.

These investigations also reveal that women farm land that has been inherited. Customary law continues to determine the way in which a household head divides the land. For a son to inherit land from his father, the land has to be sub-divided for each son and his family. Thus, to inherit land, each male member of the family can only be supplied with a plot of arable land by subdividing the land into smaller and smaller plots. This sub-division of land already adjudicated and registered is most of the time never recorded with the land registry. Sons and their wives were found to live and use land which is not legally registered as theirs. Registration by itself is therefore not a conclusive indication of what is actually taking place on the land.

Use rights   Under customary law, daughters were found not to have land for use. A daughter can only use land allocated to her mother to help produce food for the family until such time as she gets married. Thus daughters' rights to use land are limited to food cultivation. Sons, however, have full use rights of the land allocated to them. Wives have their rights to land use restricted to food production.

Table 8.4 shows that 78.6 per cent reported that their customary land use rights were only limited to cultivation, 15 per cent enjoyed certain rights through their husbands, 2.3 per cent did not have rights at all and only 1.8 per cent had full rights because they owned the land.

Since food production and providing for the family remain the responsibility of women, it is necessary that they have land on which to grow food. Men are obliged to allocate their wives certain plots to use, although the rights to these plots are not definitive. Thus, married women were found to depend upon the good will of their husbands and the availability of the land to grow food.

TABLE 8.4 Customary land use rights for women

Use rights	Frequency	Percentage
Cultivation	173	78.6
No rights	5	2.3
Has through husband	33	15
Owns the land	3	1.4
Not applicable	6	2.7

Men allocate the most remote and least fertile land, keeping the best for themselves to grow cash crops.

Rights of land allocation Women come to possess the land they use through their parents-in-law. Table 8.5 shows that 85.9 per cent of the respondents reported that the land they use had been allocated by father/mother-in-law. Table 8.5 further indicates that 91 per cent of family members allocating title land to wives are fathers-in-law, mothers-in-law and husbands.

This allotment to wives or children is for usufruct alone, creating no formal title. This shows that women's access to land is largely dependent upon their relationship to men. While wives have access to some land, unmarried women, who are prohibited from inheriting property, have no access to any land. Even though the majority of women have access rights to land for their food farming, it is important to make a distinction between access and control of land. While control is power, and implies the ability to dispose of land, access implies only the right to use or consume with the permission of those who hold the right to dispose of it (Mason 1984). Although women in Mumbuni do have access to land, they have no similar rights to allocate land. Determining rights of allocation in this study was important as these rights influence both the type of land and the type of crops grown. If a woman has no rights to allocate the land she farms, then her agricultural production priorities are subordinated to those with such rights, depending on what the person with the right wants to use the land for. It is important to note here that gender relations indeed attest not only to access to land, but also to the conditions under which women are able to use land. These relationships have direct impact on agricultural production.

TABLE 8.5 Who allocates wife land with title deed?

Allocator	Frequency	Percentage
Father/mother-in-law	100	54.5
Father/mother-in-law/husband	34	15.5
Husband	66	30.0
Other owners	10	4.5
Government	1	0.5
Not applicable	9	4.1

Women's rights to lease, mortgage, transfer or sale The study also reveals that women generally do not have the power and authority to lease, mortgage, transfer or sell land they use. Table 8.6 shows that 66.4 per cent, 60.5 per cent, 69.1 per cent, 45.9 per cent, 50 per cent and 90 per cent of women, respectively, had no power to mortgage, lease, sell, give out as a gift or make permanent investment in land. Further investigations showed that men, especially husbands, make decisions regarding the mortgaging, leasing, selling and gifting of family land.

The argument for individualized titles is that these would ensure rapid development as individuals could then get loans for agricultural development secured against their titles (Ingham et al. 1950). However, the links between land tenure and institutional credit in Kenya indicate that losing rights to land goes along with losing access to loans women might have. Agricultural Finance Corporation and the country's three major commercial banks (Standard, Barclays, Commercial) all require collateral, which they normally take in the form of land title (Shipton 1987: 42). Since it is men who hold titles, it is they who can get loans; women can still use their husbands' titles, though this is not common practice. Out of 220 women interviewed, only eight had used land title deeds to get credit.

The common practice in Mumbuni is that husbands use the newly acquired private land titles for loans. When they get loans, they need to develop the land more, by devoting more land to cash crops. In the process, women may lose part of the land they had for food crops without gaining access to money from cash crops. More land in Mumbuni has been converted to cash crop production; land scarcity in the area has become a reality. If this is true for most of arable Kenya, then women's role in producing food for their families is at risk since they do not have land to do it. Patrick Shipton, writing on land

TABLE 8.6 Women's rights to lease, mortgage and sell land

Rights	Frequency	Percentage
Right to raise loans	60	27.3
No right to raise loans	146	66.4
Right to rent	74	33.6
No right to rent	133	60.5
Right to sell	57	29.9
No right to sell	152	69.1
Right to gift	101	45.9
No right to gift	110	50
Right to make permanent improvement	13	5.9
No right to make permanent improvement	198	90

title deeds being used by husbands to get loans, observed: 'Husbands are using their newly private titles to seek loans over which they will have full personal control. Particularly vulnerable therefore, are the few whose husbands or fathers are able to mortgage their land for credit for these women may have little say in how the loan resources are used, and they may be quite powerless to stop expropriation in the event of default' (Shipton 1987: 42). This means that when husbands, fathers or brothers mortgage their land for credit, the rights of the related women (wives, daughters and sisters) who use the same land are at risk. Any future farm credit that depends on land mortgages is likely to remain firmly in the hands of men. And any land-secured credit in the hands of men will threaten the land rights of related women. In the light of these considerations, it is clear that registered titles for the purpose of securing credit have and will continue to exclude the bulk of women farmers.

Duration of land use allocated to women Questions were asked about whether the land used can be reallocated for other use by the actual owner of land. Out of 220 respondents, nineteen had actually experienced their lands being reallocated. In the traditional tenure system, once land was allocated to a wife, it remained so for life, and could not be reallocated. From the study results, there is an indication that reallocation of family land is already taking place. Some reasons given for this reallocation were: the land was to be sold; it was to be used for cash crop production; it was to be given as a gift; it was to be given to a co-wife; or it was to be leased.

In Mumbuni, family land has been divided into two parts: food land and cash crop land. In essence, this has also brought about changes in the way land is controlled by individual members of the household and how decisions are made on the use of the land. In each farm, our research found that land use organization is based on the supremacy of the man as father-in-law, husband or son. Women's access to the land for food farming is not guaranteed. Out of all the cases interviewed, 74 per cent said they had access to land for food farming while 24 per cent did not have access to family land to grow food. Those who did not have land reported that the family land had been used for growing coffee or had been sold. Generally, the landless women sell their labour to coffee farms in order to buy food to maintain themselves and their families.

Inquiries on types of land allocated to women for food farms revealed that coffee farms tend to be near home and are easily accessible while food farms are not only scattered but are also far away from home. Out of those who had access to land for food, 73.4 per cent had more than one parcel. In comparison

86.5 per cent reported that the coffee farms were concentrated under one parcel. Eighty per cent had their food farms up to 7 kilometres way from home, while 12 per cent had their food farms over 7 kilometres away.

Although the average land acreage per family in Mumbuni is approximately 2 acres, women have very limited access to these family lands for food farming. Ninety-one per cent of the women who indicated they had access to food farms reported that they were using only one-eighth of family land for food farming.

Women in Mumbuni continue to provide the highest labour for both cash and food crops. Though the coffee farms are owned and controlled by men, most of women's labour is spent on their husbands' coffee farms. The distribution of labour activities between wife and husband show that women contribute over 80 per cent of their labour in food production. In coffee production, women were found to contribute over 75 per cent of their labour in manuring, 81 per cent in picking, 81 per cent transporting and 92 per cent processing. The value created by women's labour is directly appropriated and regulated by the husbands. The women reported that they have to work in their husbands' coffee farms before they can proceed to work in their own food farms. This is a major constraint on women's food production. Thus, the unequal division of labour in the farming households and male dominance in resource control further jeopardizes the family food supply. Women have to offer free labour in plots controlled by their husbands at the expense of their own food crops and other income-earning engagements. In effect, land tenure reform has transformed the role of women in the household economy and has increased the economic burdens on women instead of creating employment.

Whether women benefit from their labour inputs is another matter. Generally, women reported that they control and take responsibility for the use of food crops. Those who sell some of their food products have full control over the money earned from the sale of food. However, since food produced is generally consumed by household members, the average income from the sale of food crops is minimal. On the other hand, out of the families who had coffee farms, 94 per cent of the men as compared to 6 per cent of the women receive direct payment from them. Cash earned from coffee was reported to be generally controlled and distributed by the men.

The case of Mumbuni shows that land tenure reform is far from being able to create equity between women and men. As already mentioned, very few women were found to own land. This confirms that legal institutions per se cannot create equality as long as the socio-cultural attitudes that do not allow equality persist. By losing rights to land, women have lost access to loans they might have had if they had land to offer as collateral for credit. Although it can still be argued that women can use their husband's titles to get credit, this was not found to have been a common practice. Women generally do not have the power to mortgage the land they use. In addition, lands allotted to women are usually too small to be of any economic value for use as security.

Another reason for the registration of titles was that registration encourages an owner to make permanent improvements on his land. In turn, security of tenure leads to farmers investing their own capital in land (Republic of Kenya 1965: 87). Women farmers who have no land of their own depend on their husbands' to grow food, but lack of security denies them the freedom to make management decisions concerning the farm, which in turn affects their investment decisions (Blaike and Bookfield 1987: 27). Since the 'owner' of the land has control over its use as collateral for credit, disposal of its produce, and use of its income, the practical effect is that the wife will not make an investment in the holding unless she is secure that she will reap the benefit of her investment.

The two cases presented below convey the dynamism of women's land relations, the experiences of individual women and the structures affecting them under the land tenure reform.

Nzilani: a landless woman Nzilani was born in Mun'gala sub-location, Mumbuni Location, Machakos district. She went to school up to Form II, but had to leave because her parents had only enough money to educate her three brothers.

She dropped out of school and later became pregnant and had a child. She got employment as a housemaid in order to take care of her child. Nzilani married in 1974 and had six more children. She divorced her husband in 1985 and now lives as a single parent.

When she divorced, the land which belonged to her former husband and which she was using for subsistence farming was immediately sold by the husband. He claimed that he needed to use the money to pay his brother's school fees. According to Nzilani, this was not so, as her ex-husband used the money carelessly.

Nzilani was forced to go back to her place of birth and use her father's land. She found the land too small to share with her brothers and their wives. Her brothers have also not been willing to share land with her. They have consistently told her to go back to her husband. Before Nzilani's father died, he had given her a portion of land (0.7 acres) to use for her subsistence. After his death, however, Nzilani's brothers grabbed the portion of land that had been given to her, claiming their wives needed more land to cultivate.

Nzilani had to look for an alternative. She leased a neighbour's land, which she was to use for only four seasons. The land is 2 acres and was leased for 150 shillings a year. The proceeds from the land are not enough to feed Nzilani and her children, so she supplements her income by selling fruit and vegetables in the local market. However, farming remains her major occupation.

Nzilani feels bitter about her ex-husband who does not take any responsibility for their children's survival. Nzilani is very poor. She and her children live from hand to mouth and she cannot afford to take her children to school.

Kiatu: a woman who owns land   Kiatu was born in Misiani, Kangundo Location, Machakos district. She is eighty-one years old. Kiatu did not go to school because when she was growing up girls were never taken to school by their parents; they remained home to help with household chores. Kiatu is a widow and has ten grown-up children. Her husband was a military policeman who died in service during the Second World War.

Kiatu's main occupation is farming. She does this with the help of workers employed on her behalf by her children. Part of the land Kiatu farms was inherited by her husband. The other portion of her land was bought with shares from a cooperative society. When her husband died, since her children were still young, all the land legally owned by the husband passed to her. However, her brothers-in-law wanted to grab some of this land from her, but with determination and the help of the village elders, she managed to secure the land which belonged to her husband.

Although the 6-acre piece of land is registered in Kiatu's name, she holds it in trust for her sons. When her sons grew up, Kiatu sub-divided the land among the eight of them. Each son, then, has less than an acre. Two sons have already registered their names on the land they have inherited. The rest of the land is still in Kiatu's name.

When asked why she did not allow her two daughters to inherit some of this land like their brothers, Kiatu said that since daughters get married, they should be given land or own land where they are married. According to her, only sons should inherit land that belongs to their fathers, because immediately after they get married, their wives will need land to farm. Kiatu strongly believes that a woman should have access to her husband's land. She knows the advantages of owning land, the greatest of which is the ability to lease some of the land for cash.

Kiatu also thinks that she has an advantage as a landowner over those who are landless because she produces food crops (e.g. maize, beans, peas, cassava, arrowroot) and does not have to buy them like landless people. She proudly says that she has a place she calls her own, and when she dies she will have a burial place.

However, Kiatu does not wish to own any more land for she claims that she does not need any more. Since she is old, she cannot even use all the land she owns. She thinks, however, that her sons might need more land.

Re-examining the women's perspectives

- These cases reflect the fact that land has historically and automatically been controlled by men through the patrilineage inheritance system, and remains substantially in their control today. In practice, only men can or do own or hold land, while women do not or cannot own land. Despite new laws in the post-independence period that allow women to own land regardless of marital status, very few women in fact do own land.

- Women's access to land often depends on their relationship to men and their marital status. Their position is totally dependent on their relationship with the spouse who owns the land. That is, the women acquire land either as wives or by virtue of family ties, while men are direct holders or heirs to land.

- In the absence of personal rights to land, divorced, separated and widowed women face gross injustice. It is evident from the case presented that most often the above-mentioned category of women are forced out of their livelihood by male relatives and are often obliged to seek alternative means of supporting themselves and their children.

- Nearly all land in this study was registered in individual male elders' names, and when the elder died, little effort was made legally to transfer titles. Consequently, widows, their daughters-in-law and sons continue to cultivate the deceased man's land without transferring title. It is important to point out that once the man dies, the wife's access to land is threatened by her husband's male relatives and sons with inheritance rights. In this study, it was found that widows were actually powerless to protect their usufruct rights in the face of their husbands' adult male relatives, who may want to sell the land. Frequently, they find that the land they had access to while their husbands were still alive is suddenly taken from them when the husband dies.

- These cases also show that separated and divorced women return to their places of birth where they become dependent on their fathers' or brothers' lands. This category of women was found to form production units with their children and mothers. The mother provided security and ensured that the daughter had some land to cultivate. Once the mother died, daughters were often thrown off the land by their brothers. Lands allotted to daughters for their livelihood, in homes where they were born, are never sufficient for their needs, and most of the time they are forced to sell their labour off the farm.

- Legally, daughters, as well as sons, should inherit land. The cases show that, in practice, fathers continue to transfer land to their sons. Occasionally, a father will give his daughter a plot of land to cultivate, though he is reluctant to do so because it means that in the future there will be less land for his sons. In cases where a daughter remains unmarried, her situation regarding land becomes precarious. She must depend upon her father or brother to provide her with land for cultivation. Brothers are reluctant, however, to share their inherited land with their sisters, and, most often, daughters are forced to contribute their labour to their mothers' production unit, if they are still alive.

- Polygamy means that land must be sub-divided between wives competing for available resources within the family. Evidently, from case studies, a woman might wake up one day to find that the land she has been cultivating for her livelihood is already allocated to a co-wife by the husband.

- The prominence given to cash crops (i.e. coffee) means that only small portions of the family land are allocated to food crops. The general conclusion for these cases shows that land tenure reform has not only confirmed powers assumed by men of arranging land use and appropriation over income from cash crops, but has also constituted the end of the traditional protective measures for women's land use. It allows men to sell land without the consent of their wives.

Conclusions

This study draws out certain common socio-cultural characteristics that form a framework from which one can make general conclusions regarding the effects of land tenure reform on women and their role in food production.

These conclusions are linked to two factors. First, that the purpose of land tenure reform is to confirm to modern law ownership of individuals to whom credit and other agricultural services like information and technology might be directed. Second, modernization of agriculture strengthens private profit incentive and facilitates the use of credit, leading to greater production efficiency and greater increases in household income.

- Structural changes created land tenure reform under colonialism and post-colonialism has eroded the traditional laws that safeguarded women's rights. Adjudication and registration of land titles have been conducted on the basis that control was equivalent to 'ownership' as understood in Western laws, which has led to the transfer of land almost exclusively to men.

- It is important to note that despite new tenure laws that allow women, regardless of marital status, to own land, very few women were found to own land in this study. Nearly all land was registered in the individual male elder's name. It is also important to note that the land adjudicators, consolidators, committees and board members have been composed of men. This means that women have been totally left out of this process, thereby rendering their concerns ill-defined and compromised.

- Women usually gain access to land as wives, and have few other opportunities to acquire land. The main issue of land tenure reform, which enables any person to acquire land regardless of sex, becomes largely redundant. Fathers continue to transfer land to sons because it is assumed that daughters will get married. If women are to continue having access to a means of a livelihood only through men as the landowners, then their position in the event of marital separation, divorce or widowhood is threatened and ill-defined.

- The rights bestowed on the individual title owner have several elements: the ability to allocate, lease, mortgage, sell for cash or dispose by will. How much land and of what quality is allocated to women depends more on their husbands' separate incentive. This means that women's agricultural priorities are subordinated to those with land ownership rights (the men). Trends show men's increasing allocation of land to cash crops and the squeeze on women's food land are likely to continue.

- Women are left in the rural areas and they continue to manage land that belongs to their husbands, yet they cannot raise credit to improve the land no matter what opportunities exist for doing so. Losing rights to land for women goes along with losing access to loans they might have, since lending institutions require collateral, which they usually take in the form of land title, particularly for agricultural credit. It is men who hold titles, and therefore it is men who can get loans. Although women can use their husbands' titles, the common practice is for husbands already to use the newly private land titles. Any future farm credit based on land mortgages is likely to remain in the hands of men. And any secured credit in the hands of men will threaten the land rights of related women.

- Men are already selling land which was once, or ostensibly still is, family land. There is ready cash for land purchase, and there is a trend for poor people to raise money, sometimes for plain subsistence. The people most threatened are women and children with little or no off-farm income, who depend on land for their livelihood.

- The justification for the registration of land title is that registration leads to increased production because security of tenure makes it worth a farmer's while to undertake permanent improvement and investment of his own capital. But the woman farmer has no titled land of her own and has to depend on her husband's farm for her food. Lack of security denies her the freedom to make management decisions concerning the farm. It is this sense of insecurity of tenure which affects women's investment decisions, since the owner of the land has the ultimate legal authority over land use.

- Land tenure reform has brought about numerous changes in land use and the division of labour. The whole land use organization at the farm level is based upon the supremacy of the man as the owner of the land. In this mode of production, women have found themselves subordinate and marginalized.

- Commercialization of agriculture brought about by land tenure reform has led to women's loss of control of the family economy. At the same time they must continue to supply the labour necessary for both food and cash crops, thereby increasing their work burdens. Agricultural incentives and technologies are directed to cash crops, given their high economic status in the country. Food crop production continues to remain stymied by indigenous technology. Men continue to earn and control money from cash crops while the responsibility for feeding the family still rests primarily with women. The income-maximizing position granted by land title deeds and cash crop production has resulted in improving only two things: cash crop fields and the position of men.

- Agricultural services provided by extension officers, such as technological information, marketing and provision of inputs like fertilizers, are biased in favour of cash crops and the male farmers who are also heads of household and land title owners. Agricultural cooperatives are formed by those who own land, and wives are not automatically granted membership. In most cases, women fail to meet the criteria for membership because of outright discrimination against them, the burden of too much work on the farms making it difficult to attend meetings and the resistance of men to their admission to the cooperatives.

- This study understood as axiomatic that the objectives of land tenure reform should apply to women as well as men and that the gains are viewed as intended for women as much as for men. However, after going through this study, we realize that women have not benefited from the objectives of land tenure reform since they have not acquired the same rights which would enable them to become beneficiaries. Land tenure reform has carried the implicit assumption that the household is a primary unit of production, management and earnings. Thus reform has forgotten that there is always a sexual division of labour, and sexual division of management of certain crops and plots, as well as the rights of appropriation over produce. Gender relations will not only affect women's access to land, but also the conditions under which women are able to use land.

- Unless differential gender relations change through the reforms, the levels of agricultural production will be plagued by a dynamic which may force women to send resources outside the productive unit, or which will not allow women to take full advantage of the resources they have. Indeed, it is folly on the part of the government to believe that it can increase the productivity of agriculture by providing a natural incentive structure for men while depending on women's unremunerated labour. As rightly observed by Cloude and Knowles: 'Although women are altruistic, they are not foolish and they will not devote their total energies to their own economic disenfranchisement' (Cloude 1969; Knowles 1978: 11).

- Lack of land tenure rights is only one aspect of women's subordination. Granting women absolute ownership rights will not result in a great change in their status, but it would have considerable positive effects upon their lives. It is also very important to consider ways in which the oppression of women can be relieved, not for humanitarian reasons alone, but because of the effects it has upon agricultural production. Changes in the law will provide women with enormous potential for relieving their subordinate positions. This study has attempted to identify ways in which women can best be supported to carry out these changes. It is my belief that these changes are important advances towards the liberation of women.

Recommendations

To the Kenyan government If the government is genuinely concerned about the impact of development on women, then it should have the political will and commitment to translate the following measures into effective action:

- Create an environment that effectively empowers women through the law and provides security of expectations for women of all ages and status, supporting their rights in land as the primary resource for food production.

- Enhance efforts to involve women as owners and managers of resources and not simply relegate them to be participants in development projects.
- Pay more attention to and act upon the differential impact that agricultural policies have on men and women, even where policies are framed in gender neutral terms. Lack of inclusion of women as beneficiaries of land tenure reform can no longer be justified.
- Immediately stop treating the household as a collective unit represented by one individual. Decision-making authority and distribution of resources within the household must be reflected in policy in order to address the different needs of women and men. National land development policies should fall into two categories: policies designed to increase economic growth and efficiency, and policies designed to increase equity.
- Advance policies that make available to women, regardless of marital status, capital (in the form of loans not requiring land as collateral but instead using women's groups to ensure repayment) for the purchase of land.
- Appoint gender-balanced land board committees, from the grassroots to the national level, to ensure that women's concerns are taken care of in the process of land adjudication, consolidation, registration and distribution. The government should create an institutional channel through which women can voice their complaints and concerns. This department should be placed at the office of the president, not only to ensure that women's voices reach the right ears, but that the obstacles they may come across can be overcome.
- Immediately appoint a sub-committee (composed of women and men) within the Land Reform Commission to advise the government on how to incorporate women's equal rights in land.

To the Kenyan Land Reform Commission   The proposed Kenyan Land Reform Commission should ensure that it recommends to the government the following:

- It is important for women to have rights to property and to own land in their own names.
- In areas of customary bilateral inheritance, joint husband–wife ownership, or lifelong tenancy, is the most natural framework of land reform and will promote equity and efficiency.
- Put into practice laws that guarantee daughters' rights to inherit land.
- Legislation should be adopted that ensures that widows, who currently have no legal protection, receive the right to inherit their husbands' property.

- To achieve equality in the reform, women should be legally assured of access to a livelihood from land in the event of widowhood or divorce.
- Women need legal powers to have access to credit, new crop technologies and to prevent the alienation of income from household consumption needs.
- Another option for land tenure reform is to give women reserve powers. Such powers would ensure that no lease or sale of land is legally valid without the wife's signature, and that in the event of divorce or widowhood, the wife obtains lifelong usufruct rights over part of the land.
- To appoint a gender-sensitive sub-committee of the Land Reform Commission composed of equal numbers of women and men who have a specific duty to focus on women's concerns about land reform. This is to ensure that the Land Reform Commission provides a gender-balanced recommendation for the formulation of land policy in Kenya that takes everybody into consideration.

To women Women should not simply assume that actions will be taken on their behalf by others.

- At the individual level, women, especially those who own land and make decisions in their households, should begin to ensure that their daughters, like their sons, inherit land.
- National women's organizations should monitor and, if necessary, intervene on behalf of other women in the formulation of land tenure policy; these organizations will take into consideration the suggested recommendations of the Land Reform Commission. Women's NGOs should make it a priority to have a vertical link at the grassroots level to mobilize women to participate at all levels in order to contribute to the success of land tenure reform. It is worth bearing in mind that the mobilization should be done at different levels – through farm service cooperatives, adjudication groups, producer cooperatives and land reform committees.
- Women's organizations must contact the men who design and implement the reform to ensure the feasibility of women's economic contribution and benefits. The problem remains finding the basis for mobilizing women.
- At the grassroots level, women should organize their own agricultural cooperatives or self-help groups to raise capital to buy their own lands.
- Women must be informed of their rights and be brought into the whole process of implementation by NGOs providing civic education.

The significance of this study lies in its contribution to the general knowledge that women's economic, political and social positions are the outcome of processes of contestation and bargaining. The present analysis will indicate that change will require simultaneous struggles over property, the norms governing gender roles and behaviour, public decision-making authority, the hierarchical character of gender relations within and outside the household, based on highly unequal access of women and men to economic, political and social power. The breadth and depth of the obstacles make women's land rights for food production a critical entry point for challenging unequal gender relations and power structures.

References

Agarwal, B. (1994) *A Field of One's Own: Gender and Land Rights in South Asia*, Cambridge: Cambridge University Press.

Allot, A. N. (1958) 'Towards a Definition of Absolute Ownership', *Journal of African Law*, 5: 99–102.

Bentsi-Enchill, K. (1965) 'Do African Systems of Land Tenure Require Special Terminology?', *African Law*, 19.

Blaike, P. and H. Bookfield (1987) *Land Degradation and Society: Food and Agricultural Organization of the Nations*, Rome: Women in Developing Agriculture.

Boserup, E. (1970) *Women's Role in Economic Development*, New York, NY: St Martin's Press.

Cloude, P. E. (1969) 'Resources and Man: A Study and Recommendations by the Committee on Resources and Man', Division of Earth Sciences, National Academy of Science, San Francisco, CA: W. H. Freeman.

Davison, J. A. (1987a) 'Land and Women's Agricultural Production: The Context', in J. Davison (ed.), *Agriculture Women and Land: The African Experience*, Boulder, CO: Westview Press, pp. 1–32.

— (1987b) 'Who Owns What? Land Registration and Tensions in Gender Relations and Production in Kenya', in J. Davison (ed.), *Agriculture Women and Land: The African Experience*, Boulder, CO: Westview Press, pp. 157–76.

— (1987c) '"Without Land We are Nothing" – The Effect of Land Tenure Policies and Practices Upon Rural Women in Kenya', *Rural Africana*, 27: 19–33.

Friedl, E. (1975) *Women and Men: An Anthropologist's View*, New York, NY: Holt, Rinehart and Winston.

Gulati, L. (1978) 'Profile of a Female Agricultural Labourer', *Economic and Political Weekly* (Review of Agriculture), 13.

Gutto, S. B.O. (1987) 'Legal Constraints on Female Participation in the Economy', MA thesis, University of Nairobi.

Guyer, J. I. (1984) *Family and Farm in Southern Cameroon*, African Research Studies, 15, Boston, MA: Boston University African Studies Centre.

Howard, R. E. (1986) *Human Rights in Commonwealth Africa*, Totowa, NJ: Rowman and Littlefield.

Ingham, J. H. et al. (eds) (1950), *Report of Committee on Agricultural Credit for Africans*, Nairobi: Republic of Kenya Government Printer.

International Labour Organization (1972) *Employment, Incomes and Equality: A Strategy for Increasing Productive Employment in Kenya*, Geneva: ILO.

Jiggins, J. (1988) 'Women's Access to Land as a Strategy for Employment Promotion, Poverty Alleviation and Household Food Security', Harare: ILO Regional Workshop.

Kaberry, P. (1952) 'Women of Grassfields: A Study of the Economic Position of Women in Bumenda, British Cameroons', Colonial Research Publications 14, London: HMSO.

Kibwana, K. (1990) 'Land Tenure', in W. R. Ochieng (ed.), *Themes in Kenyan History*, Nairobi: Heinemann, pp. 230–41.

Knowles, J. C. (1978) 'A Micro-analysis of Female Labour Force Participation in Kenya', Population and Employment Project, Working Paper 62, Geneva: ILO.

Kumar, D. (1978) 'Agrarian Relations: South India', in D. Kumar and T. Ray Chaudhuri (eds), T*he Cambridge Economic History of India, c.1757–c.1970, Vol. II*, Cambridge: Cambridge University Press, pp. 207–41.

Mason, K. O. (1984)'The Status of Women: A Review of its Relationship to Fertility and Mortality', paper prepared for the Population Science Division of the Rockefeller Foundation.

Mathangani, S. W. (1989) *Information for Women in Food Production*, Ottawa: International Development Research Centre.

Meek, C. K. (1946) *Land, Law and Customs in the Colonies*, London: Frank Cass.

Mitsud, F. M. (1967) *Customary Land Law in Africa: With Reference to Legislation Aimed at Adjusting Customary Tenures to the Needs of Development*, Rome: United Nations, Food and Agricultural Organization.

Moyana, H. V. (1984) *The Political Economy of Land in Zimbabwe*, Gweru, Zimbabwe: Mambo Press.

Mwaniki, N. (1975) 'Social and Economic Impact of Land Tenure Reform in Mbeere', Nairobi: University of Nairobi Institute for Development Studies.

Nadine, R. H. (1989) 'Women and Food Security in Kenya', Washington, DC: World Bank, Population and Human Resource Department.

Nangendo, S. M. (1994) 'Daughters of the Clay, Women of the Farm: Women, Agricultural Economic Development and Ceramic Production in Bungoma District, Western Kenya', PhD dissertation, Bryn Mawr College.

Nasimiyu, R. (1984) 'The Participation of Women in the Political Economy: A Case Study of Bukusu Women in Bungoma District, 1902–1960', MA thesis, University of Nairobi.

Ndumbu, A. (1985) *Out of my Rib: A View of Women in Development*, Nairobi: Press Trust Printers.

Noronha, R. and F. J. Lathem (1993) 'Traditional Land Tenure and Land Use Systems in Design of Agricultural Projects', Washington, DC: World Bank.

Obi, S. N. C. (1963) *The Ibo Law of Property*, London: Butterworth.

Okere, L. C. (1983) *The Anthropology of Food in Rural Igboland, Nigeria*, Leinham, MD: University Press of America.

Okoth-Ogendo, H. W. O. (1974) 'Property Theory and Land Use Analysis (An Approach to the Study of Law in the Peasant Land Use in Kenya)', Nairobi: University of Nairobi Institute for Development Studies.

— (1976) 'African Land Tenure Reform' in J. Heyer, J. K. Maitha and W. M. Senga (eds), *Agricultural Development in Kenya: An Economic Assessment*, Oxford: Oxford University Press, pp. 152–86.

— (1979) 'Land Tenure and its Implications for the Development of Kenya's Semi-arid Areas', paper for the Workshop on the Development of Kenya's Semi-arid Areas, Nairobi: University of Nairobi, IDS.

— (1981) 'Land Ownership and Land Distribution in Kenya's Farm Areas', in T. Killick (ed.), *Papers on the Kenyan Economy*, London: Heinemann, pp. 329–38.

— (1982a) 'Property Systems and Social Organizations in Africa: An Essay on the Relative

Position of Women Under Indigenous and Received Law', in N.P. Takirambudde (ed.), *The Individual Under the African Law*, All Africa Conference.

— (1982b) 'The Perils of Land Tenure Reform: The Case of Kenya', in J. W. Arntzen, L. D. Ngoongo and S. D. Turner (eds), *Land Policy and Agriculture in Eastern and Southern Africa*, Tokyo: United Nations University, pp. 79–92.

— (1989) 'Some Issues of Theory in the Study of Tenure Relations in African Agriculture', *Africa*, 59: 6–12.

Pala, A. O. (1978) *African Women in Rural Development: Trends and Priorities*, Washington, DC: American Council of Education, Overseas Liaison Committee.

— (1980) 'Women's Access to Land and their Role in Agriculture and Decision-making in the Farm: Experiences of the Jolou of Kenya', *Journal of African Research*.

— (1983) 'Women's Access to Land and their Role in Agriculture and Decision-making in the Farm: Experiences of the Jolou of Kenya', Nairobi: University of Nairobi, Institute for Development Studies.

Republic of Kenya (1965) *Development Plan, 1965–1966*, Nairobi: Republic of Kenya Government Printer.

— (1984) *Development Plan, 1984–1988*, Nairobi: Republic of Kenya Government Printer.

— (1986) *Economic Management for Renewed Growth*, Nairobi: Republic of Kenya Government Printer.

— (1989) *Development Plan, 1989–1993*, Nairobi: Republic of Kenya Government Printer.

— (1994) *Kenyan Population Census*, Vol. 1, Nairobi: Republic of Kenya Government Printer.

Republic of Kenya and UNICEF (1988) *Situation Analysis of Children and Women in Kenya*, Nairobi: GOK/UNICEF.

Riddell, J. C. and C. Dickerman (1986) *Country Profiles in Land Tenure: Africa, 1986*, Madison, WI: Land Tenure Center.

Sacks, K. (1979) *Sisters and Wives: The Past and Future of Sexual Equality*, Westport, CT: Greenwood Press.

Schapera, I. (1955) *A Handbook of Twana Law and Custom*, London: Oxford University Press.

Sheddick, I. G. J. (1953) *The Southern Sotho*, London: Oxford University Press.

Shipton, P. (1987) 'The Kenya Land Tenure Reform: Misunderstanding in the Public Creation on Private Property', Cambridge, MA: Harvard University Institute for International Development.

Simpson, S. R. (1986) 'Towards a Definition of "Absolute Ownership"': A Commentary'. *Journal of African Law*, 5: 145–50.

Sorrenson, M. A. K. (1968) *Land Reform in Kikuyu Country: A Study of Government Policy*, Nairobi: Oxford University Press.

Swynnerton, R. J. M. (1954) *A Plan to Intensify the Development of African Agriculture in Kenya*, Nairobi: Republic of Kenya Government Printer.

United Kingdom (1955) *East Africa Royal Commission (1953–1955): A Report*, Cmd 9475, London, HMSO.

Verhelst, T. (1970) *Land Tenure as a Constraint on Agricultural Development: A Reevaluation*, Los Angeles, CA: University of California School of Law, African Studies Center,

Wanjala, S. C. (1995) 'Background to the Land Question, Problems in Kenya: An Historical and Anthropological Point of View', Nairobi: University of Nairobi.

Wanjala, S. C. and N. Musymi (1990) 'Land Ownership and Use in Kenya: Past, Present and Future', Nairobi: University of Nairobi.

Index